This is the first of two volumes on the causes and cure of Stagflation —
the two-headed monster combining mass unemployment with rapid
inflation that is currently afflicting the mixed economies of the industrially developed world. Professor Meade deplores the unemployment
due to the failure of governments to adopt Keynesian measures for the
expansion of economic activity, but he recognises that in present conditions such measures would lead to an unacceptable and explosive
inflation of   qual
strategy o   y
incomes   e
employm   l
companic   )
financial

Profes   d
Great Slu   n
comparin   s
the New   s
various p   s
the limit   r
policy, I   .
subsidy   .
He argue   y
settleme   n
financial   d
moderat

This   e
theory   al
relations   t
the gene   al
reader a   e
mathem   is
based ar

Professo   ,
after ha   r
Researc   f
Hertfor   e
of Nati   e
Cabinet   r
Meade i   y
and po   ic
Policy   n
and Un

Stagflation. Volume 1
WAGE-FIXING

Forthcoming: *Stagflation Volume 2 – Demand Management*
by David Vines, Jan Maciejowski and James E. Meade

BY THE SAME AUTHOR

Efficiency, Equality and the Ownership of Property
Planning and the Price Mechanism
The Geometry of International Trade
Problems of Economic Union
A Neo-Classical Theory of Economic Growth
Principles of Political Economy
The Stationary Economy
The Growing Economy
The Controlled Economy
The Just Economy
The Intelligent Radical's Guide to Economic Policy

The Control of Inflation (CUP)
Introduction to Economic Analysis and Policy (OUP)
Theory of International Economic Policy (OUP)

also
The Structure and Reform of Direct Taxation
Report of a Committee chaired by Professor J. E. Meade
(The 'Meade' Report for the Institute for Fiscal Studies)

WAGE-FIXING

James E. Meade, C.B., F.B.A.
Emeritus Professor of Political Economy
University of Cambridge

Stagflation

London
GEORGE ALLEN & UNWIN
Boston   Sydney

George Allen & Unwin (Publishers) Ltd,
40 Museum Street, London, WC1A 1LU, UK

George Allen & Unwin (Publishers) Ltd,
Park Lane, Hemel Hempstead, Herts, HP2 4TE, UK

Allen & Unwin Inc.,
9 Winchester Terrace, Winchester, Mass 01890, USA

George Allen & Unwin Australia Pty Ltd,
8 Napier Street, North Sydney, NSW 2060, Australia

First published in 1982
Second impression 1983

British Library Cataloguing in Publication Data

Meade, James E.
    Stagflation.
    Vol. 1: Wage-fixing
1. Inflation (Finance)   2. Unemployment
I. Title
331.13'7   HD5707

ISBN 0-04-339023-4
ISBN 0-04-339024-2 Pbk

Library of Congress Cataloging in Publication Data

Meade, J. E. (James Edward), 1907-
    Stagflation.

    Contents: v. 1. Wage fixing.
    1. Unemployment – Effect of inflation on.   2. Wage-
price policy.   I. Title.
HD5710.M4   339.5   81-12717
ISBN 0-04-339023-4   AACR2
ISBN 0-04-339024-2 (pbk.)

Set in 10 on 11 point Press Roman by the Alden Press
and printed in Great Britain
by Billing and Sons Ltd
Guildford, London and Worcester

Contents

Preface   *page* xi

I   Stagflation, or Making the Worst of Both Worlds   1
     1 The Nature of the Disease   1
     2 The Causes and Consequences of the Disease   2
     3 The Cure of the Disease   5
     4 Orthodox Keynesianism and New Keynesianism   8
     5 Keynes versus the Monetarists   11
     6 The Transitional Problem   12
     7 The Meaning of Full Employment   13
     8 Wages and the Distribution of Income   15
     9 Conclusion   20

II   Effects of Wage-Fixing on Unemployment and Inflation   21
     1 Wage-Fixing and Demand Management   21
     2 Over-Ambitious Wage Claims   26
     3 The Effect of the Oil Crisis   28
     4 The Distribution of Wage Income   30
     5 Wages and the Cost of Living   33
     6 Conclusions   36

III   Other Criteria for Fixing Rates of Pay   37
     1 Comparability   37
     2 Productivity   39
     3 Low Pay   42
     4 Conclusions   43

IV   Imperfect Competition and the Case for Wage-Fixing
Institutions   44
     1 The Fairyland of Perfect Competition   45
     2 Monopolistic and Monopsonistic Features of the Real
       World   47
     3 A Single Employer in an Imperfect Labour Market:
       A Numerical Example   49
     4 The Application of the Analysis to the Whole Economy   53
     5 The Distribution of the Gains   55
     6 Conclusion   55

V	The Existing Monopolistic Powers of Labour Organisation in the UK	*page* 58
	1 Individual Contracts of Employment and Contracts to Perform a Service	58
	2 Statutory Wage-Fixing Bodies	61
	3 Statutory Provisions Directly Affecting the Individual Contract of Employment	61
	4 The Formation of Trade Unions	66
	5 The Membership of Trade Unions: The Closed Shop	67
	6 The Exemption of Trade Unions from Certain Restraints of Monopolistic Action	70
	7 Extension of the Scope of Wage Bargains	77
	8 Picketing	78
	9 Adjudication and Enforcement	80
	10 Social Security Provisions	83
	11 Conclusion	84
VI	The Role of Competition in the Labour Market	85
	1 Some Further Reasons for Intervention in the Labour Market	85
	2 The Case for a Decentralised System for Wage-Fixing	88
	3 One Union for Each Employer	91
	4 A General Limitation of Trade Union Powers	92
	5 Increased Mobility of Labour	95
	6 Conclusion	97
VII	A Centralised Incomes Policy	98
	1 Centralised Wage Guidance	98
	2 Centralised Wage-Fixing	100
	3 The Adjustment of Relativities	102
	4 An Intermediate System	104
	5 Conclusions	106
VIII	Not-Quite-Compulsory Arbitration	108
	1 The Promotion of Employment through Arbitration	108
	2 The Need for a Single Permanent Arbitral Body	110
	3 Avoidance of Abrupt Changes	112
	4 Two Possible Variations on the Scheme	113
	5 The Need for General Acceptance	114
	6 The Problem of Sanctions	115
	7 Conclusions	117
IX	Labour Co-operatives, Labour–Capital Partnerships, and Profit-Sharing Schemes	119
	1 The Case for Competitive Labour Co-operatives	119
	2 Labour Co-operatives and the Scale of Production	121

3 The Implications of the Egalitarian Principle *page* 124
4 Labour Co-operatives and Capital Intensity 126
5 Competitive Labour Co-operatives as a Cure for
  Stagflation 127
6 The Crucial Role of New Co-operatives 131
7 The Case for Inegalitarian Labour—Capital Partnerships 133
8 Conflicts of Interest in Labour—Capital Partnerships 134
9 Conclusions 136

X   Fiscal Devices for the Control of Inflation 138
1 A Great Variety of Devices 138
2 A Scheme for Control of Price Inflation 140
3 Administrative Problems of a Price-Control Scheme 143
4 A Self-Balancing Scheme 144
5 The Efficacy of a Scheme for Control of Price Inflation 146
6 A Scheme for the Control of Wage Inflation 147
7 The Direct Effect of the Schemes on Money Wage
  Settlements 149
8 Conclusions 151

XI   Summary of Conclusions: The Way Ahead 153

Appendix A The Inflationary Implications of Orthodox
Keynesian Demand Management for Full
Employment Combined with Wage Settlements
Designed to Achieve an Over-Ambitious Real Wage 159

Appendix B The Effect of New Keynesian Demand Management
Combined with Wage Settlements Aimed at (1) an
Over-Ambitious Standard of Living or (2) the
Promotion of Employment 182

Appendix C Two Models of Fiscal Devices for the Control of
Cost-Push Inflation 188

Appendix D The Legal Background to the Restraint of
Monopolistic Behaviour in the UK 207

Appendix E Further Problems of Labour Co-operatives and
Capital—Labour Partnerships 217

Index 227

Preface

This book is the first of two volumes on the causes and cure of stagflation. It deals with Wage-Fixing, and will be followed by a second volume on Demand-Management. Stagflation is a two-headed monster combining mass unemployment with rapid inflation. It is the thesis of the present work that the monster can be destroyed only by a combination of two weapons, namely: (1) institutional arrangements for wage-fixing which avoid inflationary rises in costs and (2) demand-management arrangements (i.e. fiscal, monetary, and foreign-exchange rate policies) which keep the total money demand for goods and services on a steady expansionary path. These two aspects of analysis make up a single unified whole.

The project as a whole has been sponsored by the Department of Applied Economics of the University of Cambridge. It has been supported by the Social Science Research Council who have financed the secretarial expenses, the appointment of Mr David Vines, Fellow of Pembroke College Cambridge, as a Research Officer of the Department of Applied Economics, and the assistance of Dr J. M. Maciejowski, Lecturer in Mathematical Engineering at the University of Warwick and sometime Fellow of Pembroke College Cambridge, on the problems of controlling a dynamic economic system. Professor J. E. Meade has worked on the project as an Honorary Research Associate of the Department of Applied Economics.

David Vines, in co-operation with Jan Maciejowski, will be primarily responsible for the second volume, on demand management. James Meade carries the responsibility for the present volume, though he has been greatly helped in its construction by David Vines. He is also much indebted to Professor Sir Henry Phelps Brown with whom he has continually discussed the problems covered in the present volume. Dr P. Elias, Fellow of Pembroke College Cambridge, has read and commented extensively on Chapter V on labour law while officials at the Departments of Industry and Trade read an earlier draft of Appendix D on the law relating to monopolies, mergers, and restrictive practices and corrected a number of inaccuracies. To all these the author of the present volume is most grateful, but he alone remains responsible for the analysis of this volume, some aspects of which he knows to be not completely acceptable to some of the people who have helped him so generously. He had the privilege of being a member of a small informal seminar arranged by Professor Richard Layard at the London School of Economics to discuss with Professor Abba Lerner his Market Anti-Inflation Plan (MAP). Chapter X and

Appendix C on fiscal devices for the control of inflation have been written on the basis of work done in that seminar.

Some passages in the present book are reproduced from papers by James Meade which have already been published elsewhere, namely: 'The Meaning of "Internal Balance"', *Economic Journal,* September 1978, © Nobel Foundation, 1977; 'On Stagflation', Snow Lecture, *The Listener,* 14 December 1978; 'Labour Co-operatives, Participation, and Value-Added Sharing', in *The Political Economy of Co-operation and Participation,* edited by Alasdair Clayre, Oxford University Press 1980; 'The Fixing of Money Rates of Pay' in *The Socialist Agenda,* edited by David Lipsey and Dick Leonard, Jonathan Cape, 1981; and 'Note on the Inflationary Implications of the Wage-Fixing Assumption of the Cambridge Economic Policy Group', *Oxford Economic Papers,* March 1981. He is grateful for the necessary permissions.

The author would like to express his thanks for the efficient, patient, and good humoured way in which the staff of the typing pool of the Department of Applied Economics have treated his manuscript.

Department of Applied Economics   JAMES E. MEADE
Cambridge
May 1981

To
EMM

CHAPTER I

Stagflation, or Making the Worst of Both Worlds

1. The Nature of the Disease

The purpose of this introductory chapter is to outline very briefly the nature, the cause, and the possible cure of stagflation, a nasty economic disease with an equally nasty name. The main symptom of the disease is a state of the economy which is at one and the same time stagnant and inflationary, that is to say, suffering simultaneously from heavy unemployment and from a rapid rate of rise of money prices and so of the cost of living. The disease in its acute form has inflicted society only in recent years. For some quarter of a century after the Second World War (1945–1970) economic policy was generally discussed under the assumption that there was a choice between unemployment and inflation. Should we adopt expansionary budgetary and monetary policies which give people large amounts of money with which to purchase goods and services, in which case we would have high production and employment but at the risk of driving up selling prices? Or should we adopt a restrictive financial policy in order to put a downward pressure on prices, but at the risk of creating insufficient jobs to maintain full employment?

Our trouble is that during the 1970s we have experienced much heavier unemployment than in the earlier decades and have combined this with much more rapid rates of price inflation. We have managed to make the worst of both worlds. This development is shown in Figure 1. During the 1950s and 1960s the unemployment percentage varied between 1 per cent and 3 per cent while the rate of price inflation lay generally between 1 per cent and 5 per cent per annum. In the 1970s the unemployment percentage rose to 6 per cent and the rate of price inflation fluctuated greatly between 7 per cent and no less than 24 per cent per annum.

This relatively new disease has recently spread as an epidemic through the community of countries of which we are a part, namely, the industrially developed, free-enterprise, liberal, mixed-economy democracies; and its possible consequences should be taken very seriously.

For if one wished to undermine the structure of a liberal society one might find it difficult to choose between a policy of debauching the currency by a runaway inflation or a policy designed to ensure a prolonged period of heavy unemployment. Germany in the early 1920s experienced a complete runaway inflation which reduced the value of the mark virtually

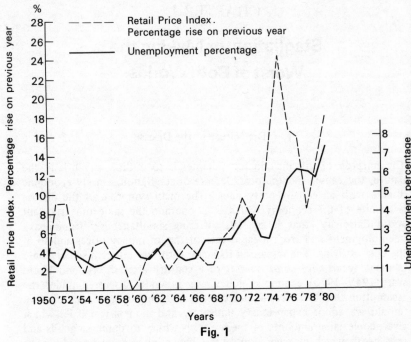

Fig. 1

to zero and ruined many members of the middle class; and this was followed in the early 1930s by a horrific period of mass unemployment
which impoverished practically the whole community. Runaway inflation
followed by mass unemployment brought the curse of Hitler upon
Germany. To combine inflation and unemployment simultaneously could
be an even surer recipe for disaster.

Our immediate danger is, of course, in no way comparable to that of
the dreadful interwar German experience, when the rate of explosive
price inflation and the level of mass unemployment were of quite different orders of magnitude from anything which we are at present experiencing. But there is one ominous feature of the experience of recent
years which does suggest that the position should be taken very seriously,
particularly in the UK. Not only do we suffer from a more virulent attack
of the disease than do other countries; but above all in this country over
the last decade or two, each level of unemployment has been associated
with ever higher rates of inflation as the years have passed.

2.   The Causes and Consequences of the Disease

It is the thesis of the present work that the disease of stagflation is basically caused by the combination of two developments: (1) the general

adoption of a Keynesian policy of expanding total money expenditures, through budgetary and monetary policies, to whatever level necessary to maintain full employment; and (2) the increased ability and willingness of trade unions and similar monopolistic pressure groups to aim at given increases in real standards of living even though they exceed the available increases in real output; combined with (3) failure in the UK to achieve a rate of growth of productivity, and so in the available real output, comparable to that achieved in other similar industrial countries.

Many factors have been suggested as the cause of this comparative failure — bad and unenterprising management, lack of suitable education and technical training, restrictive labour practices, lack of adequate investment in suitable new capital equipment, and so on. A solution of these problems is, of course, of fundamental importance, since it is these real factors which set limits on real standards of living. Incidentally, however, a solution of these problems could in addition afford relief to the problem of stagflation by increasing the real output available relative to the claims made on it. But it is by no means certain that the result would be a complete or lasting disappearance of stagflationary conditions. Other countries which have enjoyed higher rates of productivity growth have also experienced the evils of stagflation, though to a lesser degree than the UK. Moreover, so long as institutional arrangements are such that individual groups can make separate claims which together exceed real resources, appetites may well grow as rapidly as supplies expand so that the totality of claims continues to be excessive.

This volume is not about the basic and all important problems of raising productivity. It is concerned with the stagflationary effects of situations in which total claims exceed available supplies. The process will be discussed at length in Chapter II; but the general nature of the problem is clear. If demands for increases in money incomes which exceed the increases in real output available for consumption are made and satisfied, the money cost per unit of output is bound to rise; and if financial policies are simultaneously designed to provide sufficient demand to purchase the whole available output as prices which cover costs, selling prices must be inflated. The consequential rise in the cost of living will have frustrated the attempts to obtain over-ambitious increases in real incomes; and this frustration can lead to attempts to obtain even more rapid increases in money incomes. The inflation will then threaten to explode.

A most acute form of this phenomenon probably occurred in the early 1970s when the price of oil was abruptly raised by the oil-producing countries. The consequential abrupt rise in money costs and so in the cost of living meant an abrupt worsening of real incomes in the oil-importing countries and so triggered off an especially large rise in wage claims in an inevitably ineffective attempt to offset an inevitable rise in real costs of production.

Such threats of an explosive inflation mean that the authorities must do something to prevent its getting out of hand, one possible line of policy being to restrict money expenditures through restrictive fiscal and monetary policies in an attempt to discourage the raising of money prices and wage rates.

This state of affairs leads to a cruel dilemma for those who are responsible for the country's financial policy. Before each budget the Chancellor of the Exchequer can rely nowadays upon receiving much conflicting advice, some urging expansive monetary and budgetary policies designed to stimulate monetary expenditures on goods and services in order to create jobs and reduce unemployment and other advice urging restrictive policies to reduce money expenditures in order to keep down prices and fight inflation. And this conflict of advice shows itself not only within the country but also internationally between countries. Thus so long as a country like Germany had a lower rate of price inflation and a favourable excess of exports over imports, the authorities in other countries like the UK with their higher rates of price inflation and an excess demand for imports urged it to expand its domestic demand for goods and services. Surely, it was argued, it was the duty of Germany which had only a moderate rate of domestic price inflation to adopt an expansionary domestic policy that would help to increase the demand for its own products and also for imports from countries like the UK; for this would help to reduce unemployment both in Germany and the UK and at the same time to correct an imbalance in international payments by increasing the imports of the surplus country, Germany, and the exports of the deficit country, the UK. But the Germans were understandably reluctant to expand their own domestic demands because they wished above all not to stoke up their own domestic price inflation. And in the light of their past history who can blame them for that?

Such is the cruel dilemma with which we are now faced. The ultimate horror to anyone brought up in the Keynesian tradition is that we now experience a world recession and accept its coming as an act of God against which we are powerless to fight. We busy ourselves in making forecasts of how much our employment and output is likely to fall – and in waiting patiently for an economic recovery. But Keynes pointed out in the 1930s the basic absurdity of men simply assuming that they could do nothing to prevent the waste of their resources in idleness when there were so many real needs still to be satisfied.

There is, however, one outstanding difference between the Great Slump of the 1930s and the Great Stagflation of the 1970s. Heavy unemployment was accompanied in the 1930s with falling money prices and wages, but in the 1970s with rapidly rising money prices and wages. In the 1930s, unlike the 1970s, there was no dilemma for Keynesian financial policies – expansion of money expenditures was needed both to give employment and to stop deflation.

This contrast is illustrated in Figure 2 which compares what happened to the total money national income (i.e. the net amount earned from the money expenditures on the country's products) between 1925 and 1936 with what happened to it between 1965 and 1976. The onset of the Great Depression and heavy unemployment of the 1930s was accompanied by — indeed, it may be said to have been caused by — an absolute fall in the money expenditures on the country's products. The onset of heavy unemployment in the 1970s was by contrast accompanied by an explosive growth in the total of such money expenditures. There was an acute dilemma between the need to expand demand to absorb the unemployed resources and to contract demand to prevent runaway inflation.

3.   The Cure of the Disease

Is it possible to escape from this dilemma? What general set of economic and financial institutions and policies would enable us in our type of society to maintain full employment without experiencing a runaway inflation? It is the thesis of this work that escape from the dilemma of stagflation can best be achieved by a combination of two fundamental changes.

First, we need to impose some form of financial–monetary restraint in our society and to rid ourselves of the idea that whatever may happen to the rate of rise of money wage rates spenders will always be supplied with sufficient confetti money to cover the resulting cost of production, however rapidly the inflation may be developing. It is suggested that for this purpose monetary and budgetary policies should be consciously so designed as to lead to a moderate but steady rate of growth — let us say, by way of example, a rate of growth of 5 per cent per annum — in the total of money expenditures on goods and services and so in the total demand for labour to produce those goods and services. Figure 2 shows how such a 5 per cent per annum growth path would fall between the deflation of the 1930s and the explosive inflation of the 1970s.

Second, against the background of this steady 5 per cent per annum growth in the total money demand for labour it would be necessary to have some methods for fixing rates of pay which ensured the attainment and preservation of full employment.

An appropriate solution would be some form of wage-fixing arrangements which in each sector of the economy would restrain wage increases in so far as they would increase unemployment or prevent the expansion of employment in that sector. In any occupation, trade, industry, or region in which there was a scarcity of labour relative to the demand, a *rise* and not a *fall* in wage rates is needed to attract workers to that sector and so to *increase* employment in that sector; and since the system

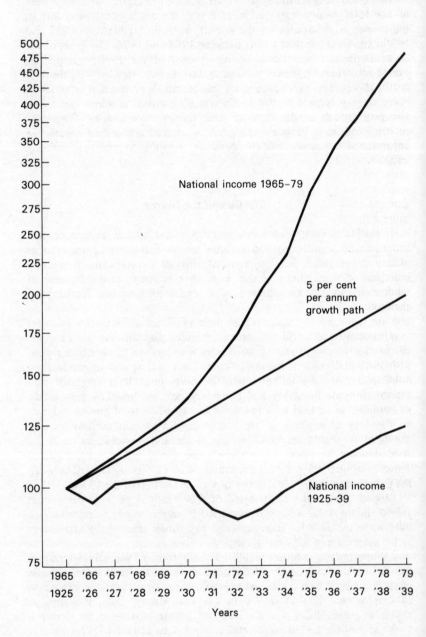

Fig. 2

would be operating against a background in which on the average over all the sectors of the economy the money demand for labour would be expanding at a steady rate, it would follow that sooner or later there would be a competitive need in each typical sector to raise its wage rates to maintain its labour force. In any sector in which labour was specially scarce wages would need to rise faster than this average. In any particular sector in which there did still exist an excess supply of labour any rise in wage rates should be avoided or moderated in order not to accentuate the problem of unemployment. The cure for unemployment in such sectors must rely partly upon a gradual improvement in that sector as it enjoyed some share of the general steady 5 per cent per annum expansion in the total demand for labour and partly upon redundant labour being attracted by, and being helped to move to, those other sectors in which employment opportunities were expanding and in which the competitive demand for labour was bidding up the wage rate and making employment more attractive.

If this system were in effective operation, full employment could be attained and maintained with only minor and temporary lapses from grace. At the same time inflation would be contained within very moderate limits; if total output was growing at, say, 2 per cent per annum, while total money expenditure on the output was growing at 5 per cent per annum, the price level would be rising by no more than 3 per cent per annum.

The devising of a set of monetary and budgetary policies to keep the level of total money expenditure on a steady 5 per cent per annum growth path raises a number of important issues. By what means should total money expenditures be controlled? By monetary policy? By fiscal policy through raising and lowering rates of tax and levels of public expenditure? By changes in the rate of foreign exchange or other measures to affect expenditure on UK exports and UK import-competing products? What should be the precise measure of total money expenditures which it was aimed to keep on a steady growth path? Should it be the Gross Domestic Product (i.e. the value of all goods and services produced for consumption, investment, government use, and exports)? Or would it be preferable to aim directly at keeping the total money demand for labour (i.e. total wage and salary earnings) on a steady growth path? Above all, in view of the dynamic interrelationships in the economy between taxes, interest rates, foreign exchange rates, prices, outputs, and employment, what are the best rules for operating the monetary, fiscal, or other controls for the purpose of keeping the chosen measure of total money expenditures on its target growth path? None of these questions will be discussed in the present volume but will be the subject matter of a subsequent volume on 'Demand Management'.

It will be a main thesis of that volume that control of *domestic* expenditures on goods and services is best achieved by frequent and prompt changes in certain tax rates. In that case interest rates as set by monetary policy could be used primarily to influence the flow of capital funds into or out of the country and so to affect the capital account of the balance of payments, while the foreign exchange rate could be used primarily to influence the balance of trade and so the net *foreign* demand for the country's products.

In this volume, however, we are not concerned with the way in which financial controls are handled. We simply start with the assumption that financial policies can be, and indeed are, so devised as to maintain the total level of money demand for the products of labour on a steady growth path. Against this background we shall discuss the economic and administrative (but not the political) problems involved in devising a set of institutions for settling money rates of pay which will attain and maintain a high and reasonably stable level of employment − what we shall call 'full employment'.

4.   Orthodox Keynesianism and New Keynesianism

The thesis of this work is thus to use demand-management policies (through monetary policy, fiscal policy, and exchange rate policy) to maintain a steady rate of growth in the total money expenditure on the products of industry, and against this background to use wage-fixing institutions and policies to maintain full employment. Many admirers of Keynes will argue that this is to stand Keynes on his head. 'Did not Keynes suggest', they will ask, 'that the control of demand should be used to influence the total amount of real output and employment which it was profitable to maintain, while the money wage rate was left simply to determine the absolute level of money prices and costs at which this level of real activity would take place'? This was in fact the way in which Keynes looked at things in the 1930s when it could be assumed that the money wage rate was constant or in any case rather sluggish in its movements. What he would be saying today is anybody's guess, but of one thing one can be certain; he would be appalled at the current rates of price inflation. It is a complete misrepresentation of the views of a great and wise man to suggest that in present conditions he would have been concerned only with the maintenance of full employment and not at all with the avoidance of rapid inflation of money prices and costs.

But whatever Keynes's policy recommendations would be in present circumstances, the policy recommendations in this work are in no way incompatible with Keynes's analysis. In the 1930s Keynes argued, rightly or wrongly, that cutting money wage rates would have little effect in expanding employment because its main effect would be simply to reduce the absolute level of the relevant money prices, money costs, money incomes, and money expenditures, leaving the levels of real output and employment much unchanged. It is a totally different matter, wholly consistent with that Keynesian analysis, to suggest that the money wage rate might be used to influence the level of employment in conditions in which the money demand was being deliberately and successfully managed through monetary and fiscal policies in such a way as to prevent changes in wage rates from causing any offsetting rise or fall in total money incomes and expenditures.

As far as the overall effects on real incomes, outputs, and employments are concerned, it makes no essential difference whether a given expansion is obtained (1) by an incomes policy, which limits the rate of rise of money wage rates and so of costs and prices to a given extent, combined with demand-management policies which raise total money expenditures to the extent needed to promote the desired expansion of output and employment, or (2) by demand-management policies, which expand total money expenditures at a given steady moderate rate, combined with wage-fixing institutions which restrain money costs to the extent needed to promote the desired expansion of output and employment. Both strategies are essentially Keynesian. We may call the former (which uses demand-management policies to maintain full employment and wage-fixing policies to control inflation) 'Orthodox Keynesianism' and the latter (which uses demand-management policies to control the inflation of money expenditures and wage-fixing policies to maintain full employment) 'New Keynesianism'.

The attainment of a high and stable level of employment and production by either means brings with it great advantages. There is the obvious elimination of waste of resources in idleness and their use to satisfy real needs. Moreover, in the modern economy there are important private and public elements of overhead cost which can be spread over a larger output. In private industry a 1 per cent increase in employment may produce more than a 1 per cent increase in output because certain 'overhead' activities need not be expanded with output. In the public sector, certain services (e.g. police, defence, education, etc.) do not need to be expanded with output, with the result that as incomes are expanded in the private sector of the economy rates of tax can be reduced to raise the same revenue to finance the same level of public 'overhead' expenditures. These advantages of full employment are to be enjoyed whether such economic activity is achieved by expanding money demand to the extent needed to cover controlled money costs or by restraining money costs to the extent necessary to match a controlled expansion of demand.

Are there then any valid reasons for preferring a 'New Keynesian' strategy (i.e. the use of the 'weapon' of demand-management policies to hit the 'target' of keeping total money expenditures on a steady growth path and the use of the 'weapon' of wage-fixing institutions to hit the 'target' of full employment) over the 'Orthodox Keynesian' strategy of the 1930s (i.e. the use of the 'weapon' of demand management to hit the 'target' of full employment and the use of the 'weapon' of an incomes policy to hit the 'target' of control of price inflation)?

The immediate reaction of a control engineer would be to ask whether this did not pose an unnecessary and indeed harmful choice. One should not pair each particular weapon off with a particular target as its partner, using weapon A to hit target A, weapon B to hit target B, and so on. Rather one should seek to discover what pattern of combination of simultaneous use of all available weapons would produce the most preferred pattern of combination of simultaneous hits on all the desirable targets. With this way of looking at things no particular weapon is concentrated on any particular target; it is the joint effect of all the weapons on all the targets which is relevant. There is no doubt that this is the way in which a control engineer would look at the problem and that in a technical sense it is the correct way to find the most preferred pattern of hits on a number of targets simultaneously.

The implication for the problems discussed in this work would be as follows. A restraint of wage rates may help both to control inflation (by restraining money costs) and to promote employment (by enabling a given level of money expenditure to purchase more output). An expansionary demand-management policy may help to promote employment (by increasing the demand for the products of labour) but it may also stoke up inflationary pressures (by enabling producers to sell at higher prices). Therefore the best strategy is to study carefully the dynamic interrelationships in the economy; and as a result of such a technical exercise to find that combination of feasible changes in wage rates and in financial policies which will provide the best possible approximation to a combination of full employment and price stability.

But it is most desirable in a modern democratic community that the ordinary man or woman in the street should as far as possible realise what is going on, with responsibilities for success or failure in the different fields of endeavour being dispersed but clearly defined and allocated. To treat the whole of macro-economic control as a single subject for the mysterious art of the control engineer is likely to appear at the best magical and at the worst totally arbitrary and unacceptable to the ordinary citizen. To put each clearly defined weapon or armoury of weapons in the charge of one particular authority or set of decision makers with the responsibility of hitting as nearly as possible one well-defined target is a much more intelligible arrangement; and if one is going to aim particular weapons at particular targets in the interests of democratic understanding and responsibility, it is most appropriate that the Central Bank, which creates money, and the Treasury, which can control the spending of it, should be responsible for preventing monetary inflations and deflations, while those who fix the wage rates in various sectors of the economy should take responsibility for the effect of their action on the resulting demands for labour.

There is a second and more substantial reason for the choice of strategy advocated in this volume. To use wage-fixing or an incomes policy as the sole or as an important contributory weapon for avoiding inflation inevitably implies the development of a detailed centralised control of a massive range of particular wage rates, as will be argued at length in Chapter VII below. It clearly involves somehow or other putting an extra *restraint* on all particular wage claims just at the time when the cost of living is *rising* rapidly; and if at the same time there is full employment resulting from demand-management policies and, as a result, no difficulty for workers in finding jobs but some difficulty for employers in finding workers, this could be done only with some system of extensive centralised control. On the other hand, a system that relies on institutions to set each particular wage rate separately with a view to the promotion of employment in each particular occupation, industry, or locality concerned could avoid the intimidating problems of a centralised incomes policy. It will be a main theme of the present volume to stress this aspect of the problem.

5. Keynes versus the Monetarists

It has been claimed above that the strategy proposed in this volume is in its real effects a Keynesian policy. But it may well be asked in what ways it differs from the proposals of the monetarists who after all argue that the control of the money supply (i.e. financial policy) should be used as the weapon to prevent inflation and that wage-bargaining should then be left free as the weapon to determine the level of employment. The term 'monetarist' can be used to cover a wide range of varieties of opinion. But in its strictest form one may perhaps interpret it as referring to those who hold (1) that the authorities should take steps to keep the total stock of money on a steady growth path and (2) that otherwise, in so far as general problems of employment, output, and price levels are concerned, decisions should be left to the market without governmental intervention.

From any such pure monetarist strategy the New Keynesian strategy advocated in this work differs in three essential ways.

First, it is not assumed that financial policy should be aimed solely at keeping the *stock* of money on a steady growth path but that it should be aimed at keeping the *flow* of money expenditures on goods and services on a steady growth path. This matter is one of the topics to be discussed in the subsequent volume on 'Demand Management'.

Second, it is not assumed that this demand management should rely solely on monetary policy, but that it should rely also — and indeed mainly — on fiscal policies. This matter will also be a topic discussed in the subsequent volume.

Third, it is not assumed that there is no need for any major reform of wage-fixing institutions. On the contrary it is a basic assumption of this work that the feasibility of any set of monetary and fiscal policies that would in effect keep the total money demand for labour on a steady 5 per cent per annum growth path depends upon its being accompanied by a suitable reform of arrangements for fixing rates of pay. If money rates of pay could be pushed up by 15 per cent in any year, total money earnings could be restricted to a rise of 5 per cent in that year only by a devastating deflation of the total demand for the products of industry sufficient to reduce by 10 per cent the number of persons in employment over whom the restricted total of money earnings was to be spread, or, in other words, to add a net figure of some two million to the number of unemployed. The two suggestions, (1) that financial policies should be designed to maintain a steady 5 per cent per annum growth in the total money demand for labour and (2) that against this background of a steady growth in the total demand for labour rates of pay should be set so as to maintain full employment, make up a single package. The financial policy is not to be attempted without suitable reform of arrangements for settling rates of pay.

6. The Transitional Problem

This means that any set of financial policies to restrain the growth rate of total money earnings to a steady 5 per cent per annum would need to be introduced in stages. Expectations of inflation cannot be removed over night. Starting from a position in which rates of pay and the cost of living were rising by 15 per cent or more a year it would be most unwise to attempt suddenly to introduce the full restraint on money earnings. Rather it would have to be done in stages. Financial restraint might be reintroduced by the announcement of a firm fiscal and monetary programme that was to limit the rate of growth of total earnings to 12.5 per cent in year 1, 10 per cent in year 2, 7.5 per cent in year 3, and 5 per cent in year 4 and every subsequent year. The successful carrying out of some such programme would be necessary to damp down inflationary expectations.

This volume is not, however, primarily concerned with these difficult and important transitional problems. It is aimed basically at answering the question: 'What sort of wage-fixing arrangements would ultimately be suitable to maintain full employment in an economy in which by monetary and fiscal policies the total money demand for labour were being consistently and successfully maintained on a steady growth path of 5 per cent per annum'? The transitional problems are, of course, of the utmost importance and present great difficulties for their solution. Reference will accordingly be made to them as the analysis proceeds.

7. The Meaning of Full Employment

There are at any one time many influences affecting the level of money
wage claims. It will be suggested in the following chapters that two important factors are: (1) the current rate of price inflation, and (2) the
general level of the current demand for labour. The higher the rate of
inflation, the higher the money claim that will be made to offset or to
anticipate the rise in the cost of living; and the higher the general level
of demand for the products of labour, the more willing will employers
be to grant any given claim and the less concerned will the workers be
about the possibility of pricing themselves out of a job.

If one considers these two factors in conjunction, there would result
at any given time a certain unemployment percentage at which the current
rate of price inflation might be expected to remain unchanged; at levels
of demand for labour greater than this the rate of price inflation might
be expected continually to accelerate and at levels of demand for labour
less than this the inflation rate might be expected to decelerate. A numerical example may serve to explain the relationship.

Suppose (1) that the current rate of inflation is 10 per cent per annum
and (2) that the rate of increase of productivity per unit of labour is
2 per cent per annum. If in these circumstances the money wage rate was
going up by 12 per cent per annum one might expect the rate of inflation
to remain at (approximately) 10 per cent per annum; for in that case
productivity would cover 2 per cent of the 12 per cent rise in wage rates
so that wage costs per unit of output would be rising by 10 per cent.
There would be a certain level of the demand for labour − that is to
say, a certain unemployment percentage − which, with the cost of living
rising at 10 per cent, would result in rises of wage rates by 12 per cent.
An unemployment percentage lower than this would represent an increased demand for labour; and this would result in rises of the rate of
pay of more than 12 per cent, in which case costs per unit of output and
so prices would start to rise by more than 10 per cent. There is thus at
any one time an unemployment percentage (what in their hideous jargon
economists have come to call the NAIRU or 'non-accelerating inflation
rate of unemployment') at which the current rate of inflation will be
maintained; if the demand for labour is raised above this rate, the rate of
price inflation will start to explode; if the demand for labour is reduced
below this level, the rate of price inflation will be damped down.

But this critical rate of unemployment at which the rate of inflation
is likely to be constant, neither accelerating nor decelerating (i.e. the
NAIRU), will itself be much affected by the wage-fixing institutions
which are currently operative. We will distinguish between two extreme
types of wage-fixing institutions: (1) those in which the primary objective
in each individual wage claim is to achieve the highest possible real wage
for the workers who are actually in employment in the occupation or

firm in question, with little or no concern for promoting the numbers employed; and (2) those which are concerned primarily with the maintenance and expansion of the volume of employment in the occupation or firm in question.

Strong monopolistic trade unions or similar organisations of workers are likely to fall more readily into the first rather than into the second of these two categories. A substantial rise in the rate of pay for their employed members is very often likely to be preferred to a smaller rise for their existing members, but one which would enable more persons to find employment in the industry or firm in question. This lack of interest in the scope for employment of persons who are not already employed in the concern or concerns covered by the wage negotiations is clearly illustrated by the current attitude to redundancies. If at the existing wage rate the size of a particular labour force must be reduced, efforts are likely to be made to achieve the run down by not replacing workers as they retire, combined perhaps with measures to encourage voluntary early retirement. This is, no doubt, a sensible arrangement, but it is wrong to represent it as being one which hurts no one − an attitude which completely ignores the welfare of the young school leavers who might find jobs in replacement of the retiring members of the workforce if the rate of pay in the firm concerned had been set at a level low enough to maintain or to expand the demand for the firm's product.

Consider then an economy in which for the vast majority of occupations and industries there are strong monopolistic trade unions, which in each particular case are making wage claims to achieve the maximum real wage for their employed members with little or no regard for the creation of new job opportunities for any unemployed outsiders. Some of these outsiders find jobs by competing with each other for places in unorganised low-paid occupations. But such occupations may be insufficient to absorb all the unemployed at rates of pay which compare favourably with the current levels of unemployment benefit or supplementary benefit available to the unemployed. In such circumstances the unemployment percentage which is needed to prevent the rate of money wage claims in the main highly organised sectors of the economy from causing an acceleration of wage costs in those sectors (i.e. the level of NAIRU) may be very high.

If, to go to the other extreme, throughout these organised sectors of the labour market the wage-fixing institutions had all been devised to set rates of pay at levels that would in each case promote the maximum level of employment in that sector, the unemployment percentage that would be compatible with no acceleration in the rate of inflation would be much lower. The rate of pay that is needed to maximise employment in any sector must, of course, be sufficiently high to attract labour to that sector. In an economy in which demand management through financial policies is successfully maintaining a steady rate of growth of 5 per cent

per annum in the demand for the services of labour, a point will necessarily be reached at which employers will need to be bidding up the
money wage rate in competition with each other in order to make their
individual offers of employment attractive. In any one sector at any one
time there will be a rate of pay that will maximise the prospect of jobs
in that sector, high enough to attract the labour force but not so high
as to restrict the demand for labour in that sector below the numbers
who would seek employment there.

If this second employment-promoting principle were adopted for
wage-fixing arrangements, the NAIRU rate of unemployment needed
to prevent an explosive inflation would be much less than it would be
if throughout the economy wages were being fixed in each sector to
maximise the standard of living of those who were already employed
in that sector. Thus, to revert to our previous example, if the rate of
inflation were 10 per cent and the rate of productivity increase were
2 per cent, wage claims at 12 per cent would be appropriate to contain
the rate of inflation at its existing rate of 10 per cent per annum. If
wage-fixing arrangements in each sector aimed at the maximisation of
the standard of living of those in employment in that sector, an unemployment percentage of 15 per cent might be necessary to prevent
wage claims from exceeding 12 per cent. But if in each sector wage rates
were set so as to maximise employment, an unemployment percentage
of only 5 per cent might be compatible with keeping wage claims down
to 12 per cent.

We will define as full employment that level of employment that would
result if, against a background of a steady growth in the total money
demand for the services of labour, the principle of wage-fixing institutions
in each sector of the economy were the promotion of employment in
that sector. The inevitable accompanying level of frictional, seasonal,
and similar unemployment we will call the full-employment rate of unemployment (or FERU). This we will contrast with the higher non-
accelerating inflation rate of unemployment (NAIRU) which would
result with wage-fixing institutions that were not designed to promote
employment. We may in fact say that FERU is what NAIRU would be
if wage-fixing institutions were reformed so as to aim throughout the
economy at the promotion of employment in each sector of the economy.

8. Wages and the Distribution of Income

If wage-fixing institutions could be so reformed that their primary function was to promote employment, the rate of pay could not simultaneously be used as a main instrument to promote a socially desirable
distribution of income. That is not to say that every wage set to promote
employment would always have undesirable distributional effects. On the

contrary, the two *desiderata* would often coincide, as for example when wage restraint in the case of a highly paid occupation would enable employment in that sector to be expanded to the advantage of less highly paid workers who could now find a job in more highly paid employment. But this coincidence of *desiderata* would not always be the case; and the setting of wage rates in each sector to promote employment in that sector would mean that the wage rate could not be used primarily either to redistribute income as between wages and profits or to offset differentials which were due to unavoidable differences in the relative scarcities of persons available for employment in different occupations, regions, or industries.

Let us consider first the distribution of income between wages and profits. As will be explained in length in Chapter II and Appendix A, inflation will result if the claims on the national output exceed the available output. Suppose wage earners claim and receive a large increase in money payment and/or profit makers greatly increase the mark-up on the labour costs of production which they use for the setting of selling prices. In so far as the money wage costs plus the increased profit margin set on those costs exceeds any increase in productivity the result will simply be an inflation of money prices. Such inflation could thus in principle arise from an excessive claim by profit makers as well as from an excessive claim by wage earners.

The figures shown on Figure 3 make it clear that the great inflation of the 1970s was not caused by a general increase of profit margins. During the 1970s there was an explosion of average weekly money earnings, which in the 1950s and 1960s had been rising at rates between 2 per cent and 8 per cent per annum and which in the 1970s rose at rates between 8 per cent and 22 per cent per annum. There seems in fact to have been in the United Kingdom and in other similar countries at the end of the 1960s a marked change in the attitude of employees, with increased pressure for rises in rates of pay; and this was much reinforced in the 1970s by the effect of the rise in the price of oil on the cost of living and thus on wage claims. The net national income is the sum of earned incomes and of incomes from property such as profits. Figure 3 shows that there was a marked reduction in the ratio of income from property to earned income during the late 1960s and 1970s. The picture is clearly one of a situation in which the upward pressure of money wage rates ate into profits, the fall in profit margins actually mitigating the rise in prices, rather than of a situation in which an increase in profit margins caused a rise of prices.*

Figure 3 shows clearly that in the 1970s it was the upward pressure of wage costs and costs of imported materials such as oil which caused

---

*The process by which an explosive upward pressure of wage claims can erode profit margins is discussed in greater detail in Appendix A.

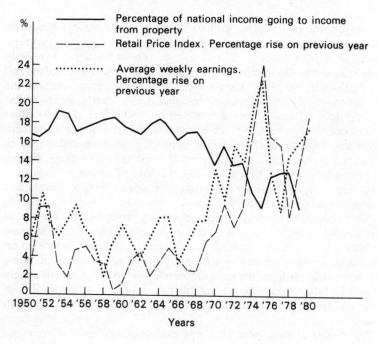

Fig. 3

the inflationary explosion and led to some erosion of incomes from property. It may be argued that an inflation of wage rates, which has the unfortunate effect of causing a price inflation, does incidentally have the desirable distributional effect of causing a shift of income from profits to wages, and is to be commended on this account. It is most desirable on grounds both of economic efficiency and of distribution that excess monopolistic profits should be avoided. There are a number of measures which are appropriate for this purpose. Wherever possible it is desirable to keep prices down through competition. For this purpose measures can be taken to prevent business restrictive practices and to control the formation of monopolies; and in Appendix D an account is given of the arrangements at present in force in the United Kingdom for this purpose. Competition can also be very effectively promoted by freedom of imports of competing foreign products. In cases where large-scale monopolistic concerns are unavoidable some form of price control may be appropriate to keep selling prices in line with costs. Nationalisation and the appropriate setting of the prices charged by the nationalised concerns is a further effective method. Action on these lines is most desirable and important.

But to rely on cost inflation as a means of eroding profits is most undesirable for two reasons. In the first place it relies upon the continuation of explosive inflationary conditions; and this is found sooner or later to lead to deflationary and restrictive financial policies in an attempt to put a stop to the inflationary explosion. There will result a reduction in employment and output; and the evil of the unemployment which will be a feature of this stagflation situation will certainly outweigh any distributional advantage from the erosion of profits. But, secondly, there is no reason to believe that the erosion of profits will not go too far. Profit is needed to meet the capital costs of production and to give an incentive for investment and enterprise in risky undertakings; and for this purpose profit must represent an adequate rate of return on the capital employed. Only if this is so will production and development take place efficiently and on a desirable scale.

This work is about wage-fixing rather than profit margins because, as is clear from Figure 3, it is wage-fixing rather than the setting of profit margins which is under present conditions the crucial matter for the control of inflation. But this does not imply that the restraint of excessive monopolistic profit is unimportant. It is of great importance mainly for other economic reasons, though it will of course incidentally make its limited contribution to keeping down the general level of selling prices.

The setting of wage rates for the promotion of employment, combined with (1) financial policies for the maintenance of a steady rate of growth in total money expenditures on goods and services and (2) effective policies for the restraint of excessive monopolistic profit margins, will result in a certain distribution between earned incomes and incomes from property. There will be inequalities as between the wealthy and the poor in the ownership of property and as between the incomes of different types of wage earners, skilled and unskilled and so on. If the setting of wage rates is to be based primarily on the promotion of employment, it cannot be used primarily for equalising the incomes as between different individuals or different families.

There is a whole battery of measures other than the fixing of wage rates which can and should be used for influencing the distribution of income and property between individuals and families. As will be argued in Chapter VI impediments to the movements of persons from low-paid to high-paid jobs should be removed. Tax measures should be taken to mitigate inequalities in post-tax incomes and to promote a wider dispersal of the ownership of property. Social benefits and welfare services such as education and health should be developed. With our present legislature, elected by adult franchise, all these measures are indeed being applied. To what extent they could be better and more effectively applied is an important matter which cannot be discussed in this book. But conditions at present are already such that there does not exist any large untapped reservoir of excess profits from which any really substantial increases in the general level of real earnings can be financed; and whether, and if so how, policies for the redistribution of income and wealth between rich and poor should be reformulated, improved, or strengthened is a matter to be determined by the action of our democratically elected Parliament and government rather than through the uncontrolled industrial action of independent monopolistic groups enabling those in the strong bargaining positions to gain at the expense of the weak.

There are great advantages in making use of fiscal and similar measures outlined in the previous paragraph rather than of wage-fixing as the basic means for influencing the distribution of income and wealth and for dealing with problems of poverty.

It releases the use of wage-fixing for its proper effective purpose, namely, for the promotion of employment in the various sectors of the economy. As we shall argue in Chapters III and IV, this is compatible with − indeed it implies − setting minimum wage rates to prevent the exploitation of low-paid workers by monopsonistic employers. But any general attempt beyond that point to improve the distribution of income by pushing up low rates of pay will make the employment of some of the persons concerned uneconomic and will thus push them into unemployment which may well be even less rewarding.

Moreover, any attempts to relieve poverty by setting a minimum wage rate raises the question whether it should be the hourly rate of pay or weekly earnings or some other measure to which the minimum should be applied. To apply the minimum to weekly earnings would be to make it impossible for an employer to take on many part-time workers (such as a married woman who wishes to supplement the family income by working for a limited number of hours each week), whereas to set the minimum for the hourly rate would not protect those who could find some work but not enough to prevent them from falling below the intended minimum.

On the other hand, fiscal and similar measures can be more effectively designed. Poverty depends so much upon the needs of the family (for example, the number of children or aged members to support) and upon the number of income-earners in the family (ranging from the single-parent family to families with a large number of adult wage-earners) that there is in fact strikingly little direct connection between low rates of pay and poverty.* Fiscal and similar measures can take into account such variations of needs and resources; simple wage-fixing for all employees in a given grade or occupation cannot do so.

---

*Professor Richard Layard summarises the statistical evidence with the statement that 'it is not true that the workers in the poorest families are mostly low-paid, nor that low-paid workers are mostly in the poorest families'. See R. Layard 'Wages policy and the redistribution of income', in D. Collard, R. Lecomber, and M. Slater, (eds.), *Income Distribution: The Limits to Redistribution,* Colston Papers No. 31 (Bristol: Scientechnica, 1980).

Political as well as economic developments have transformed the functions of the trade unions and the strike weapon as instruments for the distribution of incomes. In the early days of the nineteenth century the worker was the underdog politically as well as economically. Parliament was the preserve of the masters; legislation and its administration were heavily biased against servants and workers; the idea of achieving any decent settlement of wages through impartial arbitration based on principles acceptable to the workers or of obtaining a redistribution of income other than through industrial action could be dismissed as a utopian nonsense. But all this is different now. With adult suffrage the worker is no longer, thank goodness, politically an underdog. Through Parliament, the trade unions have in the past obtained legislation which greatly increases their monopolistic bargaining strengths. Parliament could just as effectively be used by organised popular vote to take other measures for the redistribution of income and wealth and to introduce alternative acceptable methods of fixing rates of pay.

9. Conclusion

The cure of stagflation requires action in four main economic fields.

(1) Financial policies (fiscal, monetary, and foreign exchange) should be so designed as to keep the total money demand for goods and services on a moderate steady growth path.

(2) There should be a set of policies for the promotion of competition, the control of prices and the setting of charges by nationalised concerns in order to restrain excessive monopolistic profit margins.

(3) There should be a battery of fiscal, social security, and welfare meaures to influence the distribution of income and wealth between individuals and families.

(4) There should be a radical reform of wage-fixing arrangements such that the primary concern of wage-setting in each sector of the economy will be to promote employment in that sector.

This volume is concerned solely with the fourth of these problems, not because the others are unimportant but because the radical reform of wage-fixing arrangements is the crucial element in the whole structure which is much the most difficult to achieve politically and about which there is the most uncertainty.

CHAPTER II

Effects of Wage-Fixing on Unemployment and Inflation

In the preceding chapter we expressed the opinion that one of the main factors leading to the present combination of unemployment and inflation was the increased ability and willingness of trade unions and similar monopolistic pressure groups to aim at increases in real standards of living which exceed the increases in real output available after deduction of an acceptable profit margin. In this chapter we will examine more closely the causes and effects of this wage-fixing phenomenon, which operates through uncontrolled monopolistic wage bargaining and which results, with or without the concomitant of strikes, lock-outs, or similar industrial dislocation, in the setting of fixed minimum wage rates in the various sectors of the economy.

1. Wage-Fixing and Demand Management

Such wage-fixing has some very important implications for the general working of the economic system.

A first and basic implication is the Keynesian one, namely, that the impact effect of a fluctuation in the general level of money demand for goods and services is likely to be a variation in the quantities of goods and services produced rather than a variation in the price at which a given quantity will be provided. Thus suppose that for some reason or another the total money expenditure on the products of industry falls. Producers may shade down somewhat the prices which they charge for their products. But if the money wage which they have to pay remains obstinately fixed, they will necessarily have to maintain their prices in order to cover their costs and as a result will have to reduce their output and their employment of labour, selling a smaller output at a maintained price rather than a maintained output at a lower price.

And it is of the essence of present arrangements that the money wage rate should be fixed so that employers cannot obtain a reduced wage rate simply by employing fewer workers; and in Chapter IV we will explain why wage-fixing institutions of this kind have an important role to play in our economic system. It is possible that after a time, when a reduced demand for the products of industry has thus led to heavy and continuing unemployment, new and lower money wage rates will be fixed, as the

pressure of the unemployed in the labour market in search of jobs under-
mines the power of the wage-fixing trade unions concerned. But by that
time the damage will have been done; the economy will be in recession
with low output and a number of workers involuntarily unemployed, as a
result of a decline in the money demand for the products of industry.

Conversely, starting from a position of considerable unemployment of
labour and other resources, in an economy in which money wage rates
are fixed by the action of trade unions or similar organisations the impact
effect of an increase in the total level of money expenditure on the
products of industry is likely to be an increase in the quantity produced
rather than an increase in the price charged for an unchanged quantity.

For this reason, in building any simplified model of a modern industrialised economic system as a whole it is important to allow for the fact
that the impact effects of changes in the total level of money demands for
goods and services will be upon the levels of output and employment
rather than on the levels of money prices and money wage rates. Changes
in the general level of money prices and costs can then be regarded as
occurring as the result of changes which may occur from time to time in
the levels at which money wage rates are fixed.* Such changes may, of
course, be influenced by the level of unemployment in the economy,
wages being fixed at rather higher or lower rates accordingly as the amount
of involuntary unemployment persists at a low or high level. Indeed, it is a
main thesis of this book that they should be so set.

If that were the end of the matter, there would be little to worry about.
Techniques of monetary policy and of fiscal policy for stimulating or
restraining the total level of money expenditures on goods and services can
be devised; and the obvious policy would be simply to expand or contract
total money expenditures so as to maintain a steady demand for goods and
services at a level sufficient to provide full employment without causing
any inflationary excess demand. Indeed this is the simple Orthodox
Keynesian prescription; and it is of interest to trace its development in
order to understand why it is not itself a sufficient answer to our present
discontents.

For this purpose we must go back to the great depression of the 1930s
in order to trace the history of the Keynesian ideas. At that time there

---

*Models of the economy which are constructed on this basis may be called
'Keynesian'. Other models – often called 'equilibrium' models – have been constructed which assume that it is prices rather than quantities which respond to
fluctuations in demand. Those who construct such models are logically compelled to
conclude, as indeed they expressly do, that all unemployment is voluntary in the
sense that the unemployed person prefers unemployment rather than reducing the
wage which he demands to the level needed to find himself a job. I find this a strange
way of describing the world and repeat my desire that on my tombstone should be
inscribed the words "He tried in his time to be an Economist; but Commonsense
would keep breaking in".

developed a great deficiency of effective demand for goods and services throughout the world economy. Men and machines lay idle and foodstuffs and raw materials piled up in unused heaps, although at the same time impoverished citizens throughout the world were in crying need of food, shelter, warmth, and clothes, to say nothing of some of the amenities of life. This poverty in the midst of potential plenty was a phenomenon which many regarded as both foolish and wicked. It was in these circumstances that Keynes elaborated his system of thought whereby in such conditions the governments of the world might in concert stimulate effective demands for goods and services — demands the satisfaction of which would relieve poverty and the fulfilment of which would at the same time provide work for the unemployed.

The weapons recommended for this process of stimulating effective demand were of three kinds. First, public authorities might themselves spend more on public works of various kinds — road-making, housing projects, capital development in nationalised industries, and so on. Second, the Central Bank could take steps to increase the supply of money and to reduce the rates of interest at which funds could be borrowed for investment in capital development of every kind in the private sector of the economy. Third, rates of tax might be reduced and social benefits and similar governmental outlays increased in order to leave the ordinary tax-paying citizen with a larger amount of tax-free income to spend on goods and services. The immediate increases in incomes caused by these initial increases in expenditures on goods and services would lead to further secondary increases in expenditures and so in incomes, which in turn would lead to further tertiary increases, and so on.

This Keynesian technique of demand management, as it came to be known, was never designed to cope with all forms of unemployment. In a dynamic economy there will always be some people on the move from contracting to expanding activities, and they will be without work during this frictional process of movement. Moreover, structural industrial situations can arise in which workers remain unemployed in spite of a strong demand for their products because of an inadequate supply of specialised machinery or of a few specially skilled workers needed to cooperate with them in the productive process.

Keynes never intended that his demand-management techniques should be used to cope with such frictional and structural unemployment, but only with what we may call general unemployment; namely, with those situations in which there is widespread unemployment of labour and of capital equipment of all kinds, due to a general deficiency of demand for the products of industry.

It is, of course, impossible to draw a hard and fast line between these different types of unemployment. Even at the bottom of the most severe general depression there may be some few industries producing new products in which the available specialised equipment and specialised labour force are insufficient to cope with the demand. As general demand is stimulated, there will be more and more particular bottlenecks of this kind where demand is excessive in relation to potential specialised productive resources. If demand-management policies were being used to control the level of *real* output and employment rather than the level of *money* expenditure, it would be difficult to say at what precise point one should regard general unemployment to have disappeared and the remaining pockets of unemployment to be wholly frictional or structural cases; but at some point the line would have to be drawn.

Keynes was a practical man. He did his great work on these subjects in the 1930s when there was heavy unemployment in an atmosphere of falling rather than rising money costs and prices. He was not then concerned with the danger that a policy of demand management for the reduction of unemployment might be frustrated by an explosion of money wage costs. But in the discussions of plans for postwar reconstruction he was very conscious of this danger for the post Second World War economy.

Thus during the 1930s Keynes was preaching the doctrine that governments should take on one more important function; namely, that of demand management. During the war, thought was given to postwar reconstruction; and in the White Paper of 1944 on Employment Policy* general demand management for the maintenance of full employment was officially recognised by the all-party government in the UK to be a proper governmental function. Nor was this great revolution of thought confined to the UK. In the United States a similar governmental obligation to be concerned with maintaining a high level of employment was recognised by an Act of Congress. Indeed, when Keynes died in April 1946, at the very moment of a transition from war to peace economy, he left a world in which virtually all the governments of our type of country were explicitly or implicitly committed to Keynesian policies of demand management.

There followed a quarter of a century of the most unparalleled economic growth and prosperity. We in the UK are sometimes apt to think of it as a period of failure. This is the exact opposite of the truth in that our standards of living have never grown at a faster rate. Our problem during those years was that other countries were doing even better than we were.

But over the last few years it has all turned sour, and we are now cursed with the epidemic of stagflation. What has happened? There are two main factors at work: first, the temptation for the politicians to use the tools of demand management for the overstimulation of the economy and, second, the uncontrolled power of labour monopolies to press for wage increases.

In the old days of the Gold Standard and of Balanced Budgets, there was little or no opportunity for the authorities to exercise discretionary power over the level of total demand. The supply of money and the

*Government White Paper. Employment Policy. Cmd 6727. May 1944.

consequential ease or tightness of funds on the capital market had to be managed by the Central Bank with the overriding purpose of keeping the sterling price of gold fixed in a free world market for gold. The rigid conventional requirement that the government's budget should be balanced except in extreme crisis such as that of a major war made it impossible to vary government expenditures and taxes so as to stimulate demand through budget deficits. The Keynesian revolution replaced both these rigid conventional constraints — indeed, one might almost call them constitutional constraints — with the simple hope that politicians would have the good sense to use their discretionary powers over monetary and fiscal policies in a disciplined manner.

But expansion of demand is always more attractive politically than contraction. Making funds available at cheaper rates for house purchase, paying larger child benefits or old-age pensions, reducing the rate of income tax — all these are policies which provide immediate specific benefits to specific groups of voters. The inflationary dangers which may result are vague, dispersed, and delayed; and a week is a long time in politics. On the contrary, to contract demand hits certain specific citizens clearly and immediately, and the advantages of avoiding inflation are vague, dispersed, and delayed. As a result the stimulation of the economy through demand-management techniques has on balance been overdone.

After 1922 in the interwar period in the UK the unemployment percentage (except for one or two months) never fell below 10 per cent and in 1932 rose to 23 per cent. After the Second World War for many years the economy was driven at unemployment percentages of between 1.5 per cent and 2.5 per cent (see Figure 1), while 3 per cent was regarded by some as a threat of serious unemployment. There is no doubt that Keynesian stimulation of demand has been used to tackle frictional and structural as well as general unemployment.

Trouble of an explosive–inflationary kind then arises because of the combination of the adoption of such Keynesian policies of expanding demand for the maintenance of very low levels of unemployment with methods of wage-fixing through trade unions and similar monopolistic pressure groups, which enable them to aim at increases in real standards of living which exceed the available increases in real output.

For many years after the Second World War there was in fact strong pressure on Keynesian grounds to design monetary and fiscal policies in such a way as to maintain very low levels of unemployment with little regard to what was happening to money rates of pay. On this principle, however rapidly money pay was being pushed up, demand-management policies were to be sufficiently expansionary for the whole output of goods and services to find purchasers even though their money costs and prices might be much inflated. Policies with this effect have been promoted not only on the general, or 'macro', level of monetary and budgetary strategy but also in particular, or 'micro', cases of lame ducks such as

British Leyland, where from time to time government funds have been provided to maintain output and employment somewhat independently of the level at which rates of pay might be set.

2. Over-Ambitious Wage Claims

This expectation that very full employment would be maintained by monetary and fiscal policies with little regard to the level of money pay has encouraged the idea that it is the duty of the financial authorities rather than of the wage-fixing institutions to cope with unemployment. Monopolistic organisations of workers are able, and are thus encouraged, to make wage claims which are not designed to promote employment but rather simply to improve the standard of living for the employed members of the particular group of workers in question; and there have been many developments which have increased the bargaining powers of trade unions and similar monopolistic pressure groups and have encouraged the use of such powers:

(1) The legal position of trade unions has in recent years been such as to endow them with very extensive monopolistic powers to reinforce their wage claims. The position will be described in Chapter V.

(2) Developments of modern technology have increased the power of small compact groups of workers to hold up large ranges of economic activity: a few computer operatives to put a stop to large governmental processes, a limited number of producers of a vital component to halt important assembly lines, a few air traffic controllers to close a major international airport, a limited number of electrical engineers to cripple industry, and so on, with the result that at a very small cost in strike pay for a small number of strikers a very large amount of economic loss can be inflicted.

(3) At the same time markets for the products of individual manufacturing concerns have become more differentiated, with the result that individual productive concerns face less perfectly competitive markets for their products. Each individual enterprise is *pro tanto* less averse to granting a pay rise and to covering the consequential rise in its cost by an offsetting rise in the price charged for its product. The resistance of the employing enterprise to a pay claim is thus reduced.*

(4) The development in some cases of wage-bargaining for whole sectors of the economy rather than for smaller competing parts of it means that individual employers will be less hesitant to grant wage increases since they know that their immediate competitors will be facing similar cost increases.

*See Tibor Scitovsky, 'Market power and inflation', *Economica*, August, 1978.

(5) The very marked rises in real rates of pay and standards of living which have taken place since the bad old days of the 1930s have meant that workers have more capital resources behind them and thus a greater staying power if they do decide to strike or take other industrial action which will cause a temporary decline in their incomes.

(6) Rates of unemployment and supplementary benefit have also improved since the bad old days of the 1930s. This development, which is greatly to be welcomed, has probably had the incidental effect of reducing somewhat the pressure from unemployed workers to seek jobs even at low rates of pay.

The result has been on the part of the trade unions the formulation, and on the part of the employers the concession, of money wage claims which aim at an over-ambitious rise in the real standard of living of the workers. Wage claims may be described in general as being over-ambitious if for the economy as a whole they represent a demand for a rise in the real standard of living which exceeds the rise in real output per head and so in the real supply of goods and services available, after making allowance for an acceptable profit margin, to satisfy the desired higher level of consumption. Each separate group may be demanding a real rise in earnings (e.g. of 10 per cent) which it knows well exceeds the general increase in goods and services which will be available for real consumption; but each group may feel that it is entitled to an improvement in its own standard even if this means an improvement at the expense of some other group. However, if all or most groups are simultaneously making real demands which exceed the real available supplies, they obviously cannot all be satisfied. They will in fact be frustrated by an unanticipated degree of inflation of the cost of living which unexpectedly reduces the real value of their money wage claim.

There are many particular forms which this system of over-ambitious wage claims may take and many ways in which the consequential inflation may develop.* But in essence the process is a simple one which may be illustrated by the following numerical example.

Suppose that we are all organised into powerful pressure groups of trade unions, professional associations, giant business corporations, industrial cartels and the like, each tight group prepared to use its monopoly powers to enforce its own claims on the national income. Suppose that we all demand a rise in our real standards of pay of, say, 5 per cent a year; but suppose that productivity per head is rising only by, say, 2 per cent a year. We all start this year by demanding our 5 per cent rise in money pay. This causes money costs per unit of output to go up by 3 per cent, since improved productivity will account for only 2 per cent of the 5 per cent rise in money wage costs. Except in so far as

*The matter is analysed in more precise detail in Appendix A.

profit margins are excessive, reductions in output and increases in un-employment can be avoided only if total money demands for goods are allowed to expand so that producers can sell their outputs at prices inflated by 3 per cent to cover the 3 per cent rise in their costs. In this case, the cost of living will go up by 3 per cent. Next year we will demand an 8 per cent rise in pay of which 3 per cent is designed to offset the current rate of inflation of the cost of living and 5 per cent to give us the real rise in our standards which we are demanding. But this 8 per cent rise in money wages will cause a 6 per cent rise in money costs on our assumption that improved productivity continues to reduce costs by only 2 per cent per annum. If selling prices are to keep in line with costs and unemployment is thus to be avoided, selling prices must rise by 6 per cent. The following year, therefore, we all demand a wage increase of 11 per cent, of which 6 per cent is designed to offset the inflation of the cost of living and 5 per cent to give us our real rise. And so on. Each year the rate of price inflation increases probably in an explosive manner as soon as we start to put forward wage claims designed not merely to make up for past rises in the cost of living but to anticipate future increases in the rate of inflation.

Attempts to get a quart out of a pint pot will, of course, always be frustrated; but the process can have some very unfortunate side effects. It leads to an increasingly serious problem of uncontrolled inflation or an increasingly serious problem of unemployment or some combination of the two.

3.　The Effect of the Oil Crisis

This quart-out-of-a-pint-pot syndrome can arise either because our thirst expands from a pint to a quart or because the capacity of the pot shrinks from a quart to a pint. Our present severe attack of stagflation was triggered off by the shrinkage of the capacity of the pot which occurred as a result of the fourfold increase in the price of oil in the mid-1970s.

From a Keynesian full-employment point of view this led to a deficiency of total effective demand; the oil producers refrained from spending and saved much of the abrupt increase in their incomes; the consumers paid more for oil and had so much less to spend on their own outputs of goods and services; the maintenance of full employment called for a Keynesian stimulation of demand.

On the other hand, from a cost–price–inflation point of view the situation called for anti-inflationary policies. The change was equivalent to a reduction of real output per head in the oil importing countries, since each unit of their manufactures would exchange for less imported oil. For full employment this called for some reduction in the real wage rate. The cost of living rose because of the rise in the price of oil; and to maintain employment without any additional inflation of money costs and prices it would have been necessary to resist increases in rates of pay in spite of the increase in the cost of living. But there was a natural attempt to maintain previous rates of increase in real pay and to push up pay increases sufficiently to take into account the increased cost of living due to the increased price of imported oil.

The result was a sudden intensification of the dilemma of stagflation as the capacity of the pot suddenly shrank from a quart to a pint.

The continuing oil crisis is a very serious matter. If it were true (1) that there was a rigidly fixed ratio between the oil required for each person's employment and (2) that there was a definite fixed reduction in the supply of oil, a predetermined increase in the level of unemployment would be inevitable. The situation is, however, not as traumatic as that, since there are many ways in which oil use per man employed can be reduced. There are a number of uses of oil which are not tied to employment levels, such as the use of the private motor car and the domestic heating of dwelling houses; some forms of employment (e.g. many services) require much less energy per person employed than do other industrial processes; there are many ways in which in industry energy used per man employed can be reduced by using alternative technologies which depend more on labour and less on other forms of energy; there are alternative sources of energy to be developed. To set in motion and to make profitable the various economies and substitutions requires that the price of oil should be allowed to rise relatively to the price of other goods and services, including the price of labour. The real wage rate must be reduced, or at least rise less rapidly than it would have done in the absence of the oil crisis, if employment is to be maintained and indeed expanded. The oil crisis greatly increases but does not totally transform the problem of stagflation.

The rise in the price of oil implies a redistribution of real income. Out of the sale proceeds from any given real output a larger proportion must go to the owners of the oil and a smaller proportion to the workers who have produced the product with the aid of the oil. In the mid-1970s the initial oil crisis implied a redistribution from the citizens of the UK to the Arab owners of the imported oil. But in the present continuing crisis, with North Sea oil coming to cover the whole of UK requirements the redistribution is from UK citizens as workers to the UK-owned North Sea Oil. In so far as this means that the revenues of the UK government from royalties and taxation of oil are increased, the redistribution is from UK citizens as workers to UK citizens as taxpayers. In so far as this is the case, it means that there is no need for a reduction in real *post-tax* earnings, though it does not modify the fact that there must be a reduction in real *pre-tax* earnings. Wage costs must go up less than the cost of oil to give the necessary incentives to economise in the use of oil; in other words pre-tax rates of pay must not rise in such a way as to offset the rise in the cost of living due to the rise in the price of oil. But in so far as the increased price of oil reverts to the UK government the revenue could be used to reduce rates of tax and thus to sustain post-tax increases.

4. The Distribution of Wage Income

In addition to the quart-out-of-a-pint-pot syndrome, there is another kind of explosive mechanism which may also be at work and which we may call the keeping-up-with-the-Joneses syndrome. People are very concerned with wage differentials. Smith feels badly used not simply because his pay is low but also because he has lost out in comparison with Jones. Suppose that candlestick makers consider that they should be paid 5 per cent more than butchers and bakers and that at the same time butchers and bakers consider that they should be paid at least as much as candlestick makers. Starting from the same wage the candlestick makers demand a 5 per cent rise. The butchers and bakers respond quickly with a demand for a similar 5 per cent rise in order to keep in line with the candlestick makers. The candlestick makers then respond with another 5 per cent demand in order to get ahead once more, to which the butchers and bakers respond with another 5 per cent demand in order to catch up once more. And so on. In vain attempts to escape from the frustration of this leap-frogging process each group may put forward its claims more and more rapidly and may put forward on each occasion larger and larger claims in an attempt to offset in advance the anticipated counter-claims of the other group. In these conditions the rate of wage inflation will quickly explode.

As explained above, recent developments have increased the ability and the willingness of groups of workers to press for ambitious wage claims; and as one group after another has successfully exercised its increased muscle power, the message has spread. Group after group has come to realize that it has latent monopolistic bargaining powers, the extent of which it had not previously appreciated; and group after group has come to be willing to use such powers with less and less regard for their unfortunate effects upon the community.

This presents a difficult moral issue in the case of groups of workers in particularly sensitive sectors of the economy. Should they be less free than others to exercise their muscle power? Consider the case of the hospital nurses or the police who have refused to take industrial action, though their latent bargaining power may well be as great as, or even greater than, that of, for example, the coal miners. With a three-day week in industry and a certain amount of shivering at home the community can sit out quite a lengthy coal strike. But how long could it hold out if all hospitals and police services were completely closed down?

Before one is free with one's condemnations of any such group which has not refrained from action one needs to consider carefully the pressures on a group which sees other groups receiving large increases of pay by the exercise of monopolistic bargaining power and which is asked to deny itself a similar rise in pay by refraining on humanitarian grounds from exercising its own even greater bargaining power. School workers, hospital workers, and social workers cannot, like miners and lorry drivers, confine their activities to crippling industry and causing widespread unemployment; they have the stark choice between hurting the children, the sick, and the deprived or doing nothing.

Or consider the case of such trade union leaders as Mr Tom Jackson of the Post Office workers or Mr Sidney Weighell of the Railway workers who at the Trade Union Congress in 1978 opposed the return to uncontrolled monopoly bargaining and who with other trade union leaders have argued for an alternative Better Way for fixing money wage rates at fair and uninflated levels. When later they in turn put forward claims for large percentage pay increases on behalf of their own members, backed by the implied threat of industrial action, they are accused of humbug and hypocrisy, of talking big about moderation in general and then putting in excessive claims for their own members. But such accusations are grossly unfair. There is nothing at all hypocritical or inconsistent in arguing for an alternative method to be applied simultaneously to all groups for the attainment of fair but moderate pay settlements, and at the same time making sure that, if there is to be a continuation of uncontrolled monopoly bargaining, then in the consequential free-for-all their own members — in the immortal words of Mr Frank Cousins — are going to be part of the all. A statesman who argues for an international disarmament treaty is not a hypocrite because, in the absence of such a treaty, he maintains the armed power of his own country.

The free-for-all devil-take-the-hindmost that results from the present methods of settlements of pay through uncontrolled monopoly bargaining inflicts severe moral damage on society. The spread of the ideas that each group should be free to form a powerful independent monopoly, should be judge in its own cause as to what its pay ought to be, should be given special legal privileges to enable it more effectively to inflict damage on others until its aims are achieved, and, if it is to compete successfully in its claims *vis-à-vis* other monopolistic groups, must be ready to become less and less compassionate, scrupulous, and conscience-stricken in the means that it chooses to employ — all this encourages the present increasing disregard of the rule of law and thus helps to undermine an essential foundation for a decent society. This damage to the fabric of society may well be the most important aspect of the matter. To have one's rate of pay determined by impartial arbitral award rather than by causing discomfort and distress to one's fellow citizens would be to respect the rule of law in preference to the methods of unarmed guerilla warfare.

The distress and discomfort which is caused when one group of workers takes industrial action is no longer confined to the employers of those workers. Indeed it falls nowadays primarily upon other groups of wage earners.

In the bad old days of the early nineteenth century the strike was the only weapon available to a group of workers; it was aimed at an employer or a limited group of employers whose profits were to be hit by the discontinuance of production and who might, therefore, stand to lose less by accepting the strikers' demands than by the continuation of the strike. Workers could make real gains at the expense of the excess profits of a group of employers who were in open or tacit combination to hold wages down.

This is no longer the typical situation. It is manifestly not so in the case of a nationalised industry or of public employment. If the miners obtain a higher wage, then either the government's budget revenue suffers through the reduced profits or increased losses of the National Coal Board — in which case it is the general taxpayer or those whose welfare depends upon government expenditures who suffer — or else the price of coal is raised and the miners gain at the expense of the general consumers of coal. Similarly, if school workers and hospital workers receive higher wages, there is no Gradgrind unscrupulous employer at the expense of whose excess profits they can be paid. In fact the increase in their wage will be at the expense of the rate payers or taxpayers or, if increased wage costs lead to some reduction of service, at the expense of the school children or the hospital patients.

Even in the private sector of the economy any gains in real earnings to be achieved in today's conditions from a further general squeeze in profits are very limited. Of the net national income no less than 90 per cent now accrues to earned incomes* leaving only 10 per cent for incomes from property of all kinds. Thus a 20 per cent cut in total incomes from property would be needed to obtain a once-for-all increase of 2 per cent in earned incomes, a rise which could be obtained continually year after year by a normal increase in productivity. These figures are for incomes before tax; the distribution of incomes after tax is even more heavily weighted in favour of earned incomes. Moreover a substantial part of company profits and other forms of incomes from property accrue to pension funds and thus to the support of retired workers. Indeed no less than 50 per cent of the securities quoted on the Stock Exchange are now held by pension funds and other similar institutions. And some level of profits is in any case necessary to meet necessary capital costs, to maintain incentives in industry, and in particular to promote investment and capital development. The level of real earnings today is dependent above all on the size of the national cake rather than on its distribution, on output per worker rather than on any reduction of excess profits.

*Income from Employment (employed plus self-employed) as a percentage of Gross Domestic Product less Capital Consumption, Average 1975–1977. See Figure 3.

This means that, if any one group does succeed in obtaining an exceptionally large increase in pay, any resulting real rise in its standards in excess of the general increase in productivity in the country as a whole is likely to be achieved primarily at the expense of other earners. It will result in the inflation of the prices of its products which are charged to other earners, the extent to which it can be financed by a further squeeze on profits being very limited.

Uncontrolled monopoly bargaining by labour organisations is not the appropriate means for correcting any undesirable distribution of income between rich and poor, between the low-paid and the high-paid members of society. It is true that in its idealistic political mood the trade union movement as a whole presses for improvements for the low-paid. In their realistic down-to-earth bargaining mood the particular unions which represent the better paid press for a restoration of their differentials. As we have seen, these leap-frogging movements intensify the problem of stagflation; and there is no reason to believe that the low-paid will beat the strong and highly organised in the rat race. Successful monopolistic action by any one highly organised group to maintain relatively high rates of pay either by restricting entry into the trade or by compelling employers to refrain from offering additional jobs at a somewhat lower rate of pay will involve pushing some workers out into the cold of unemployment or of employment in less attractive jobs at lower rates of pay.

This does not imply that we should be unconcerned about the distribution of income and property between rich and poor. On the contrary, as has been argued in Section 8 of Chapter I, there is much that can and should be done by alternative measures which would in fact be more effective instruments than would the use of wage-fixing for the purpose of obtaining a more satisfactory distribution of income and wealth.

5. Wages and the Cost of Living

The transformation that is needed in the principles on which rates of pay should be set if they are to be used to promote employment is a radical one. In particular it means that less emphasis must be put upon the attainment or preservation of a given real wage and much more on the level of the money wage which, given the steady 5 per cent per annum growth in the total demand for labour, will promote employment in any given sector of the economy.

This basic fact is perhaps most vividly illustrated by the effects of the dramatic rise in the price of oil, which were described above. For full employment real wage rates must vary with changes in real productivity, including changes in the terms of trade between the products of the country's labour and other products. If full employment is to be maintained with a steady rate of growth of the total *money* demand for labour, then the *money* wage rate must grow in a corresponding steady manner. It must not be sharply raised because the cost of living has gone up as a result of some drastic deterioration in productivity or in the terms of trade; and conversely, of course, the money wage rate need not be cut because costs and prices have fallen as a result of an improvement in productivity or the terms of trade.

A similar consideration can arise from variations in tax rates resulting from changes in the finance needed for schemes of government expenditure. Thus a rise in indirect taxes imposed to finance some increased programme of public expenditure will raise the cost of living. If there is a steady rate of growth in the total money demand for labour, any abrupt rise in the money wage rate to offset the rise in the cost of living will cause unemployment. In fact, of course, the effect of the rise in the cost of living due to the increased level of indirect taxation in reducing the level of *real* consumption is the way in which resources are planned by the government's fiscal policy to be released for the increased programme of government expenditure. Once more the converse proposition is also true. There is no call for a reduction in money wage rates to offset the fact that a fall in the cost of living due to a reduction in rates of indirect taxation will otherwise raise the real purchasing power of money wage incomes — that is precisely what it is designed to do.

There is one further reason why, if demand-management policies are effectively designed to maintain a steady rate of growth in the total money demand for labour, the wage rate must not be closely tied to the cost of living. Any such close tie of wage rates to the cost of living may in such circumstances lead to great instability in the economy. The reasons for this are formulated with more precision in Appendix B. They are of the following kind: a high money wage fixed in period 1 will lead to a high level of money costs and so of the cost of living and so to a still higher level of wage rates in period 2; but that will lead to much unemployment in period 2, since the total money demand for labour is *ex-hypothesi* not inflated to cover the higher wage rates; this collapse in the demand for labour can then cause a sharp fall in the rate of rise of money wage rates in period 3 which will lead to a lower rise in the cost of living and so to a still lower rise in money wage rates which, with a steady total demand for labour, will cause a big increase in the level of employment, which can cause a large rise in the money wage rate; and so once more around the cycle.

This means that, if demand-management policies are going to maintain a steady rate of growth at 5 per cent per annum in the total money demand for labour, there must be a corresponding normal rate of rise in money wage rates, variations of particular settlements above or below this norm in any one sector of the economy depending upon the need for larger or smaller rises to promote employment in that sector. These settlements must not be tied to current variations in the cost of living.

As will be argued at length in Chapters VII and VIII, it would be helpful if there could be a periodic authoritative statement of what the appropriate norm should be; and any such reform could be adapted for application in the transitional period. Thus, while a more or less constant 5 per cent per annum 'norm' might well be desirable as a permanent institution, a gradually falling 'norm' from year to year — for example, from 10 per cent in year 1, to 7.5 per cent in year 2, to 5 per cent in year 3 and subsequent years — could be announced as operative during the process from a period of rapid inflation to one of stability. This series of norms for wage increases during the transitional period would be geared to the transitional rates of rise of the total money demand for labour which were planned to be made operative from year to year by means of financial demand-management policies.

Thus there would be no call for any drastic slashing of real wage rates during the transitional period; the 'norm' increase in the money wage rate would broadly speaking match the transitional 'norm' increase in the total money demand for labour. There might, however, be some temporary decline in real wage rates due to the restoration of profit margins which had been eroded during the preceding process of explosive wage-cost inflation. During that process selling prices may have been adjusted to rising money wage costs only after a certain time lag with the result that money wages had at any one time risen relatively to the price of the products of industry, with the two-fold result that the real wage was unnaturally inflated and the real profit margin undesirably deflated. As the rate of cost-price inflation falls off, this distortion will be removed. (The process is more precisely formulated in Appendix A.)

But in contrast to this restoration of the profit margin there will in the transitional period be two forces working in the opposite direction which will help to maintain and to raise the real purchasing power of money earnings. In the first place, there will be the regular continuing rise in output per head due to technical progress; and, secondly, as we have explained in Section 4 of Chapter I, there will also be the special but important once-for-all rise in real spendable incomes which will result from the spreading both of private overheads in industry as total output rises, with the consequential reduction of cost per unit of output, and also of public overheads in the budget, with a consequential reduction in the need for tax revenue as the cost of unemployment relief falls and the tax base is restored from its previous low stagflationary level. Provided that profit margins are controlled by competition or other measures of the kind enumerated in Section 8 of Chapter I, the fixing of money wage rates without direct reference to the cost of living but for the promotion of employment against the background of a steady growth in the total money demand for the products of labour carries no threat to — indeed, on the contrary, it promises nothing but good for — the real purchasing power of money earnings.

6.   Conclusions

For the reasons outlined in this and the preceding chapter one may conclude that (1) the primary objective of wage-fixing should be the promotion
of employment, but (2) that this will be effective only if accompanied
by successful monetary and fiscal policies to ensure the maintenance of a
steady rate of growth in total money expenditures on goods and services
and so in the demand for labour, and (3) that it will be acceptable in a
humane, compassionate society only if it is accompanied by a battery of
other measures for ensuring a socially acceptable distribution of income
and wealth.

CHAPTER III

Other Criteria for Fixing Rates of Pay

The thesis of this work is that against the background of a battery of other measures for affecting the distribution of incomes and property and against the background of monetary and budgetary measures to ensure a steady rate of expansion in the total demand for labour, the overriding criterion for fixing rates of pay should be the promotion of employment. How far does this criterion conflict with the other criteria which are often considered for this purpose? Three alternative criteria are often proposed, namely:

(1) comparability with the rates of pay of other workers;
(2) the linking of rates of pay with improved productivity;
(3) the special improvement of conditions for low-paid workers.

1. Comparability

It has been fashionable in the UK to consider the fixing of wage rates in particular sectors of the economy by the institution of special independent commissions to make comparability studies with the pay of similar workers in other sectors. But in an economy with free and costless movement and freedom from any unnecessary restrictions on entry into alternative occupations, industries and regions, the institutionalisation of this principle would be unnecessary; the primary basic comparability could be left to the individual worker to vote with his or her feet. To set wage rates and conditions of employment in the various sectors of the economy which would recruit sufficient, but not more than sufficient, workers to meet the demand for labour in that sector would serve to promote employment without causing unemployment; and with free and costless movement of workers it is the same thing as setting wage rates and conditions which compare adequately with wage rates and conditions in the other sectors which compete for similar workers. All that one would need do would be to let the individual workers do their own comparability studies and let wages and conditions of work then be set at levels sufficient to man up or to woman up the various competing sectors of the economy.

If movement from one job to another were in fact easy and costless that would be all that one need say on the subject of comparability. Let the individual workers compare and choose for themselves. But movement is not completely free and costless and, as a result, is slow and sluggish. As will be argued later, this makes it desirable to pay regard not only to the immediate current situation but also to probable future developments in an employment situation, in order to judge whether a wage is appropriate to maintain a balance between supply and demand over a reasonable period of time. Judgements of this kind should properly rest on comparability studies in the sense that it is necessary to judge whether a given wage level in one sector of the economy, when compared with the wages and conditions likely to be available for similar workers in other sectors of the economy, would be appropriate over the longer run to attract and retain the labour force that would be needed to maintain a balance between supply and demand in the sector concerned.

Whether or not a present wage offer needs to be improved in order to avoid a future deficiency of labour is, of course, a matter on which opinions can differ and which inevitably rests upon hypothetical judgements. It is just the sort of question which calls for an impartial, expert assessment of the kind which will be discussed in Chapter VIII. To this extent, the principle of comparability is needed in order to set wage rates which will balance supply and demand in the various sectors of the economy. But to press the principle of comparability beyond that is to embark on a mysterious metaphysical exercise. How is one to balance job security and pension rights against high immediate pay, or how to balance a quiet life at a routine job against a tiring but exciting job but with longer holidays? Different individuals have different valuations of the different characteristics of different jobs. One can do no more than try to assess whether at given relative rates of pay sufficient individuals prefer one job to another.

This distrust of what may be called administrative comparability has some rather far-reaching implications, which can perhaps best be illustrated by reviewing it in its most extreme form. Consider then a system of national job evaluation which by giving marks to every relevant aspect of every job — responsibility, unpleasantness, degree of skill, dexterity, etc. — produced a national rate of pay for every job or rather a national scale of relativities of pay between all the jobs in the community. Jobs could be compared on the job-evaluation scale and it would be clear which jobs were to be regarded as meriting the same rates of pay and which were not.

But how would one fix the absolute level of money rates of pay? There would have to be some centralised method for fixing the level of a basic wage or of some particular rate of pay, which, since the relativities would be settled by the job evaluation scales, would peg all the rates of pay. In other words, there would be a complete centrally determined wages policy. Less extensive systems of administered comparability would not lead to this extreme result. But the problem remains. The more extensive the system of administered comparability between a large range of occupations, the more important and the more difficult becomes the problem of deciding how and by whom the absolute level of any given group of comparable jobs is to be settled.

Less complete and more *ad hoc* arrangements for comparability studies which are unrelated to the balance between the supply and demand for labour in the sector of the economy under examination are a sure way of organising an inflationary upward pressure of money wage rates. Such exercises are never addressed to the question whether the wage rate in Sector A should be reduced because it is higher than the rate paid for so-called 'similar' labour skills and conditions in Sector B; they are addressed to the question whether the rate in Sector B should be raised to the rate in Sector A, even though at the current rate in Sector B there are more persons seeking work than can be employed there.

A process which is based on the assumption that the rate of pay for a particular type of work in a particular sector of the economy must not be less than the average pay for 'similar' work in the other sectors of the economy is bound to be inflationary. So long as there remains any inequality in rates of pay, some must be below the average; the continuous jacking up of those below the average will necessarily raise the average and thus go on until all are equated at the top rate. But in a changing world there will always be occurring some events (e.g. an increased demand for a particular product) that will promote some special increase in pay in some particular sector and will thus promote once more the general equalising upward thrust for all 'similar' workers.

2. Productivity

It would, of course, be most undesirable to introduce any system of wage-fixing which prohibited any group of employers and workers from reaching a voluntary agreement that the workers should receive some increase in pay in return for undertaking additional duties or changing their methods or conditions of work in such a way as to increase their output. But it is quite a different matter to introduce, as was at one time the case in the UK, the principle that workers can receive an increase in wages above some stated norm (for example, a 5 per cent annual increase) only in so far as they increase their output per head in such a way as to cover the additional wage cost. As anything more than a very temporary emergency measure any such rule is grossly unfair. There are many industrial processes where technological conditions make increases in output per head relatively easy; in other cases increased productivity may be very difficult; and in many cases, particularly in service industries, increases in output per head may be impossible or, even if possible, may be incapable of measurement. Any long-run application of the principle that wage increases should be tied to increases in measured productivity would thus be grossly unfair; it would cause those who happened to be employed in sectors where output per head could be measured and for technological reasons could be increased to grow richer and richer, at the expense of those who happened to be employed in the other sectors of the economy where such measured increases in productivity were technologically impossible. The system would quickly collapse. Indeed past experience has shown how necessary it would be to invent bogus measurements of productivity increases to allow those in the less favoured occupations to remain in line with their more fortunately placed fellow workers. For this reason productivity deals have in the past rapidly degenerated into slightly camouflaged but basically bogus ways of avoiding general restrictions on wages increases.

The unfairness of wage increases that were restricted to true increases in output per head is apparent. But the inefficiencies that would result from the application of such a principle are equally horrifying. The history of agriculture in the progressive industrial economies of the West serves to illustrate the point. In agriculture throughout the Western world there have over the last decades been exceptionally great increases in productivity. But food is a product for which the demand is inelastic in respect of both income and price. When people get richer they spend a smaller proportion of their income on food; when the price of foodstuffs falls relative to the price of other things, they do not greatly shift their expenditure from other things on to additional consumption of food. As a result, as output per head increased in agriculture fewer people were needed in agriculture to produce the food needed by society. Indeed the reduction in the relative size of the agricultural population throughout the economically progressive Western world has been one of the most dramatic changes over the last two centuries. Increased productivity in agriculture means that fewer resources are needed in agriculture. Economic efficiency requires, as has indeed happened, that the redundant workers should move from agriculture into industry and other services. The reduction in the demand for agricultural workers due to the increased output per worker has caused agricultural wages to be depressed relative to wages and incomes elsewhere. On social and distributional grounds it may well be right and proper for the state to take measures to slow down and mitigate this process. But if there is an exceptionally high rate of increased productivity in the production of something for which the demand is inelastic economic efficiency requires that, sooner or later, there should be an exceptionally large reduction in the selling price of the product so that there is an incentive to move out of the occupation. Rates of pay there should be relatively low rather than relatively high.

On the other hand, if the increase in productivity occurs in an industry for whose product the elasticity of demand is high and if the new technology is not of an exceptionally labour-saving type, a higher rate of pay will be appropriate, since a larger labour force will be needed. The basic analytical principle is simple. Increased productivity may cause an excess supply or an excess demand for labour in a particular set of jobs. There is no analytical need on special grounds of productivity to modify the rule that rates of pay should be set so as to help to balance supply and demand in each sector of the economy.

Nevertheless, changes in productivity do introduce very real complications and difficulties which may require some modification of the general principle of fixing wage rates so as to maintain over the longer run a balance between the supply and demand for labour in any particular sector.

In order to give an incentive to introduce new and more efficient methods of production it may be desirable to offer increases in pay and/or to allow increases in profitability where productivity is increased. In some industries there will then be a conflict between the need to offer rewards for greater productivity and the need to contract the total labour force which is still needed in the industry. An ideal solution might be to allow for some increases in pay as an incentive for those who are already employed in the industry but to offer less attractive terms to new entrants to discourage persons from seeking employment in an industry in which the demand for labour had contracted.

Such a solution would involve old and new workers being paid at different rates even though they were doing precisely the same job. In an economy in which there was a continuous general rise in output per head in the economy as a whole an arrangement of the following kind might provide a workable compromise between the conflicting desiderata. An immediate rise in pay might take place in order to give the incentive for the needed innovations. The rate of pay would then be higher in that industry than was in fact needed over the longer run to maintain a balance between the supply and demand for labour. The relative height of the rate of pay in the innovating industry might subsequently be eroded by allowing the rates of pay in the rest of the economy (which would be rising in line with the general overall increase in productivity) to rise up to and, if necessary, ultimately to overtake the exceptionally high rate in the innovating industry, which would be kept rather stagnant so long as there was an excess supply of labour in that industry. With the passage of time the older workers in the innovating firm would gradually be replaced by new entrants so that in a rough and ready way the workers who were employed at the time of the innovation would in fact gain relatively to those who entered the industry after the change.

This compromise process would be very possible under the institutional arrangements outlined later in Chapter VIII, which would permit employers to offer any wage increases which they judged desirable to encourage any innovation but which would also increase their ability to resist

further subsequent claims so long as there was an excess supply of labour
in their sector of the economy.

In any case it remains of crucial importance that in the long run, by
some process or another, reduced costs should lead to reduced prices
to the consumer rather than to abnormally high incomes to the particular
producers and that the consumer's response should then be allowed to
determine the ultimate expansion or contraction of the labour force in
the industry.

3. Low Pay

The basic cure for low pay is to make it easy for the workers concerned
to move from the low-paid to the higher paid occupations by increasing
their knowledge of the possibilities of employment in the better paid
occupations, industries and regions, by increasing the opportunities for
training for the better paid jobs, by removing obstacles to movement
from one region to another (such as the present difficulty for a worker
with security of tenure in a rented house in one district to find alternative
accommodation elsewhere), and by removing artificial monopolistic restrictions against entry into other sectors of the economy. In spite of
policies of this kind there may, of course, remain some pockets of sweated
labour where, through ignorance and apathy, freedom to take voluntary
trade union action has not been effective in preventing exploitation by
monopsonistic employers, resulting in unnecessarily low levels of pay.
In the limited range of such cases it is the right and duty of the state to
intervene by the operation of compulsory Wage Councils or otherwise
to ensure that adequate wages are paid. The need for some form of wage-
fixing in such cases will be analysed in more detail in Chapter IV.*

Moreover, as we have already argued in Section 8 of Chapter I the
suggestion that the primary function of wage-fixing in each sector of
the economy should be to promote employment in that sector by taking
account of the conditions of supply and demand for labour in that sector
does not mean that one should not be concerned about the distribution
of income and wealth. But it does mean that for this purpose the main
reliance must be placed on governmental policies of the kind which have
already been enumerated in Chapter I rather than on a general squeezing
of profits through an inflationary upward pressure of wages with the
consequent risk of unemployment; and we have already explained why
such measures constitute a more effective method for the relief of poverty.

---

*In terms of Table I (in Chapter IV) the absence of trade union organisation
will require a governmental wage-fixing authority to cause a shift from Situation I
to Situation IV of that table.

4.   Conclusions

One may summarise these conclusions about the criteria on which rates of pay should be fixed as follows:

First, against the background of financial policies to ensure a steady annual rate of growth in the money demand for labour as a whole and of a battery of fiscal and other policies for the redistribution of income and wealth, the basic criterion for fixing rates of pay should be to promote employment by restraining wage rates which restrict employment below the numbers who seek work in the occupation concerned, but raising rates where this is necessary to attract labour to maintain or expand a needed labour force.

Second, comparability studies may be needed to aid judgements whether particular rates of pay are appropriate to maintain future recruitment at an adequate level; but comparability should always be based on the attractiveness of various jobs, revealed as far as possible by individual choices between jobs.

Third, as far as low pay is concerned, there is a case for special state intervention in exceptional cases of exploited workers; and, as will be argued later, it is particularly important to avoid measures which are aimed at protecting high-paid workers from the competition of other less well paid workers.

Fourth, there should be no impediment to individual productivity deals between workers and employers, but this should not involve any general regulations which tie increases of wages to increases in productivity. It is appropriate that existing workers in any set of jobs that is adversely affected by new technologies should enjoy some protection in their pay or indeed even experience some immediate incentive bonus; but it is inappropriate that such protection or bonus should be perpetuated for all time and for all new entrants.

CHAPTER IV

Imperfect Competition and the Case for Wage-Fixing Institutions

We have stated the case for an economic system which ensures (1) a steady rate of growth in the level of the total money demands for the economy's goods and services and (2) the setting of money wage rates at levels which, against this background of a steady expansion of demand for the products of labour, promotes the full employment of the available labour. We are considering these arrangements in a mixed economy in which free enterprise plays a leading role.

The forces of competition play a basic role in a free-enterprise system, as one enterprise searches for profit by expanding into a market against other competing enterprises. Steps are accordingly properly taken to prevent restrictive practices and the formation of monopolistic cartels among producers. Some simple minded persons may suggest that the same principles be applied in the labour market by outlawing the formation of similar labour monopolistic cartels and restrictive practices in restraint of trade. In other words, why not preserve full employment, against the background of a steady rate of growth of the total money demand for the products of labour, by a process of trade union bashing? Why not let the competing employers faced with the growing demand for their products bid against each other for the services of the available supply of workers, and let any workers who are still unemployed offer their services at wage rates at which it becomes profitable for the competing employers to employ them?

It is the purpose of this chapter to argue that any such solution is unacceptable because wage-fixing arrangements of one kind or another play an essential role in the imperfectly competitive world in which we live. There are, however, some very important and beneficial forces at work in a competitive system; and although these forces are impeded and maimed in the real world in which competition is imperfect, yet they are potentially very beneficial and should be utilised as far as is compatible with the imperfections of the competitive system. Accordingly it is our intention in this chapter to outline the effects of the forces of competition in the fairyland of a perfectly competitive world, to explain in what respects the beneficial effects of competition are inevitably impeded, and in what respects they may still be promoted, in the real world of imperfect competition, and to apply this analysis to the problem of determining the proper functions of labour monopolies or other wage-fixing institutions in a mixed economy with an extensive free-enterprise sector.

1. The Fairyland of Perfect Competition

The full and unimpeded effects of competition would occur only if there were (1) a large number of independent competing producers of every product, (2) a large number of independent individual competing workers in every grade of work, (3) no obstacles to the free movement of goods and persons, and (4) well organised markets for the purchase and sale of goods and services.

Such a state of affairs would promote full employment. As long as any individual was involuntarily unemployed he could offer his services at a fractionally lower rate in competition with other workers; and since we are assuming that employers would be competing with each other to expand their demands for labour as the total level of money expenditures was expanded by monetary and fiscal policies on its steady growth path, the result would be that everyone would find employment.

The real income of the community and so of the individual citizens would thus be raised by the avoidance of unemployed resources. It would, perhaps more importantly, also be raised by using those resources in the most efficient ways for a number of reasons. First, the competing producers would be searching for the most profitable markets; and that would imply expanding the production of those goods which the consumers most needed and for which they were, therefore, offering the highest prices relatively to the costs of production. Second, workers would be attracted to these desirable lines of production which, being the most profitable, would offer the highest wages. Third, producers would make use of the most efficient methods of production; for if there were any better method of production which enabled cost per unit of output to be reduced, it would pay any individual producer to adopt it and to increase his profit by reducing his cost; and with workers competing for jobs this would not be impeded by demarcation rules and other monopolistic restrictive practices in the labour market.

Thus the perfectly competitive system would maximise the real income per head of the community by the full and the most efficient employment of the community's resources. It would not, however, necessarily lead to an equal, or to any other socially desired, distribution of the real income between the various individual citizens. The owners of property would be in receipt of interest and rents on the capital and land used in production; and the distribution of this investment income would depend upon the actual distribution of the ownership of property. Moreover, the distribution of wage earnings between the workers would be equal only in so far as all workers were endowed, both genetically by birth and in an acquired way through training and upbringing, with the same skills and abilities and had the same luck in finding themselves in the right place in the right occupation at the right time. In fact those with luck and with the skills and abilities which at any one time were scarce relative to the demands for them would earn higher rewards than those who were less lucky and who possessed less scarce skills and abilities.

Would there, therefore, be a case even in an otherwise perfectly competitive economy for the formation of labour monopolies to force up real wage rates in order to improve the distribution of real income?

Consider first the possibility of pushing up the general level of real wage rates throughout the economy by the simultaneous use of trade union pressure in all sectors of the economy. A rise in the money wage rates relative to the selling prices of the products produced (the necessary condition for a rise in the real wage rate) would, in the conditions under examination, make employers less willing to expand their production; they would take on labour so long as the wage which they had to pay was less than the price at which they could sell the additional output produced, and with a higher wage rate this productive margin would be reached at a lower level of employment; and the result would be to cause unemployment. There would be a rise in the real incomes of those workers who were still employed but at the expense both of the profits of the producers and also of the unemployed.

A similar result would occur if any one particular group of workers alone formed a monopoly and pushed up its real wage rate above the competitive level. Such workers (who might or might not be those with low earnings) could improve their real earnings at the expense of their employers or of the customers who had to pay a higher price for their products — but also at the expense of those individuals in this group of workers who lost their employment or were barred from employment in this sector of the economy. The higher wage for this group of workers would, for the reasons given in the preceding paragraph, reduce the demand for workers in this group. Those who were thus excluded from this line of employment would have to seek employment elsewhere; and in the perfectly competitive economy under examination this would necessarily mean employment on terms less favourable than before, since *ex hypothesi* they had previously been free to move into the employment which offered the most attractive terms for their skills and abilities.

Thus in a perfectly competitive economy an upward pressure on real wage rates by monopolistic labour organisations necessarily worsens conditions for some workers who are pushed out into the cold. For this reason it is desirable to rely on measures other than the fixing of wage rates (e.g. on social security arrangements, progressive taxation, and the other measures mentioned in Section 8 of Chapter I) to improve the distribution of real income and to use the fixing of wage rates primarily as an instrument to promote the full employment and efficient deployment of the labour force.*

2. Monopolistic and Monopsonistic Features of the Real World

So much for the fairyland of perfect competition. There are a number of reasons why in the real world it is not possible to rely fully on the forces of competition in the organisation of the productive process. Technical economies of large-scale production mean that in many cases the size of an efficient productive enterprise is large relative to the market for its products; and in such cases there may be room for only one or at the most a few producers. Differentiation between similar branded products by significant differences of real characteristics or by imaginary differences due to advertisement and packaging may make it impossible for one producer to invade another producer's market merely by a fractional reduction in the price charged for the product. Real costs of movement of goods and/or of workers from one place to another may mean that local markets for goods and for workers enjoy some protection from each other. Absence of organised markets may mean that workers and producers are ignorant of the possibilities of selling their services or their products in alternative markets.

Consider then a producer who for one or other of these reasons — for example, because of economies of large-scale production — is producing and selling in an imperfectly competitive market. If he expands his output he may have to cut his price and so his profit margin significantly in order to increase his sales; and by restricting his output for sale in his protected market he can raise his selling price and so his profit margin. He has a *monopolistic* incentive to restrict output and sales.

He may also have an additional incentive to restrict the scale of his operations, if he is the only or the main employer of labour in the occupation or district in which he produces; for if he took on more workers

*Thus even if the conditions which made for perfect competition in the productive processes of the economy were fulfilled there would be a strong case for governmental intervention (e.g. by fiscal policy, social security measures, etc.) to influence the distribution of income and wealth. Nor would this be the only reason for governmental intervention. There are certain 'public goods' (e.g. law and order and defence) which can be 'enjoyed' by the community only if they are centrally acquired on behalf of the whole community, even though in this case needed supplies (e.g. police cars) could be competitively produced and supplied to the public authority concerned. Measures to avoid pollution provide yet another example of the need for governmental interventions. In this chapter we are concerned not with the whole question of *laissez-faire* versus government action in economic matters, but with the narrower question of the role of competition and of monopolistic arrangements in the organisation of the productive processes.

he might have to offer a significantly higher wage rate to all his employees in order to attract more workers into his localised labour market; and, conversely, by taking on less labour he may be able to exploit at a lower wage rate all the workers whom he does still employ. In these conditions he has what is known as a *monopsonistic* incentive to restrict the scale of his employment.

These two powers — monopolistic and monopsonistic — may well go together, though they are not necessarily connected; where they do go together, the producer has a double incentive to restrict his employment and output, both in order to raise the price charged for his product and also in order to reduce the wage rate paid to his employees.

Important measures can be devised to reduce the monopolistic powers of producers: freedom of import of competing products; regulations against producers' cartels and other similar restrictive practices; arrangements which restrict the formation of monopolies and business mergers where there are no real efficiency arguments to outweigh the resulting increase in monopolistic power; these and similar measures can be taken to reduce monopolistic influences. Where substantial monopoly power is inevitable, measures can be taken by the control of selling prices to remove the ability of the producer to increase his profit margin by raising prices through the restriction of output; and in the extreme cases (such as the inevitable total monopoly of a railway system or road network or electricity grid) the activity can be nationalised.*

Measures can also be taken to reduce the monopsonistic powers of producers in particular by making it easy for exploited workers who are badly paid in any district or occupation to move easily (by retraining and geographical movement) into better paid jobs. This is a most important matter to which we will return in Chapter VI.

But when all is said and done, very significant elements of monopsonistic power will remain; and this provides the basic economic justification for trade union organisation. Monopolistic power on the part of workers can restore their bargaining position *vis-à-vis* a monopsonistic employer. It is not only that it is unfair that a single employer confronted by a large number of competing workers whom he can play off against each other in a monopsonistic market should be enabled to grab an unfair share of the product. That is true and important. But there is another and more sophisticated justification. The trade union will set a given wage rate which the employer can no longer reduce by taking on less labour; the employer's incentive to restrict employment in order to reduce the wage rate is removed; and thus the volume of employment which the employer will offer at any given wage rate will be increased by the monopolistic wage-fixing of the trade union.

*The legal curbs on the use of monopolistic powers in the UK are outlined in Appendix D.

3. A Single Employer in an Imperfect Labour Market: A Numerical Example

This last consideration is of such basic importance that it is worthwhile analysing it in some detail by means of the arithmetical example given in Table I. We are considering the case of a single employer* who is employing the number of men shown in column a. Column b then measures what the employer will add net to the total receipt from the sale of his products by producing and selling more as a result of employing the last additional man; this in the jargon of the economist is called 'the marginal revenue product of labour'.† Thus, for example, for purposes of illustration we are assuming that by taking on the 15th man, that is, by employing 15 instead of 14 men (column a), the employer will add £13 to his total receipts (column b). The marginal revenue product of column b is assumed to fall as more and more workers are employed. This may be due to either or both of two developments: first, because less and less output may be added to production as more and more men have to work with the given equipment and other resources of the firm; and, second, because the employer may be selling his product in an imperfect market so that if he produces and sells more he may have to lower his selling price (or incur greater selling costs) in order to dispose of the increased output.

Our present concern is, however, not with the market in which the employer is selling his product but with the market in which he is hiring labour. For the purposes of Situation I illustrated in columns (c), (d), and (e) we assume that the employer has a monopsonistic power which is not offset by any trade union or other wage-fixing institution. Because of the cost of workers moving to another district or another job, the employer will lose some but not all of his labour if he pays a lower wage; because of the cost of new workers moving into the district or occupation, the employer will have to pay a higher wage rate if he wishes to attract more persons into his employment. Column c gives a numerical illustration of this phenomenon; thus, for example, a wage rate of £10.2 is assumed to be needed to attract 12 workers but a wage rate of £10.3 would be needed to attract 13 workers. Column d then shows the total wage bill incurred at different levels of employment; thus with 14 workers employed (column a) at a wage rate of £10.4 (column c), the total wage bill will be £10.4 × 14 = £145.6 (column d). Finally column e then shows what the employer adds to his labour cost by taking on one more

---

*By 'single employer' we mean the agent that is ultimately responsible for the decisions which affect the scale of employment in any concern. Thus the term covers a wide range from the single individual who owns and manages a small private business to the board of a gigantic corporate concern.

†This measures what is added *net* to the employer's receipts by taking on an additional worker, that is, the addition to his *gross* receipts less any addition to the cost of raw materials, etc., needed to produce the additional output.

Table I

		I No Wage-Fixing			II Minimum Wage Rate Fixed at 12.5			III Minimum Wage Rate Fixed at 14.5			IV Minimum Wage Rate Fixed at 10.7		
Employment	Marginal Revenue Product of Labour	Wage Rate	Wage Bill	Marginal Labour Cost	Wage Rate	Wage Bill	Marginal Labour Cost	Wage Rate	Wage Bill	Marginal Labour Cost	Wage Rate	Wage Bill	Marginal Labour Cost
a	b	c	d	e	f	g	h	i	j	k	l	m	n
No:	£	£	£	£	£	£	£	£	£	£	£	£	£
10	18	10.0	100.0	—	12.5	125.0	12.5	14.5	145.0	14.5	10.7	107.0	10.7
11	17	10.1	111.1	11.1		137.5			159.5			117.7	
12	16	10.2	122.4	11.3		150.0			174.0			128.4	
13	15	10.3	133.9	11.5		162.5			188.5			139.1	
14	14	10.4	145.6	11.7		175.0			203.0			149.8	
15	13	10.5	157.5	11.9		187.5			217.5			160.5	
16	12	10.6	169.6	12.1		200.0			232.0			171.2	
17	11	10.7	181.9	12.3		212.5			246.5			181.9	
18	10	10.8	194.4	12.5		225.0			261.0		10.8	194.4	12.5
19	9	10.9	207.1	12.7		237.5			275.5		10.9	207.1	12.7
20	8	11.0	220.0	12.9		250.0			290.0		11.0	220.0	12.9

worker, which in the economist's jargon is called 'the marginal labour cost'. Thus by employing 14 workers instead of 13 (column a) the wage bill is increased from £133.9 to £145.6 (column d), so that the increase in labour cost due to taking on the 14th worker is £145.6 − £133.9 = £11.7 (column e).*

It will pay the employer to expand his employment, output, and sales so long as what he adds thereby to his net revenue is greater than what it adds thereby to his labour costs.† In Situation I he will therefore employ 15 workers, since employing 15 rather than 14 adds more to his net revenue (£13) than to his wage bill (£11.9), while employing 16 rather than 15 workers would add less to his net revenue (£12) than to his wage bill (£12.1).

Suppose now that by trade union action or some other institutional change a minimum wage rate of £12.5 was imposed, as shown in columns f, g, and h of Situation II. At this fixed wage rate of £12.5 (column f) the marginal wage cost will be £12.5 (column h) because taking on one more worker simply adds the constant wage rate of one worker to the total wage bill. It will still pay the employer to employ 15 rather than 14 workers, since he will thereby add less to his wage bill (£12.5) than he will add net to his net revenue (£13); but by taking on a 16th worker he will add more to his wage bill (£12.5) than to his net revenue (£12). Thus by fixing a wage rate which the employers cannot reduce by restricting their demand for labour, the wage rate has been raised from £10.5 to £12.5 between Situation I and Situation II without any decline in the level of employment.

There is, however, one obvious possible snag. The employer's total wage cost has gone up between Situation I and Situation II by £30, from £157.5 to £187.5, as a result of the extra £2 paid to the 15 workers in employment. It is possible that this extra cost unmatched by any extra revenue will bankrupt the employer. This is by no means certain.

---

*The marginal labour cost of £11.7 is greater than the wage rate of £10.4 needed to attract 14 workers, because in addition to the £10.4 paid to the 14th worker there is also a rise of wage rate from £10.3 to £10.4 payable to all the existing 13 workers. The additional wage cost is thus £10.4 + (£0.1 × 13) = £11.7.

†This is a formalistic way of describing a balance of considerations which is important in the real world, though it will never in fact be assessed with the arithmetical precision illustrated in the table. In reaching a business decision that involves expanding the labour force those in charge of the concern will in fact need to balance the expected net increase in the concern's receipts (after allowing for any extra expenditures on raw materials, on advertising, or any cutting of selling price to expand the market) against the expected increase in the wage bill. In an unorganised labour market, one question which must arise is whether and, if so, to what extent a higher wage rate will have to be paid in order to achieve the planned expansion of the labour force. Table I is devised to highlight the implications of this very real problem. The reader should not be put off by the fact that in order to do so it employs an over-simplified, over-precise numerical example.

The monopsonistic power of the employer in Situation I (together with any monopolistic power exercised by him in the market for his products) may have enabled him to earn a profit from which he can afford to lose £30 without having to close down his activities. But the danger of killing the goose that lays the golden eggs is a real one.

If the trade union wage negotiators are more concerned with the wage rate earned by those in employment than with the volume of employment provided by the firm concerned, they might exert their monopolistic power still further. Situation III shows the position if the minimum wage rate (and so the marginal labour cost) is set at £14.5 instead of £12.5. Employment up to the 13th worker will now add more to the employer's net revenue (i.e. £15) than to his marginal labour cost of £14.5; but the 14th worker would add only £14 to revenue but £14.5 to labour cost. There is, of course, in Situation III a greater danger than in Situation II that the employer will be driven out of business by the high labour cost. The wage bill at £188.5 is £1 higher than in Situation II; and at the same time the employer's net revenue will be £27 less than in Situation I or Situation II, since he will have lost £13 in net revenue by reducing his employment from 15 to 14 and a further £14 in net revenue by reducing his employment from 14 to 13, as is shown in column b. Thus comparing Situation III with Situation I the employer will have lost £31 + £27 = £58 in total profit, £31 being the increase in the total wage bill from £157.5 to £188.5 and £27 being the loss of net revenue by £13 + £14 = £27. However, if the employer's monopsonistic–monopolistic position was sufficient to absorb this loss of profit, the wage rate could be raised to £14.5 with a reduction of employment from 15 to 13.

Situation IV shows the case in which the monopsonistic power of the employer is removed by the fixing of a minimum wage rate, but in which this minimum is set at a level which maximises the level of employment provided by the employer. This position is achieved by setting a minimum wage rate of £10.7. This wage is sufficient (see column c) to attract 17 workers to the firm. It would have to be raised to £10.8 in order to attract an 18th worker. At £10.7 the wage (and so, if it is fixed, the marginal labour cost of £10.7) is less than the £11 which is added to net revenue by taking on the 17th worker. So a wage of £10.7 will cause employment to be increased to 17. A further rise in the wage rate to £10.8 would be needed to attract the 18th worker; but this would be higher than the 18th worker's marginal revenue product of £10 (column b). Thus a wage of £10.8 would not promote employment by the firm, but might attract more workers to the occupation than could find employment in it. The wage of £10.7 of Situation III can thus be regarded as the wage that would most promote employment; it would maximise employment in the occupation in question without the danger of causing unemployment by attracting an excess supply of labour to the occupation.*

If we compare Situation IV with Situation I, the wage rate has been raised from £10.5 to £10.7 and the volume of employment has simultaneously been increased from 15 to 17. The employing concern will as a result be somewhat less profitable. Its total wage cost will have risen by £24.4 (i.e. from £157.5 to £181.9); but at the same time its revenue will have increased by £12 + £11 = £23 (i.e. by £12 as a result of taking on the 16th man and by a further £11 as a result of taking on the 17th man). Thus its profit will have fallen by only £24.4 − £23 = £1.4.

4. The Application of the Analysis to the Whole Economy

The situations illustrated in Table I refer to the experience of a single employer for whom, for example, in the shift from Situation I to Situation IV, wage-fixing arrangements are introduced for the first time, these arrangements being designed to promote employment by that single employer. The analysis of the table is based on the assumption that there is no concomitant change in the wage-fixing institutions for any other employers in the economy. The purpose of the table has thus been solely to illustrate by the example of a single employer the fact that wage-fixing institutions can, if properly used in a world of imperfect competition in labour markets, simultaneously both promote employment and raise wage rates.

If the change of institutions is generalised for all employers in the economy, the picture is much changed and becomes much more favourable to the general body of wage earners.† Thus suppose that all employers

---

*In contrast with Situation IV, Situation II leaves two workers out in the cold of unemployment or of less attractive jobs, since the 16th and 17th workers would prefer jobs in this firm at a wage rate of no more than £10.7. Situation III leaves no less than four workers out in the cold.

†The generalisation of the change will, as we shall see, affect the level of the economy's total employment and production. What happens as a result to the level of *money* wages, *money* prices, and *money* incomes will depend upon the general financial policies involved. We are, however, in the present analysis interested in certain underlying relationships between *real* wages, *real* productivities of labour, and the *real* volumes of employment. These real relationshisp are not affected by whether, for example a 10 per cent rise in the real wage rate is produced by a 10 per cent rise in the money wage rate (money prices constant) or by a corresponding fall in money prices (money wage rates constant). All that is necessary is that some financial policy should be adopted which does enable changes in real wage rates to be effected by changes in money wage rates; and this would be achieved (though not with an absolutely constant level of money prices) by the adoption of financial policies, such as those advocated in this work, designed to keep the general level of the total money demand for the products of labour or for labour itself on a steady growth path. The alternative assumption of a constant level of money prices is adopted in the following analysis purely for the purpose of simplification of exposition, so that a change in the real wage rate can be represented by a change in the money wage rate.

simultaneously shift from the absence of wage-fixing institutions (as in Situation I) to the introduction of the wage-fixing institutions of a type designed to promote employment by each employer (as in Situation IV). The particular employer depicted in Table I in his attempt to take on the two additional workers will be attracting them either from an existing pool of the unemployed or from other employers; but at the same time each of the other employers will be attempting to attract additional workers either from an existing pool of the unemployed or else from other employers including the particular employer depicted in the table. As a result of the greater competition between employers the supply curve of labour to each individual employer will be raised. For example, the particular supply curve of labour depicted in column c would be raised since the employer in question would no longer be able to attract as many as 17 workers for a wage of £10.7, because other employers had now made offers which attracted some of these 17 workers away on better terms elsewhere. Thus the effect of generalising the shift from Situation I to Situation IV would be partly to increase the general level of employment at somewhat improved wage rates (corresponding to the £10.7 of Situation IV) and partly, in so far as the unemployed could not satisfy the employers' combined demands for labour, to raise the general level of wages still further through the increased competition for labour between the various employers (i.e. to raise still further the wage corresponding to the £10.7 of Situation IV).

This phenomenon would in certain aspects be even more marked with a general shift from Situation III to Situation IV (i.e. a shift from wage-fixing institutions which attempted to obtain the highest wage for those employed by the employer in question to wage-fixing institutions which attempted to promote the volume of employment offered by each employer). The shift from Situation III to Situation IV would in itself increase the demand for labour by the particular employer depicted in Table I by 4 workers, that is, by twice as much as the shift from Situation I to Situation IV. A simultaneous shift by many employers from wage-fixing institutions designed to raise the wage rate of those employed to wage-fixing institutions designed to promote the number of workers employed would thus have an even more marked effect in increasing the demand for labour, an increased demand which would have to be met either by a reduction in unemployment or by the attraction of labour from other less rewarding sectors of the economy or by some general increase in wage rates.

The shift of certain employments from Situation III to Situation IV implies an initial reduction in the wage rates of those concerned. But the generalised wage increases that would result from the resulting increased competition by employers for each other's labour would restore to some extent the wage rates for those who had made the shift. This would occur in so far as there were no unemployed workers to be absorbed or workers to be attracted from employers who had not been subject to the change. It is not, therefore, at all certain how far the wage rates would in fact have to be reduced in the employments making the shift. The probable outcome is that the wage rates which had been most effectively raised by monopolistic action on the part of the workers under Situation III conditions would be reduced by the change, while those which had not been much raised by monopolistic action would in the final outcome enjoy a net increase.

5. The Distribution of the Gains

It is not, therefore, to be asserted that a generalised shift from Situation III principles of wage-fixing to those of Situation IV would automatically improve the situation for everyone. On the contrary, it might well worsen the position for a limited number of workers who had previously exercised the most effective monopoly powers. It is, however, safe to reach the following conclusions about the effect of the change:

(1) It would result in increased employment if there were initially any substantial group of available unemployed persons.
(2) It would increase the wages for those workers who were not initially able to exercise much or any monopolistic powers of wage-fixing.
(3) It would thus tend to equalise earnings by increasing the demand for those workers who had been excluded from privileged monopolised occupations relative to those who had been included in these privileged groups.
(4) Among those who would gain would be the employers of labour, the unemployed, and workers who had not been employed in the occupations most effectively protected by monopolistic wage-fixing. There might be some losses among those who had been most effectively protected.
(5) The gains would certainly outweigh the losses, since the total national product would be increased partly by increasing the general level of employment and partly by the attraction of workers from positions of low pay and productivity into previously protected positions of high pay and productivity. There would thus be a larger total cake available for the redistributive effects of taxation, social welfare services, social benefits, etc.

6. Conclusion

The basic philosophy that will permeate the treatment of these labour problems in the rest of this book may thus be summarised under four main headings.

First, in order to enable the fixing of wage rates to be used as a main instrument for promoting the full employment and the efficient deployment of labour it is desirable to shift the emphasis on to other instruments (such as the measures discussed in Section 8 of Chapter I) for the achievement of a desirable distribution of income and wealth.

Second, in order to be able to make the most of the powerful, though necessarily imperfect, forces of competition in a free-enterprise system it is desirable to take measures to reduce the monopolistic and monopsonistic powers of employers wherever this can be done without serious offsetting disadvantages. As far as monopolistic powers are concerned this implies measures such as: the free import of competing products; the restraint of restrictive practices and of the unnecessary formation of monopolies and mergers; price control; and nationalisation. Employers' monopsonistic powers can be reduced by measures which increase the mobility of labour between districts and occupations, thus enabling workers to play one employer off against another. We will return to this problem in Chapter VI.

Third, there remains, however, a basic need for the offsetting of employers' monopsonistic powers in labour markets through the fixing of wage rates by the monopolistic action of organised labour or by some other means.

Fourth, even though competition will in many respects be imperfect, nevertheless in a free-enterprise economy there remain some very powerful competitive forces the operation of which should be impeded as little as possible. Competition among employers will increase the demand for labour. But while wage-fixing by monopolistic labour organisations is needed to promote employment in otherwise monopsonistic markets, the level of the wage rate so fixed should be restrained (by competition between groups of workers or otherwise) in order that it should not restrict employment in that sector of the economy and thus push other workers out into the cold.

This last point expresses the great labour market dilemma which it will be a main purpose of the following chapters to discuss. On the one hand, where many workers face a single employer in a monopsonistic market, organisation is needed to prevent the exploitation of the workers through the restriction of employment and the reduction of the wage rate. On the other hand, any minimum wage rate which is set for this purpose should not be raised to a level which is itself so high as to restrict employment and to push some workers out into the cold of unemployment or less preferred employment.

The powers needed for the first legitimate purpose are the same as those which can be misused for the second undesirable end. Thus a powerful trade union can lead to an undesirable privileged position for the group of workers which it protects, leading to a position of the kind depicted in Situation III of Table I. It may be able to do this simply by organising a sufficient body of workers who will withdraw their labour *en bloc* if the wage on which they insist is undercut; or it may back up its insistence on this wage by restricting the number of persons who can be admitted to the employment in question (e.g. by unnecessary apprenticeship requirements or demarcation rules or by a pre-entry closed shop arrangement whereby the employer agrees to employ only trade union members and the trade union limits the numbers it will admit to membership).

The basic question, therefore, remains. Can wage-fixing institutions be devised which will make possible the employment-promotion objectives of Situation IV of Table I without leading to the monopolistic restrictions of Situation III of the table?

CHAPTER V

The Existing Monopolistic Powers of Labour Organisation in the UK *

In the preceding chapter we gave reasons for the view that wage-fixing institutions of one kind or another are a necessary and desirable feature in our economy. This function is in general at present performed by collective bargaining between employers and trade unions, a function which cannot be performed without the possession and exercise of monopolistic powers by the organised groups of workers. But, as was argued in the preceding chapter, these powers must in each instance be used with restraint in the interests of the rest of the community. Accordingly, in the present chapter we will give an account of the existing monopolistic bargaining powers of labour organisations; and in Chapters VI, VII and VIII we will consider what restraints, if any, might usefully be imposed in the social interest on the use of such powers.

The bargaining power of trade unions does not depend solely upon the legal provisions concerning their formation and their activities. In Chapter II we have already enumerated some other factors: technological developments which have increased the ability of small groups to disrupt a large range of activities; market developments which have made employers less hesitant to raise prices to cover increased wage costs; and the increased economic resources and staying power of those individuals who are taking or threatening industrial action. But these powers are all dependent upon the underlying legal provisions which regulate or affect the exercise of bargaining power. Accordingly the present chapter presents a brief survey of the implications of the relevant legal provisions as they existed at the time when, in 1979, the Conservative government took over from the Labour government, together with an account of the subsequent alterations made by legislation in 1980.

1. Individual Contracts of Employment and Contracts to Perform a Service

In the fairyland of perfect competition which we described in Chapter IV

---

*This chapter is based upon B.A. Hepple and Paul O'Higgins, *Employment Law*, 2nd ed (London: Sweet & Maxwell, 1976); Otto Kahn-Freund, *Labour and Law*, 2nd ed (London: Stevens & Sons, 1977); and Patrick Elias, *Trade Disputes (Law at Work)* (London: Sweet & Maxwell, 1980). I have in addition had great help from discussion with Dr Elias who has commented on an earlier draft.

the basic legal arrangement would be freedom of individual contracts between a person who wanted a job done and the person who was to do the job. An employer would, for instance, contract with an employee to work for him for a certain payment for a certain time at certain tasks. The law would be invoked to enable either party to the contract who felt aggrieved to ensure that the terms of the contract were fulfilled or to seek damages in case of a breach of the contract. Individual workers would be free, having fulfilled the terms of any particular contract, to seek a more favourable contract with an alternative competing employer; and an individual employer, having fulfilled the terms of a contract with an individual employee, would be free to replace him with an alternative competing employee.

This conception of freedom for individual contracts is fundamental in UK labour law. As will be explained in later sections of this chapter, much superstructure has been built on this basic legal concept to meet the real-world conditions of imperfect competition, with the result that many of the relevant relationships in practice are not between two contracting individuals but between organised groups; but it is on the basis of such individual contracts − an exchange of work for a payment − that the legal structure of rights and duties in labour relationships is constructed.

Individual labour contracts may take either of two forms. The first is a contract of employment whereby an employer contracts with an employee to work for him. The individual contract of employment is not necessarily or normally expressed in detail in a written document. Many of its terms will be held to be implied because they are part of the normal custom and practice in the industry or occupation in question or simply because they are needed to make sense of the purpose of the contract. But perhaps the most important source of contractual terms is the collective agreement. A collective agreement between an employer, or an employer's association, and a trade union is not normally itself intended to constitute, or treated as constituting, a binding contract; it is in the nature of a gentleman's agreement which expresses the intentions of the parties concerned about the terms and conditions of work. But the terms of a collective agreement (e.g. as to the rate of pay) may well be held to be an implied term of the individual worker's contract of employment or the parties may agree expressly to incorporate them.*

---

*There is an express statutory provision which ensures that the terms of any collective agreement which restricts the right to engage in industrial action shall not form part of any individual contract of employment unless the agreement is with a union which is officially certified to be independent of the employer's control, is in writing, expressly allows incorporation into individual contracts, is reasonably accessible, and is in fact expressly or implicitly incorporated into the individual contract.

An employer is now under a statutory obligation to provide written particulars to each employee about certain terms of the contract of employment, such as rates of pay, hours of work, holidays, sick pay, pensions length of notice, and disciplinary procedures. These written particulars are not themselves a contract; they express the employer's view of the contract. They may, however, provide evidence for the interpretation of the contract, and, if not contested by the employee, their terms may well be treated as part of the implied terms of the individual contract of employment. These written particulars must be provided within thirteen weeks of the start of the employment and thus must cover all but casual labour.

Work may, however, be done not under a 'contract of employment' but by a self-employed person under a 'contract to perform a service'. At the extremes the distinction between the two types of contract is a clear one, for example, between, on the one hand, a regular weekly wage earner who is an integral part of a business organisation and doing his job under the direct control, orders, and management of the employer, and, on the other hand, an expert who is called in temporarily to do a special task at a fixed fee under his own control and management.

In the fairyland of perfect competition the distinction would not have any important economic implications. But, as will be seen in later sections of this chapter, much of the superstructure of labour law designed to meet the needs of the real world of imperfect competition relates only to contracts of employment; and thus in the actual world the distinction between employees and self-employed does have some very important implications. Self-employment may be a way of avoiding collective bargaining agreements about wage rates, holidays, sick pay, pensions, etc. It may also be a means of avoiding certain statutory requirements which apply only to employees, namely, in regard to: National Insurance contributions, redundancy payments, industrial training levies, compulsory liability insurance, preferential claims on liquidation, requirements for minimum lengths of notice of termination of employment, and remedies for unfair dismissal. A worker as well as his employer may have some incentives to prefer self-employment; there may be some income tax advantage in being taxed as a self-employed person (under Schedule D) rather than as an employee (under Schedule E), quite apart from any greater opportunity to evade tax; he may share directly or indirectly in some of the immediate gains arising from the avoidance of the statutory requirements enumerated above; and he may avoid trade union restrictions which could make it difficult for him to find employment, or to earn as much, in the occupation in question.

There is at the present time a tendency in some sectors for the growth of self-employment, which raises the question whether and, if so, how any particular legal provision which at present applies only to employees should be extended to cover all workers, whether self-employed or employees.

2.   Statutory Wage-Fixing Bodies

In Chapter IV we argued that the reason why some form of wage-fixing institution was desirable was in order to offset the monopsonistic bargaining power which a single employer might exercise in conditions of imperfect competition over a large number of competing workers. In the UK the main wage-fixing institution is the collective bargaining between an employer or a group of employers and the workers organised and represented as a group by a trade union. But certain employments are covered by statutory bodies which, in place of normal collective bargaining, lay down minimum rates of pay and other terms of employment which override any inconsistent terms in the individual contracts of employment of the workers concerned. Such bodies are operative to prevent monopsonistic exploitation in employments where collective bargaining is non-existent or rudimentary and ineffective. But the general policy is to encourage the growth of effective collective bargaining to replace such bodies.

Wages Councils and the Agricultural Wages Boards are bodies with independent members as well as representatives of workers and employers, the independent members having the effective power of arbitration. Statutory Joint Industrial Councils which are composed only of representatives of the workers and employers without the addition of independent members but which can appeal to the Central Arbitration Committee (see Section 9 below) for a compulsory arbitral award are intended to work as a half-way house on the road to independent collective bargaining. This arrangement clearly illustrates the general preference in the UK to operate wage-fixing through independent collective bargaining.

3.   Statutory Provisions Directly Affecting the Individual Contract of Employment

The main relevance of labour law in promoting wage-fixing in the UK lies in the provisions, examined in later sections of this chapter, which enable the trade unions legitimately to organise monopolistic groups of workers in order to exert power in wage bargaining. But there are also a number of other statutory provisions which take the form of a direct limitation of the freedom of the individual employer and employee in the terms of the individual contract of employment or which in some direct or indirect way affect the individual contract of employment.

Some of these statutory provisions affect matters which it is not proposed to discuss in this chapter, though they are in some cases of the greatest importance. Such matters include: safety at work; restrictions on hours of work and conditions of work for women and children; equal pay for equal work for men and women; many questions concerning pregnancy, confinement, and maternity; the prevention of discrimination by employers on grounds of sex or race; and the special treatment of certain groups of workers such as registered dockworkers. Such statutory provisions may, of course, raise labour costs, and they may affect the terms of collective wage agreements. But we leave them on one side in order to concentrate attention on those which more directly affect the normal basic structure of bargaining power between employers and employed.

(i) *Guaranteed Work*

Many collective agreements contain arrangements for the payment of a guaranteed amount in any week in which work is short. But there is also a statutory provision which entitles an employee to a minimum guaranteed daily payment for up to five days in any three-month period in which he is not provided with work. This guarantee does not apply if the employee has unreasonably refused suitable alternative employment or if the failure to provide work is due to a trade dispute in which the employer is involved; but the obligation to pay is still operative if the failure to provide work is due indirectly to some other trade dispute, for example, due to a strike elsewhere which cuts off the employer's supplies of necessary raw materials.

(ii) *Length of Notice*

There are statutory provisions which set rules for the minimum length of notice which must be given for the termination of a contract of employment. The individual contract of employment may require longer periods of notice than these statutory minima; but the parties to the individual contract have a right to the statutory minima whatever the terms of the individual contract. The minimum notice to be given by an employer to any employee who has been continuously employed for four weeks or more rises from one week's to twelve weeks' notice according to the length of time which he has been continuously in the employer's employment. The minimum period of notice which the employee must give is constant at one week.

The determination of what constitutes a break in the continuity of employment is important not only for determining this statutory minimum length of notice but also, as is shown later in this section, for determining compensation for redundancy and for unfair dismissal.* The general rule is that if a week passes without employment this does not count as a period of employment and it destroys the continuity of employment. A very important exception to this rule is that absence during any week from employment due to a strike or lock-out means that that week does not count for the length of period of continuous employment but does not break the continuity of employment. There are also some periods which count as periods of employment even in the absence of actual employment, namely, some periods of sickness, temporary cessation of work, and pregnancy or confinement. In certain cases a change of employer (e.g. a takeover of a business by one employer from another) does not break the continuity of employment.

(iii) *Redundancy*

An employee who has become redundant and whose contract of employment is terminated on that ground (e.g. because of a decline in the employer's business or because the employee's operation is no longer needed as a result of technological change) has a statutory right to compensation. The amount of redundancy compensation depends upon the employee's rate of pay and the period for which he has been continuously in the employer's service; it is one half of a week's pay for each year of employment between the ages of 22 and 40, and one and a half week's pay for each year of employment between ages 41 and 64. There is a scaling down of compensation for workers approaching retirement; and wages over a certain figure and employment for more than 20 years are ignored. The determination of the amount of compensation raises two problems: first, the determination of the length of continuous employment discussed above; and, second, what constitutes the employee's normal week's pay, for the calculation of which there is a complicated set of rules.

The provisions for redundancy raise great difficulties in cases where the employee has been offered alternative employment by the employer, perhaps at a different place of work, or with somewhat different hours of work, or on a somewhat different task. The employee loses the right to redundancy payment if he unreasonably refuses the offer of suitable alternative employment.

Serious complications also arise where the contract of employment permits lay-offs or short time in the case of a falling off of the employer's trade.

Employers must pay a levy into a central redundancy fund; and in the case of a redundancy payment to a dismissed employee the employer

---

*It is also necessary for the determination of maternity pay, guaranteed pay, and other less important statutory rights.

can obtain a rebate from the central fund to cover part of his obligation to pay redundancy compensation. There are thus three parties concerned in any dispute about a redundancy payment: the employer, the employee, and the Department of Employment, which is concerned with the question whether a rebate is properly payable to the employer.

(iv) *Unfair Dismissal*

Statutory provisions have recently introduced the idea of 'unfair dismissal'. Provided that the employer has acted reasonably, dismissal is not to be regarded as unfair if the grounds are incapacity for the job, serious misconduct, redundancy, some statutory requirement (e.g. a driving disqualification for someone employed to drive), national security, or some other substantial reason such as the unwillingness of the worker to accept a change of working conditions (e.g. in hours worked) which has been generally accepted in a negotiated collective agreement. The dismissal of a temporary replacement of a temporarily absent permanent employee is not in general unfair. On the other hand, certain reasons for dismissal are automatically to be treated as unfair, namely, the dismissal of someone on the grounds of a past criminal conviction which is spent, the dismissal of a woman because of pregnancy or confinement, and dismissal because of membership or activity in an 'independent' trade union (i.e. one that is officially recognised to be independent of the control and influence of the employer) or because of refusal to join a trade union that was under the influence or control of the employer.

Except in the case of a closed shop, the special provisions for which will be discussed in Section 5, dismissal of a worker for not joining a union would also be unfair.* A dismissed employee's claim can lie only against the employer; but the Employment Act of 1980 introduced the further principle that, in the case in which other workers by threatening a strike or by similar action forced an employer to discharge a worker because he would not join a trade union, the employer could in turn make a claim against those who had forced him to dismiss the non-union employee.

A similar provision relating to the dismissal of a worker for not joining a union exists under the Employment Act of 1980 in respect of work done under contract. Thus suppose producer A is supplying under contract to B some component for B's use. Suppose that the employees of B insist that the contract should stipulate that the components be made

---

*Since the Employment Act of 1980 action short of dismissal to compel membership of a trade union is also unlawful. This raises a difficult question of the definition of such action. For example, in some collective bargains the union may insist that the favourable wage or other conditions should not be extended to non-union employees. Is the acceptance of such a provision by the employer to be regarded as action to compel the worker to join the union?

only by union labour and that A is employing a non-union employee on their production. If B is unwilling to waive the stipulation that non-union labour should not be employed and if A can find no alternative work for him, A may be unable to avoid dismissing the non-union worker. In this case the non-union worker would have a claim against A for unfair dismissal; but since the Employment Act of 1980 A could in turn claim against B for not waiving the stipulation forbidding the use of non-union labour; and B in turn could claim against his workers who had not allowed him to waive the stipulation, provided that they do so by threatening some form of industrial action.

The rules against dismissal for membership or activity in an independent trade union apply to all workers. The other rules against unfair dismissal do not apply to persons over normal retirement age for the job, persons employed by their spouse, persons employed outside Great Britain, and registered dockworkers. In addition, in order to make it easier to set up new businesses, the Employment Act of 1980 exempts from the unfair dismissal provisions a new business during the first two years of its operation, so long as it employs fewer than 20 persons.

For others the rules against unfair dismissal (except for the rules protecting trade union membership and activities which apply in all cases) apply only after a certain period of continuous employment with the employer, at present set in the general case at 52 weeks, but at 104 weeks for employers with fewer than 20 employees.

Cases concerning unfair dismissal fall within the jurisdiction of the industrial tribunals (see Section 9 below). In the case of a lock-out or strike or other industrial action an employer can, while the lock-out or strike is still in action, dismiss the whole of his labour force and take on a new labour force without this falling within the jurisdiction of the tribunal, with the effect that this is not treated as unfair dismissal. But this is so only if he dismisses all the relevant employees; any form of selective dismissal, whatever the process of selection, would make it liable to the jurisdiction of the tribunal and would raise the question whether the dismissal was fair or not, given all the surrounding conditions.

As a remedy against unfair dismissal the employer may be required to compensate the dismissed employee. Such compensation consists of two elements: (1) a basic compensation subject to a maximum which depends on the period of continuous employment and the level of the employee's rate of pay; and (2) a compensatory award to cover expenses, benefits lost since the date of dismissal, estimated future lost benefits, and loss of pension rights, with a certain maximum award. The calculation of such compensation thus raises the two problems of what constitutes a period of continuous employment and what constitutes an employee's normal week's pay, which we have already mentioned. As an alternative remedy the employer may be ordered to reinstate the dismissed employee. He is not, however, ultimately compelled to take back a worker; but in the case of failure to fulfil an order to reinstate, the employer is liable to pay an extra sum in compensation, additional to the two elements mentioned above.

These statutory measures of protection against unfair dismissal do not in any way reduce any right which a dismissed employee may have to claim damages from his employer for having wrongfully dismissed him in breach of some term in his individual contract of employment, though any damages which he might receive for breach of contract would be reduced by the amount of any compensation granted for unfair dismissal.

In addition to the matters discussed above the law relating to unfair dismissal contains some further provisions which have very important implications for the power of trade unions to organise their membership. We defer discussion of these till later in Section 5.

It is of interest to note that the statutory provisions described in this section, in particular those relating to unfair dismissal, represent a movement from 'contract' towards 'status' or 'property rights' in the field of employment law. A worker in a job now obtains by statute certain rights to his job which depend *inter alia* on the length of time for which he has held the job and the loss of which through redundancy or unfair dismissal needs to be compensated even if the termination of the employment in no way broke the terms of his contract with his employer.

4. The Formation of Trade Unions

In addition to the statutory provisions which affect the individual contract of employment, enumerated in Section 3, there are a number of provisions which confer a special legal status on trade unions and employers' associations.

A trade union must consist of workers and one of its principal objectives must be the regulation of relations between those workers and their employers. It can, however, have other objectives as well. If it takes part in party political activities it must set up a political fund financed by levies on its members and from which alone its political objectives can be financed; the institution of such a fund must satisfy certain requirements including a secret ballot of members to set up the fund and the right of individual members of the union to opt out of the political levy.

A Certification Officer keeps a record of 'listed' trade unions, the advantage of such certification being that it confers relief from income tax on the trade union's provident funds. An 'independent trade union' is a listed union certified to be independent of any control by an employer or employer's association. As is noted in what follows, certification of independence is needed for a trade union to enjoy a number of the favourable provisions of the law.

Before the Employment Act of 1980 one of these favourable legal provisions took the form of a procedure whereby an independent trade union could ensure effective recognition by an employer for the purposes of collective bargaining. An appeal could be made to the Advisory Conciliation and Arbitration Service (ACAS) and the Central Arbitration Committee (CAC) which are described in Section 9 below; and a recommendation could be obtained determining which union should represent a group of workers for bargaining over a given set of subjects. If the recommendation was not accepted by the employer, a final sanction was the issue of a compulsory arbitral award specifying the terms which the employer must observe. This provision was repealed by the Employment Act of 1980.

But a trade union may, of course, still induce an employer voluntarily to recognise it for bargaining purposes. In the case of an independent trade union which is so recognised the law provides a procedure for the disclosure of information by the employer to the trade union concerned. Subject to a number of safeguards covering information obtained in confidence by the employer and information the disclosure of which would cause substantial injury to the business for reasons other than its effect on collective bargaining, an employer is under a statutory obligation to disclose information which is needed by the trade union concerned for effective collective bargaining. A similar procedure (through ACAS and the CAC) to that described in the preceding paragraph can lead to a compulsory arbitral award specifying the terms which must be observed by an employer who is held to have made serious collective bargaining impossible by the failure to disclose the relevant information.

Where redundancies occur, employers are under a legal obligation to consult with any relevant independent recognised trade union about the treatment of the redundancies, in addition to an obligation to report substantive redundancies in advance to the Department of Employment.

Further statutory provisions favour trade union activity and the recruitment of members by trade unions. We have already noted in the previous section that the dismissal of an employee because of membership or activity in an independent trade union is ruled to be unfair; and in addition an employee has a statutory right not to be deterred from joining an independent trade union by sanctions short of dismissal. Officials and members of an independent trade union which has been recognised for bargaining also have a statutory right to time off with pay for trade union activities.

5. The Membership of Trade Unions: The Closed Shop

By the statutory provisions described in previous sections a trade union's ability to canvass and organise its membership has certain legal protections.

But it does not necessarily have to admit all comers to its membership.

A trade union is a voluntary club or society and like other such clubs has far-reaching powers in deciding about admissions to and expulsions from membership. An applicant who was refused membership would probably have little or no case for recourse under the common law to the ordinary courts for redress; but as in the case of other clubs or societies an aggrieved individual who had been unwillingly expelled could have recourse to the ordinary law courts for redress if the action taken by the trade union had not been in accordance with its rules or with the principles of natural justice. But this leaves many cases uncovered. To take an example, if a worker was expelled from membership of a trade union because he had refused to join in a strike action, he would have no redress if (1) the trade union rule book stated that such was the penalty for disobeying a lawful trade union call to strike and (2) his case had been fairly examined and decided, giving him a proper opportunity to defend his behaviour.

Expulsion from a trade union can in any case be an important instrument for maintaining trade union discipline and thus unified monopoly action, since, for example, loss of trade union membership may entail loss of pension rights from a trade union fund to which the worker had been contributing. But the issue becomes one of basic importance if there is a 'closed shop' (technically known as a 'union membership agreement'), that is to say, a state of affairs in which the established practice is for the employer to employ no one who is not a member of the relevant trade union. For in this case loss of trade union membership implies loss of job and thus in the extreme case loss of livelihood.

Closed shops can in fact take many forms with many varying grades of severity in their application. But they can usefully be divided into two broad groups: (1) the post-entry closed shop in which case the employer is free to engage a worker whether he be a trade unionist or not, and may continue to employ him provided that the worker when he has been engaged joins the relevant trade union; or (2) the pre-entry closed shop in which case the employer can engage only those workers who are already members of the relevant trade union. Both kinds of closed shop increase the powers of discipline which the trade union can exercise over the workers concerned and thus promote its bargaining power. They also protect the workers concerned from the competition of members of other unions which are not recognised in the closed-shop agreement and who may be less well paid. The pre-entry closed shop, if it is combined with trade union rules and practices which severely limit admission to the union, can in addition operate as a direct monopoly control restricting the supply of labour to the trade or occupation concerned.

Before the enactment of the Employment Act of 1980 there were no serious legal restraints on the formation of such closed shops. The employer who agreed to operate a closed shop was safeguarded because a worker who in such a case was dismissed because he was not a member of the relevant trade union was barred from pleading that he was unfairly dismissed, except in the extreme case in which he could show that he had a religious objection to joining any union. Any worker who was refused admission to, or was expelled from, a union which operated a closed shop would be debarred from work in that trade or occupation. Apart from the right, as stated above, for a member who was expelled to go to the ordinary courts on the grounds that the trade union's action was not in accord with its rule book or with the claims of natural justice, his only recourse was a review of the case by an informal TUC body, which was also available to consider cases of aggrieved workers who had been refused admission to a union. But even this recourse was, of course, available only if the union concerned was affiliated to the TUC.

The Employment Act of 1980 introduces four important changes restraining the operation of pre-entry closed shops.

First, it extends the protection which the law gives to those who are dismissed for not joining the relevant union. Previously only the narrow category of persons who had a religious objection to joining any union was protected; protection now covers the wider category of persons who for any deeply held personal conviction object to being a member of any trade union or of the trade union in question.

Second, an employer will no longer be protected from the charge of unfair dismissal if the employee concerned has been in his employment before the institution of the closed shop and has refrained from joining the union. In the case of such dismissal the worker concerned can claim compensation from the employer. But if the employer had in effect been compelled by the refusal of the trade union members concerned to permit the continued employment of the non-union member, the employer could in turn seek compensation from the trade union or its members who had forced his hand.

Third, in the case of any new closed shop to be instituted after the enactment of the Employment Act of 1980 the employer will be protected from the charge of unfair dismissal of a worker who will not join the relevant union, only if this closed shop has been set up after an 80 per cent affirmative vote of all the workers covered by the agreement (and not merely of all those who choose to vote).

Fourth, a worker who was excluded or expelled from a trade union which operated a closed shop is now enabled (in addition to the rights of appeal to the courts and to the TUC review body mentioned above) to complain to an industrial tribunal that his exclusion or expulsion was unreasonable; and the trade union would be liable to pay compensation if its action were found to be unreasonable.

This fourth provision comes close to the heart of the matter. But its importance depends on the interpretation put by the tribunals on the word 'unreasonable'. If it were considered unreasonable for a trade union to exclude any one from the union who was in fact able to do the job, then the provision could in operation greatly weaken the power of the union to maintain a monopolistic scarcity of labour in the trade or occupation concerned. If, however, exclusion is interpreted as unreasonable only if it is based on the colour of the applicant's hair or a personal grudge against his parents or some such personal reason, the provision, while it might prevent a few individual cases of unjust treatment, would do nothing basically to affect the monopolistic situation. It would seem inappropriate to leave unguided to a court or a tribunal the choice between interpretations of a term which has such basic economic implications.

Under the Employment Act of 1980 the minister is empowered to issue Codes of Practice which give general guidance as to what may be regarded desirable conduct or arrangements for various aspects of labour relations. The suggestions made in these codes do not constitute legal requirements but they may be quoted as evidence in court. The Code of Practice which has been issued on closed shops gives no guidance on what is reasonable or unreasonable in refusing admission to or expulsion from a union. It does, however, give one piece of guidance about dismissals by suggesting that closed-shop agreements should 'provide that an employee will not be dismissed if expelled from his union for refusal to take part in industrial action'. But this guidance is not a binding requirement; the tribunal can be properly required to consider it, but is free to ignore it.

6.   The Exemption of Trade Unions from Certain Restraints on Monopolistic Action

In the two preceding sections we have described how the law facilitates the formation of trade unions. One of these possible lawful arrangements is the initiation of a pre-entry closed shop which does confer a most important monopolistic power in so far as it can be used to restrict the quantity of labour permitted to enter a given field. But most of the arrangements described so far promote the effective formation of trade unions without in themselves conferring on them any special monopolistic powers. But there would be little in the way of bargaining power to be gained from the formation of a trade union if at the same time the law forbade the use of its monopolistic powers by any such organisation. In the case of other groups both the common law and various statutory provisions do forbid or seriously restrain, except in a few exceptional cases, the use of monopolistic powers. Thus, to take the simplest possible example, it would be unlawful for all the producers of commodity X to get together in a cartel to set quotas restricting the supply of X or to set a monopoly price for a unit of X with an agreement not to sell any X below that price; and the law would also be able to prevent them from merging into a single combined company which would give them directly the same monopoly power. But labour organisations are expressly exempted from such legal restrictions. They can organise on any scale and their activities (in fixing the price of labour, restricting the supply of labour, and so on) are not unlawful; they are exempted both from the common law decisions against restraint of trade and from the statutory provisions limiting restrictive business practices and the formation of monopolies. As we shall see, this is indeed the crux of the whole matter. If they are to fulfil a wage-fixing function, trade unions must be exempt to some extent from legal provisions against restraint of trade. But to what extent, in what particular respects, and subject to what constraints?*

In addition to these exemptions from legal provisions controlling behaviour in restraint of trade, combined action by a number of workers in contemplation or furtherance of a trade dispute is protected from liability as a case of criminal conspiracy unless the act in question would have been punishable as a crime when committed by an individual alone. This means that in the case of a trade dispute agreed action by a group of workers to injure or annoy an employer by means which would not in themselves be crimes, or to commit a tort, or to break their contracts cannot be treated as a criminal offence.

On the other hand, certain acts which may be taken in the course of a trade dispute in order to induce individual workers to join in the prosecution of a strike or other industrial action (such as persistently following a person from place to place; hiding tools, clothes, or other property or depriving a person of their use; watching and besetting the house or other place where a person resides or works; and following a person with two or more other persons in a disorderly manner) are expressly ruled by statute to be punishable as crimes, though there is some doubt as to whether these acts are in and of themselves criminal or whether they are to be regarded as criminal acts only if they are done in connection with some other civil wrong (such as an actionable nuisance to the person concerned).

---

*In Appendix D we outline the structure and operations of the Monopolies and Mergers Commission and of the Restrictive Practices Court in controlling business monopolistic practices. Ministers do in fact have the power to refer restrictive labour practices to the Monopolies and Mergers Commission for it to report whether the practice exists and, if so, what adverse effects, if any, it may have. But such references have not in fact been made; and in any case the Commission is not required to consider remedies and the government has not taken any powers to control any practices which the Commission may condemn. But, much more important, under the Restrictive Trade Practices Act, which is the effective legislation to outlaw monopolistic and restrictive practices, agreements which relate to questions of employment, pay, hours of work, and other labour matters are exempt from the provisions of the Act.

The exemptions described above will mean that certain monopolistic actions by trade unions in restraint of trade will not in themselves be unlawful. But such actions will normally damage the economic interests of other persons; and if those persons could take action in the civil courts to obtain compensation for such damages or to obtain a court order requiring the trade union or its members to desist from the damaging action, the express intention to confer effective monopolistic bargaining powers on trade unions would be wholly or in large part stultified. For this reason the trade unions and their members enjoy important legal immunities against action in respect of such damages.

Since the legislation following the Taff Vale case in 1906, trade unions and employers' associations have been (with very minor exceptions)* immune from all actions for damages in tort. These immunities mean that no action of a trade union or employer's association can be held wrongful merely because it hurts someone else by restricting the opportunities for others to buy or sell or produce or work or to take part in any gainful activity. They mean also that the funds of the trade union or employers' association are not at risk against any claims for damages caused by the trade union or employers' association or their officers or agents or members through inducing a breach of contract or interference with any contract or for any other tort committed by the officers or members of the trade union (e.g. libel, detaining the employer's or customer's goods, trespass or nuisance, physically preventing a person from working).

While, as described above, no action for damages in tort can (with very minor exceptions) be taken against a trade union or an employers' association itself, whether there be a trade dispute or not, officials and members of a trade union do not enjoy such far-reaching immunity. Actions in tort for damages against them as individuals are not ruled out in general; but statutory protection against such liability is given to them only if the act in question was done in contemplation or furtherance of a trade dispute and then only against liability for certain specified torts, namely: those connected with breach of contract (inducing someone else to break a contract, interfering with someone's contract, or threatening to do any of these things); interfering with the trade, business, employment, disposal of property, or use of labour by another person; or conspiring with other persons to damage another's interest either by means which were not unlawful in themselves (simple conspiracy) or by

---

*The exceptions are for certain damages for personal injury resulting from negligence etc. or certain damages due to the misuse of property. But even these liabilities are not incurred if the acts causing the damage are taken in contemplation or furtherance of a trade dispute.

means (e.g. inducing a breach of contract) for which immunity is given as described above for acts by individual trade union members.*

The Employment Act of 1980 removes this immunity for individual members of a trade union from tort actions for damages in three cases:

(1) where the act has resulted from someone acting as a picket at some place of work other than his or her own place of work;
(2) where the act has resulted from action in a trade dispute which has been taken against an employer who is not a party to that dispute and is not a direct supplier to or customer of the employer who is a party to the dispute;
(3) where a person induces an employee of one employer to break his contract of employment in order to compel workers employed by another employer to join a particular trade union.

The far-reaching implications of the first and second of these cases will be discussed later in this chapter.

Officials or member of a trade union are not given immunity in any circumstances against personal liability for damages for other torts such as libel, detaining the employer's or customer's goods, trespass or nuisance, physically preventing a person from working, etc.

As far as the trade unions themselves are concerned these immunities are practically unqualified which means that the trade unions' funds are protected against all such claims for damages. In the case of individual workers the protection covers only such action as is taken 'in contemplation or furtherance of a trade dispute'. For this reason the notions of a 'trade dispute' and of actions taken 'in contemplation or furtherance' of such disputes are of central importance in trade union law, since they are the basis for giving these special immunities for many acts which would otherwise be illegal. A 'trade dispute' must be a dispute either between employers and workers or between workers and workers; but disputes between employers and employers are not covered. The fact that disputes between workers and workers are covered means that if one union, for example, organises a strike to prevent an employer from recognising another union, while that other union organises a strike in order to compel its recognition, both sets of strikers will enjoy the legal immunities conferred on those acting in furtherance of a trade dispute. The employer who suffers the ill effects of the strikes has no remedy except the hope that an informal TUC committee (acting under its

---

*There is some legal uncertainty surrounding the precise scope of this last provision.

'Bridlington principles') will in due course persuade the warring unions on the division of membership and powers between them.*

For the dispute to be a 'trade' dispute for the purpose of the granting of legal immunities it must be a dispute about such matters as the terms and conditions of employment, engagement of workers, duties of employment, allocation of work between workers, discipline, membership of a trade union, facilities for officers of trade unions, machinery for negotiation, etc. The statutory protections given in cases of a trade dispute disappear if the only motive in the dispute is not about 'trade' but is some personal grudge or desire to punish someone.

The wide range of subjects thus covered by the phrase a 'trade dispute' means that trade union action can legitimately be taken not only to support claims for higher wage rates, shorter hours, or other improvements in conditions of work, but also to maintain pay by restricting the supply of labour or inflating the demand for it, for example, by restricting the number or prolonging the period of training of apprentices, by restricting entry to the unions, by demarcation rules, by rules to insist on the extra manning of operations and on uses of unproductive labour.

Before the Employment Act of 1980, the words 'in furtherance' of a trade dispute had been interpreted by the courts to cover action which is only very indirectly and remotely connected with the dispute, provided only that the person taking the action genuinely considered that it might have some effect on the settlement of the dispute, however remote that effect might be and however great the damage which it might incidentally cause to third parties. The implications of this wide interpretation of the meaning of 'in contemplation or furtherance' of a trade dispute and of the changes made by the Employment Act of 1980 can best be explained by means of an example.

A possible case would be one of three firms A, B, and C, in which A purchases supplies from B and B purchases supplies from C.

If the employees *a* of firm A were in dispute with their employer A, they might (1) strike against their employer A, (2) induce the employees *b* of firm B to threaten to strike against their employer B unless B stopped

---

*The Employment Act of 1980 may have an indirect and unintended effect on this conclusion. Suppose the workers of two unions A and B to be in dispute about recognition by their employer C, who as a result of their action is forced to break a contract with one of his customers D. Since the dispute is between workers A and B and not between them and their employer C, their interference with the contract between C and D is interference with a contract between two bodies neither of which is a party in the dispute. It may thus be held to fall into the category of what below we call 'tertiary' action, which no longer enjoys the legal immunities against tort action. Thus D might take action in the civil courts against A and B in respect of the damage caused to him by their interference with his contract with C.

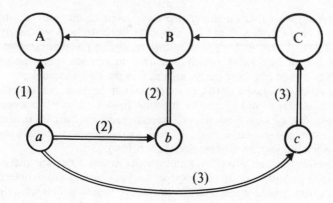

supplying goods to A, or (3) induce the employees *c* of firm C to threaten to strike against their employer C unless C stopped supplying to B so long as B was supplying A. Such actions may be called (1) primary, (2) secondary, and (3) tertiary. A similar situation might arise where C was buying goods from B who was buying from A, in which case the employees *a* might induce the employees *b* and/or the employees *c* to put pressure on B and/or C in order to stop sales by A. Before the Employment Act of 1980, provided that the employees *a*, *b* and *c* genuinely considered that their action would aid employees *a* in their dispute with A they enjoyed the immunities due to action taken in contemplation or further-ance of a trade dispute, even though much damage was inflicted on B and C in the process of giving a little help to *a*.

The Employment Act of 1980 sets out to remove the immunities against claims for damages in the case of what we have called tertiary actions while preserving them for secondary as well as primary actions. In terms of the above example the workers *c* would no longer enjoy immunities in respect of their industrial action against C, nor would the workers *a* enjoy immunity in respect of any action taken to induce employees *c* to take action against their employer C.

Such action may take the form of blacking (i.e. of simple refusal of the workers concerned to handle the goods which are directly or in-directly providing A with a market or with supplies) or of sympathetic strikes (e.g. of strikes by workers other than the employees of A in order to induce employers B or C to stop purchasing or supplying goods which are directly or indirectly providing A with a market or with supplies). Thus secondary action in the form of blacking or of sympathetic strikes in support of a particular trade dispute will be lawful if it is taken to prevent a direct supplier or customer of the employer who is in dispute from trading with that employer. However, even in that case it will no longer be lawful unless it can be judged as likely to be a reasonably effective form of support for those in dispute; and in no circumstances will tertiary action be lawful, which attempts to operate more indirectly through the trade of a third party, such as C in the above example.

The sanction against tertiary action would be that the individuals taking such action would not be immune from civil court proceedings to recover damages by those whose interests had been hurt by the secondary action, and recourse could be had to the courts to obtain an injunction to stop such action (see Section 9 below).

Neither before nor after the Employment Act of 1980 was there any statutory immunity against claims for damages arising from breach of contract. This would mean that, in the above example, if B were under a firm contract with A to supply goods to A and were induced by lawful secondary action not to supply them, A could legally obtain damages from B for breach of contract. But B may be trading with A without any such contract. If there is a contract it may well be such that damages do not arise if its fulfilment is frustrated by events beyond the control of the parties to the contract; and it is common nowadays for contracts to include such an escape clause. Even if this were not the case, B might well be prepared to risk such damages rather than face a strike, because he would be liable to a much greater loss if his business were brought to a complete standstill.

The employers A and B would also have a legal claim against any individual worker who broke his contract of employment as a result of taking industrial action. A strike would involve a breach of contract by any individual worker who ceased work without giving the length of notice required under his individual contract of employment; and most cases of industrial action do in fact involve some breach of their contracts by the individual workers concerned. The workers may, however, give due notice of their intention to strike; and in this case their action might be interpreted by the courts, according to the particular circumstances of the case, as a breach, or as a termination, or as a suspension, of their contracts. Normally, however, employers do not take court action in cases of breach of contract by their employees; and there are a number of reasons for this. First, this would require legal action against each individual worker separately. Second, any such claim against an individual worker would be for compensation for the damage caused by him alone in stopping work; and the total damage done to the concern when all workers stop work together is likely to be much greater than the sum of the individual damages which would be done by each worker alone ceasing work. Third, it is not possible to obtain a court injunction requiring a worker to return to work to fulfil his contract of employment. Finally, and perhaps most importantly, court action against workers to obtain damages would be likely to embitter relations between the employer and his labour force which he would hope to eventually employ once more.

The legal immunities of workers taking industrial action depend upon their being taken in connection with a 'trade' dispute. As we have seen, a wide scope is given to the meaning of the term to cover all matters concerned — pay, employment, conditions of work, membership of unions, etc. But there exists an increasing number of cases in which it is difficult to draw the line between action taken in furtherance of a trade dispute and action taken for a political end. Many disputes nowadays are in effect disputes with Parliament or the government. Would action taken by a group of workers to demand a wage increase with the express purpose of forcing a government to admit the need to revise or repeal some statutory restriction on pay (an official incomes policy) be a dispute about trade? Would action taken by a group of civil servants (i.e. those needed to operate the computers needed to raise revenue from the income tax) in sympathetic support of another group of workers who were taking industrial action to protest against their future redundancy which was expected to result from a change in the tax base (e.g. elimination of a tax on road vehicles) be action taken 'in furtherance of a trade dispute'? Would a strike for a wage claim in an industry which relied upon a state subsidy be action taken in furtherance of a trade dispute, if it was admitted by all concerned that the claim could be met only by a governmental decision to raise the subsidy payable to the industry? Where in the modern world is the line to be drawn? Are strikes against the policy of a democratically constituted Parliament and government in effect to be granted legal immunities?

7. Extension of the Scope of Wage Bargains

Before the Employment Act of 1980 there were statutory provisions (operated through the Advisory, Conciliation and Arbitration Service (ACAS) and the Central Arbitration Committee (CAC), which are described below in Section 9) enabling the terms and conditions of employment which were recognised in any sector of the economy (as a result of a collective bargain, an arbitral decision, or otherwise), or which were generally ruling in that sector, to be enforced against any individual employer who was not observing them. A trade union or an employer's association that was party to the generally recognised terms could claim that an employer was not observing such terms and, if the claim was substantiated, could obtain an award which caused the generally recognised terms to be incorporated into the terms of the individual contracts of employment between the offending employer and his employees.

The enforcement throughout the sector of the economy concerned of terms set by a collective agreement protects from outside competition both the employers and the employed who have reached the agreement, and thus strengthens the ability and the willingness of both sides to raise the rate of pay. Moreover the application of this power in the absence of a recognised collective agreement to cover the terms generally ruling in the sector of the economy concerned introduced a danger of inflationary leap-frogging. For if the 'terms generally ruling' is interpreted to mean 'the average of the various terms in the various firms concerned', then any group below the average would have a claim to be raised to the average. Such action raises the average, which in turn provides a new claim to all who as a result are now left below the new and higher average — a process which theoretically has no end until everyone is paid at the same, namely, the highest, rate.

The Employment Act of 1980 repealed the provisions for this procedure so that there is no longer any legal means whereby collective bargains can be compulsorily extended in this manner to cover the whole of any given trade. But it has not modified the application of the Fair Wages Resolution, that is to say, of the principle that in all work done to fulfil contracts with the government or local authorities wages should be paid at the recognised or generally ruling rates. Moreover, this principle has been interpreted to imply that if, as is often the case, the rates recognised by the relevant collective agreement refer only to minimum rates, then the wage paid must be at the higher rate which is in fact generally ruling in that sector and not simply at the recognised minimum rate.

8.   Picketing

Picketing is expressly permitted by law to allow workers who are taking industrial action peacefully to persuade others to withdraw their labour and thus to join the industrial action. On some recent occasions (e.g. the coal strike of 1972 and the lorry drivers' strike of 1979) highly organised, widespread mass picketing has been the decisive factor in an industrial dispute. In some instances action has gone far beyond 'peaceful persuasion'; but quite apart from any such unlawful acts (and it is clear that they are criminal offences), great pressure has been exerted by organising widespread mass pickets not merely to make the industrial action fully effective in the case of those directly concerned in the dispute but also to exert pressure in other sectors of the economy in support of the primary dispute. Thus, for example, the coal miners in 1972 organised pickets to prevent oil reaching oil-fired generating stations in order to reinforce the adverse effect on the supply to the community of electricity of the cessation of supplies of coal. Before the Employment Act of 1980 there was no legal bar against the use of picketing, as of other measures of industrial action, for the furtherance of a trade dispute by such indirect means; but the Employment Act of 1980 restricts picketing to picketing by a worker at his own place of work or by an accompanying relevant trade union official; and any one else who by picketing induces a breach of contract will no longer be immune from being sued for any resulting damages; and it will be open to those who are hurt by such action to seek a court injunction to put a stop to it.

We explained above how the Employment Act of 1980 outlawed what we called tertiary, but permitted what we called secondary, action in blacking and sympathetic strikes (see Section 6 above). But by confining picketing to a worker's own place of work all secondary as well as tertiary picketing is outlawed. Indeed even some primary picketing would now be unlawful; in the case of a dispute between a trade union and a group of employers in which all action was primary, being action taken by members of that union against their employers in that group, the employee of one particular employer in that group could not lawfully act as a picket at the factory of another employer in that group.

It will be no part of the duties of the police to ensure that secondary and tertiary picketing does not take place. It will be for the employers concerned to observe at each place of work whether pickets are formed by persons other than those whose place of work it is, and to take civil action in the courts to sue such persons for damages or to obtain a court order instructing such persons to desist from such picketing.

But the police have far-reaching duties in such matters as the prevention of obstruction of the highway or of a breach of the peace, and it is a criminal offence to obstruct the police in the execution of their duties. This means inevitably that it is in many respects a matter for the police to use their judgement in the light of the circumstances of each particular case as to what is permissible and what is not permissible in the organisation of a picket. For example, mass picketing is not regulated by any overriding legal limit to the size of a picket. It is true that the minister has issued a Code of Practice on Pickets which gives some guidance as to what may be considered reasonable, suggesting that in general the number of pickets at the entrance to a place of work should not exceed six; but as has been explained above, this opinion, while it can be submitted as evidence in court, does not bind the court in its judgment.

The difficulties involved in devising rules to govern reasonable picketing arrangements are well illustrated by considering the modern use of buses to take workers to their place of work and of lorries to deliver supplies to factories and to collect products from factories. Pickets may desire peacefully to persuade the workers in the bus not to go to work or the lorry drivers not to deliver the supplies or to fetch the products; but pickets must not obstruct the highway. If the drivers drive without stopping how can the pickets peacefully inform and persuade? If the pickets stand in the way of the vehicles or erect barriers, is it not the duty of the police to stop the obstruction of the highway? In fact in many cases the police and the pickets agree on commonsensical solutions, such that the police will stop each vehicle to allow one picket to speak to the driver for a short period of time. But it is practically impossible to draft precise rules which cover all possible situations for this or other similar picketing arrangements (such as what number of pickets is likely to lead to a breach of the peace), with the result that the police are necessarily left with a very wide range of discretion. The only feasible approach to a solution would seem to be, not to attempt to devise precise rules, but to define publicly by statute or otherwise the general duties of the police which they are to take into account in the exercise of their discretion, such as to allow facilities for the giving of information and persuasion by peaceful pickets subject always to the avoidance of serious threats of the breach of the peace or of unreasonable interference with the free use of the highway.

9. Adjudication and Enforcement

The implementation of the various legal provisions outlined above requires, in addition to the administrative functions of the government departments concerned, a large extension of decisions about complaints, disputes and applications under this large range of topics.

For this purpose there now exist, in addition to the regular courts of law, some special judicial or semi-judicial bodies. In general the chairman of these bodies is a lawyer, but they contain also lay members representing both sides of industry. The ordinary courts cannot be expected to have the detailed knowledge and practice of industrial matters and labour relations which are useful in settling disputes. There is thus a strong case for a set of special tribunals whose decisions remain subject to appeal on points of law to the courts, which in turn should and do remain the ultimate interpreters and guardians of the law.

It is not the purpose of this chapter to describe these bodies and their functions, composition, and procedures in any detail, but merely to note their existence.

(i) There is now a widespread structure of *Industrial Tribunals* whose functions include questions concerning: industrial training levies; written particulars of employment; redundancy payments; sex discrimination in employment; equal pay for men and women; unfair dismissal; health and safety at work; payments for a guaranteed week; maternity pay; various rights for trade unions, members, and officials; and employees' rights on the insolvency of the employer.

Above the Industrial Tribunals there is a special court called the *Employment Appeal Tribunal* to which questions of law can be referred from the Industrial Tribunals.

Questions concerning personal injuries, torts, and breach of contracts of all kinds are dealt with by the ordinary civil courts, though the Lord Chancellor has the power, which he has not yet exercised, to transfer jurisdiction in respect of certain breaches of contract of employment to the Industrial Tribunal.

(ii) There is an official service, *The Advisory, Conciliation, and Arbitration Service (ACAS),* whose function it is to improve industrial relations by being ready to conciliate in disputes, and by encouraging, extending, and reforming machinery for collective bargaining. It has the power of making enquiries and recommendations in some of the matters discussed above, such as questions concerning the obligation of employers to disclose the information needed for effective collective bargaining.

ACAS has no powers of enforcing decisions in these matters. But there exists an independent arbitration body, the *Central Arbitration Committee (CAC),* which does possess some such powers in addition to its function of operating as a voluntary arbitral body where the parties to a dispute so desire. The CAC has the ultimate power of making binding awards which an employer must observe in cases in which there has been a failure to accept an ACAS recommendation on certain matters such as the disclosure of information.

A matter of great importance is the methods and penalties by means of which the law may be enforced.

At present in matters concerning trade disputes and other trade union activities there is little recourse to the criminal law. Certain acts (e.g. of physical violence) would, of course, remain criminal in all circumstances, and, as noted in Section 6, certain specified acts connected with the conduct of trade disputes (such as hiding a worker's tools) have been made criminal by statute. But the whole corpus of criminal conspiracy in restraint of trade is no longer applicable to the purposes or activities of trade unions.

Civil proceedings for damages for breach of contract are not ruled out by any special immunities for trade unions or trade unionists. Most strikers are in fact in breach of their individual contracts of employment; but for reasons discussed in Section 6 employers do not normally sue for damages from individual employees.

Civil proceedings for damages in tort (e.g. for damages from restraint of trade or inducement for breach of contract) are in general ruled out against trade unions as such and are also ruled out against individual workers if the damaging action has been taken in contemplation or furtherance of a trade dispute. The Employment Act of 1980 would, as explained in Section 5, make trade unions liable to pay compensation for damages to a person who was unreasonably expelled or excluded from a trade union which was operating a closed shop, and in the three important cases described in Section 6 would make an individual person who was taking action in a trade dispute liable to civil actions in tort for damages.

An important factor which inhibits the suing of individual workers for damages in respect of breach of contract or of tort is the cost and difficulty of collecting any such damages, particularly if the worker is determined to defy the law. The situation would be altered in an important respect if, as was suggested by the Labour government in 'In Place of Strife',* damages or fines could be collected at source by attachment of the worker's earnings.

There remains the important and difficult problem of the use by the courts of injunctions in the case of trade union action. An injunction is an order by the court to someone or some body to desist from certain acts until by the process of a normal trial it can be determined whether the act is lawful or not. In the case of a trade dispute the following sort of situation may arise.

A trade union is taking some action against a producer; the action may do irreparable damage to the producer if it is taken; on the other hand, if the action is not taken at once its efficacy in affecting the current issue (e.g. the outcome of a strike elsewhere) will disappear. Suppose, however, that there is reasonable doubt whether the action can be judged to be lawfully taken in furtherance of a trade dispute. In these circumstances by allowing or disallowing the injunction the court is in fact deciding the issue in favour of the employer or of the trade union, even though in theory a later trial would decide the issue between them.

Injunctions are normally obeyed in our law-abiding country, though there is some reason to question whether this will invariably be the case in industrial disputes. The penalty for disobedience would be imprisonment for contempt of court, an occurrence which can be welcomed by some offenders in circumstances in which they feel strongly about an issue and judge that martyrdom will promote the cause.

The courts thus have an extremely important but difficult function in deciding whether or not to grant an injunction. They are by statute required (1) to hear both sides, and not only the party asking for the injunction, if in their opinion the other party would claim a trade-dispute defence of its action, and (2), in exercising their discretion whether or not to grant an injunction, to have regard to the probability of the party against whom the injunction is sought being able at the ultimate trial to establish his claim to a trade-dispute defence.

The problem is indeed of crucial importance. In the wider range of cases of unlawful industrial action (such as what we have called tertiary blacking or sympathetic striking, pickets operating not at their own place of work, action taken when it can be claimed that there is no trade dispute, and so on) the effective civil remedy for the employer is to obtain an injunction to put a stop to the action. The prospects and costs of

*Government White Paper. *In Place of Strife: A Policy for Industrial Relations.* Cmnd 3888. January 1969.

proceeding to obtain actual damages from the individual wrongdoers after the action may well mean that no effective remedy is to be found in that way. It is the injunction which stops the action, not the compensation for damage caused by the action which matters.

10.   Social Security Provisions

Social security provisions may have an influence on the monopolistic powers of trade unions by affecting their ability and willingness to organise industrial action; and these provisions have been changed in certain respects by a Social Security Act of 1980.

Workers indirectly thrown out of work as a result of a trade dispute, for example, those out of work in firm A as a result of a strike in firm B which stops the supply of some component vital for the maintenance of production and employment in firm A, will receive unemployment pay. But any person who is out of work directly because of a trade dispute at his own place of work is not eligible to receive unemployment benefit unless he can show that he is not directly interested in the outcome of the dispute at his place of work. In general such a person would not be eligible either to receive any supplementary benefit to cover his own needs, although, until the enactment of the Social Security Act 1980, he could in exceptional cases of dire need obtain a small amount of such benefit.

But supplementary benefit is receivable to meet the basic needs (rent, rates, food clothing) of the worker's dependants, after deduction of any other resources including strike pay otherwise available to the worker concerned (over and above a small amount of such other resources which are disregarded). Thus, for example, if the dependants' basic needs were £50 and the worker had £10 available from other sources to be taken into account, the supplementary benefit receivable would be £40. But by the Social Security Act of 1980 the worker will in all cases be deemed to be receiving £12 in strike pay, so that the above figure of £40 net receipts of supplementary benefit would be further reduced to £28 in the case of a worker who had not in fact any resources from strike pay. This would be so whether or not the worker concerned were a member of a trade union or of the trade union in dispute.

The effect of this provision would be to make the cost of strikes financially more expensive for the trade union funds or to increase the moral pressure on a trade union not to organise a strike which put such a strain on the standard of living of the workers concerned. Clearly these arrangements could impose great hardship on the families of some strikers, whether willingly or unwillingly on strike and whether trade unionists or not. A preferable arrangement might well be to provide supplementary benefit to meet basic needs, but to provide it in the form of a loan repayable by attachment from the subsequent earnings of the workers concerned. Such an arrangement would have the same ultimate effect of imposing on the workers the final cost of the strike without reducing the families concerned to immediate intolerable hardship.

11.   Conclusion

There is at present a large range of legal provisions which encourage the formation of monopolistic labour organisations and which protect their powers for monopolistic wage bargaining. These take many forms of which the most important are: the ability to control the supply of labour to a sector of the economy through a pre-entry closed shop; exemption from the common law and statutory laws which prevent restraint of trade; and various immunities from civil actions for damages caused by strikes and other forms of industrial action. In a limited number of respects the Employment Act of 1980 has reduced the scope of these legal protections of the exercise by trade unions of monopolistic powers; but it will be one of the purposes of the following chapter to consider whether in the interest of competition there should be any further reduction of these legal powers to take monopolistic action.

CHAPTER VI

The Role of Competition in the Labour Market

In Chapter IV we have considered at length the reasons why in a world of imperfect competition it is desirable that there should exist wage-fixing institutions to offset the monopsonistic powers of an employer. There are, however, some other additional reasons why it is not suitable to rely solely on the forces of competition for the setting of rates of pay.

1. Some Further Reasons for Intervention in the Labour Market

In the first place, a full return to competitive conditions in the labour market would have to involve very ungenerous treatment of the unemployed in order to ensure that the competition of the unemployed in search of work resulted in no increases, indeed in reductions, of wage rates wherever the supply of labour exceeded the demand. But in a humane compassionate society one does not want to have to rely on the threat of starvation of those who are unfortunate enough to lose their jobs in a contracting sector of the economy as the means of ensuring moderation in the wage rates set in such occupations. One needs to find some alternative method which applies supply—demand criteria for the fixing of wage rates for those in employment without inflicting needless hardship and anxiety on those particular individuals who are inevitably adversely affected by economic change.

Redundancy payments and generous unemployment benefits, in particular earnings-related benefits,* were designed to promote economic growth by reducing the resistance to loss of jobs in contracting sectors of the economy. But measures of this kind, by maintaining standards of living during periods of unemployment, are bound to make persons more choosey in their search for and acceptance of alternative jobs. They are thus likely to cause some rise in the normal level of frictional unemployment.† There is thus inevitably some conflict between generosity of treatment of the unemployed and the incentives for the unemployed to

---

*Earnings-related benefits are being abolished.
† See S. J. Nickell, 'The effect of unemployment and related benefits on the duration of unemployment', *Economic Journal*, March 1979.

search for and to move to new and useful even if less attractive jobs. Here, as is so often the case, there is need for some compromise between warm-hearted generosity and hard-headed design of incentives.*

It is worth noting in passing that certain fiscal reforms can be designed to ease this conflict. Until recently there were two particular ways in which the tax-cum-social-security system removed incentives to work.

First, social benefits to the unemployed are not liable to income tax, whereas earnings in employment are so liable. It is important, therefore, to raise the personal allowance under the income tax, that is, the first slice of a taxpayer's income which is exempt from tax, at least to the level of untaxed social benefits which the taxpayer would receive if he or she were unemployed. This should be combined with making social benefits to the unemployed liable to tax. If the unemployed had no other resource he would not be taxed because his personal allowance under the income tax would cover his unemployment pay. But if he had other additional resources he would, as indeed he should, pay tax on them.† At present however rich a man may be he receives additional tax-free benefit if he is sick or unemployed.

Second, the unemployed parent receives social benefits for the support of children, whereas until recently the employed parent had in the main to rely on earnings to support the children, though this burden was in part relieved by relatively low family allowances and by relating the first slice of earnings which was free of tax to the number of children in the family. This system is in the process of being replaced by a system of universal child benefits which will be paid in respect of all children regardless of the economic position of the parents, with the result that social benefits in support of children will no longer be lost when an unemployed parent finds work.

In Chapter IV we considered at length the case for wage-fixing institutions in order to offset the bargaining powers of individual employers in monopsonistic situations. But even if within each sector of the economy (e.g. in each industry or region separately) there were a large number of employers in full competition against each other so that no one individual employer had any significant monopsonistic power, there could still be a case for wage-fixing institutions if movement of labour between the competitive sectors was difficult. The competitive mechanism might

---

*The employers' incentives as well as the employees' incentives may be affected. Thus the prospect of possible costs of redundancy payments or charges of unfair dismissal may dissuade some employers who face an uncertain future from expanding their workforce.

†This would remove the anomaly whereby a worker may find that he is actually better off by being unemployed for a part of the year. After working for a period sufficient to earn an amount equal to his personal allowance under the income tax, any additional earnings will be taxed but a switch to unemployment benefit will not be taxed.

work with relatively little hardship if workers could move readily from those competitive sectors (i.e. occupations, trades, industries, or regions) in which pay and employment prospects were poor to those competitive sectors in which they were good. There are many things which can and should be done to make movement between sectors of the economy easier than it is. But whatever is done, movement will never be free and costless. Quite apart from any monetary costs most people feel a disturbing loss at having to leave the friends, relations, neighbourhood, and working conditions to which they have become accustomed; and where, as is increasingly the case, both husband and wife have jobs, acceptable movement may well involve both partners simultaneously finding satisfactory jobs in the new locality. As a result movement of labour from Sector A to Sector B will often be a rather slow process. Often it will have to rely not on Mr Smith moving from A to B but upon waiting until Father Smith retires from Sector A and Son Smith has finished his schooling and is recruited into Sector B.

This sluggishness in labour movements between sectors has an important implication for fixing rates of pay.

Consider the following extreme example. Suppose there to be an industry composed of many small competing firms each of which must take the ruling wage rate as given because it does not constitute a sufficiently important part of the whole market to be able significantly to affect the wage rate by varying its own demand for labour. Suppose that the demand for the industry's product is high and expanding but that there is a severe bottleneck of some form of needed capital equipment. In such an industry there may simultaneously be serious unemployment as well as a high demand for the industry's product. There could, for example, be many unemployed weavers in a fully competitive textile industry, together with a high demand for cloth, simply because there were not enough looms. If the redundant weavers could not move readily out of the industry for the time being and then move readily back again when additional looms had been installed, there would be a temporary period of severe unemployment in the industry. Textbook competition between the workers would drive pay down to starvation levels, without conferring any substantial benefits in the form of an expanded volume of employment so long as the supply of looms remained inadequate to employ all the available workers. It is true that the very low wage costs combined with the very high demand for cloth would lead to exceptional profits on the existing looms and thus to an exceptionally strong incentive to invest in additional looms. The reduction in the rate of pay might therefore help to speed up the expansion of capacity in the industry. This would inevitably take some time, possibly a long time. But as it occurred labour would in due course become scarce and, as new looms were continually installed to meet the expanding demand for cloth, the wage rate would be bid up from its starvation level to the high level needed to attract the required additional workers.

How far should the initial slump in the rate of pay be encouraged in order to speed up the investment in new looms? Or how far should it be resisted in order to stabilize the incomes of the workers concerned, particularly in view of the fact that a low rate of pay would have little or no immediate effect on the volume of employment? Such a situation would call for a difficult assessment of the possible effects of restrained wage rates now not so much in providing jobs now as in speeding up the process of providing jobs at good wages in the future.

The above example is one in which labour immobility threatens to lead to a temporary slump in a given wage rate. The opposite situation is, of course, equally possible. If it had been the weavers and not the looms that were in temporary short supply, the danger would have lain in an excessive temporary boom in the wage rate which could not be maintained without unemployment when the balance of the labour force had been restored.

These parables of the weaver's wage have been rehearsed solely in order to illustrate in a striking form the fact that impediments to rapid labour mobility could lead to marked fluctuations in rates of pay with little or no immediate advantage in maintaining and expanding levels of employment but perhaps with future advantageous effects, the scale and the importance of which it would be difficult to assess. They are only extreme examples of the fact that because of costs of movement it may in many cases be desirable to consider future developments as well as immediate present conditions in any employment situation in the search for a reasonably steady wage structure which over time would be suitable to maintain a balance between supply and demand.

2.   The Case for a Decentralised System for Wage-Fixing

The basic problem with which we are concerned in this work is how to fix money rates of pay in such a way as to promote employment against the background of monetary and fiscal policies which are so designed as to maintain a steady rate of growth of, say, 5 per cent per annum in the total money demand for labour. If all reliance on competitive forces, however much tamed or regulated, were abandoned this objective could be achieved only by a detailed, authoritarian, centralised method of wage fixing. But there would be great advantages to be gained from the use of decentralised adjustments of wage rates if it were possible to devise regulated forms of competition which could obtain the objective of full employment without the evils of unregulated competition that have been already described.

The decentralised way to achieve the objective of full employment is to ensure that in each individual occupation, industry, or region of the country the rate of pay is set in such a way as to promote employment in that sector. In any particular sector in which there was a scarcity of labour the money rate of pay would be raised to the extent needed to equate supply and demand in that sector, the higher rate of pay helping not only to reduce the demand for labour in that sector but also to attract a greater number of workers into that sector so that employment could be expanded there. In any sector in which there existed a surplus of unemployed labour, there would be no call for any absolute reduction in money rates of pay, but increases in such rates would be restrained or altogether avoided; and this would help both to maintain the demand for labour in that sector and also to make rates of pay in the other expanding sectors of the economy still more attractive. If such principles for the setting of rates of pay were applied in each individual sector of the economy against the background of a general 5 per cent per annum expansion in the total money demand for labour, the overall result should be a general rise in the level of employment and, when full employment was reached, a continuing rise in the average money rate of pay which maintained employment without any excessive or explosive price inflation and with real rates of pay rising at the underlying rate of increase in real output per head.

Such a principle for the fixing of money rates of pay would, however, involve important modifications of present practice. There is much evidence* of a widespread tendency throughout the industrially developed countries of the free-enterprise world to set rates of pay for various jobs through trade union and other institutions at levels which bear a rather stable customary relationship to each other with little or no regard to the extent to which there is a relative excess demand for, or supply of, labour in any particular sector of the economy. Nevertheless there have in fact been very considerable changes in the relative sizes of the labour force in the various sectors of the economy, some having expanded and others having contracted very markedly over the years. But this flow of labour from one sector to another does not seem to have been due in any substantial degree to the attraction of high rates of pay in expanding sectors and low rates of pay in contracting sectors. The main motive force behind the redeployment of labour seems rather to have been the attraction of good job opportunities in expanding sectors and bad job opportunities in the contracting sectors; labour has moved to where work is available.

The evidence that relative rates of pay have not in fact been a main motive force for the deployment of labour rests upon the fact that there have not been any very marked changes in relative rates of pay. But this does not in itself imply that changes in relative rates of pay would not have exerted a powerful influence if they had in fact occurred on any appreci-

---

*See OECD, Report of expert group on 'Wage and labour mobility', 1965; and W.B. Reddaway, 'Wage flexibility and the distribution of labour', *Lloyds Bank Review*, October 1959.

able scale; and there is some evidence* that choice of occupation has indeed been highly sensitive to the limited variations in rates of pay which have in fact occurred.

A decentralised adjustment of particular money rates of pay to particular conditions of supply and demand would in any case be an effective way of ensuring that the average rate of pay of the economy as a whole moved in such a way as to achieve and maintain full employment against the background of a steady 5 per cent per annum growth in the total money demand for labour. Moreover, it would also help to promote the desired movement of labour from contracting to expanding sectors. On the other hand, it would involve a considerable change in present practices for the fixing of rates of pay. Is the disturbance necessary or worthwhile?

There are a number of reasons for doing everything possible to promote the change.

First, in so far as choice of occupations is sensitive both to job opportunities and to relative rates of pay, only moderate changes in relative rates of pay would in fact be needed. When demand shifted from Sector A to Sector B there would be an immediate improvement in prospects for employment in A relative to B. Changes in relative rates of pay would be needed only to supplement the attractive force of relative job opportunities; and in so far as choice of job is highly sensitive to rates of pay, the final disturbances needed to existing relativities would not be very marked. Moreover, the application of the system should be designed so as to avoid large, abrupt fluctuations in relativities; changes should be moderate and gradual. For example, it should be agreed that there would in no case be any call for any absolute reduction in the money rate of pay; with a steady 5 per cent per annum growth of the total money demand for labour relative rates of pay could be adjusted over the course of time by differences in the rates at which money rates of pay were raised.

Second, to rely wholly on job opportunities for the redeployment of labour is wasteful and unkind. It means in fact that unemployment, that is to say the non-availability of a job in one's present occupation, must be a main driving force. And it may well be the less mobile workers who are made redundant in contracting sectors. A restraint of wage increases in such sectors will help to maintain employment in those sectors for workers to whom the cost of movement is high and will give an incentive to move to the better paid occupations on the part of those workers (the young unmarried worker, in particular) for whom the cost of movement is not so high. As a result both the total level of unemployment and also the real cost of movement of a given amount of labour from one sector to another will be reduced.

If there were literally no money or other costs of movement from

*C.A. Pissarides, 'The role of relative wages and excess demand in the sectoral flow of labour', *Review of Economic Studies*, October 1978.

one sector to another, the free flow of labour would bring about what economic efficiency would in those conditions require, namely, that the same grade of labour would charge the same price for its use in all sectors. But where there is appreciable cost of movement between an expanding and a contracting sector rates of pay for the same grade of labour would naturally vary to the extent necessary to cover the cost of movement of the more mobile workers from the contracting to the expanding sector; and this is what an efficient redeployment of labour would require.

Third, if relative rates of pay are to be maintained by custom or otherwise at given stable levels, the solution of the problem of avoiding excessive wage-cost inflation for the economy as a whole demands some alternative more centralised mechanism for determining the absolute level of money pay for the economy as a whole. The difficulties in the way of the alternative more centralised methods will be considered in Chapter VII; they provide the decisive argument in favour of the more decentralised principle outlined above.

If a decentralised method of wage-fixing is to be adopted, the basic question remains whether institutional arrangements can be devised which permit wage-fixing bargains between organised groups of workers and their employers without enabling monopolistic wage-bargaining power to set wage rates at levels which impede the promotion of employment in the various sectors concerned.

3.   One Union for Each Employer

One principle which appears logically attractive at first sight is that the immunities given to trade unions and similar labour organisations should be limited to organisations designed only to cover employment with a single employer. As we have argued in Chapter IV the fundamental economic justification is to offset the monopsonistic powers of individual employers and to remove the normal lack of balance of bargaining power where one employer employs many workers. Let the workers employed by any one employer form a monopolistic group to counterbalance the monopsonistic powers of that employer; but let there be full competition within any industry between the different independent employers and between corresponding different independent organised groups of workers. Such an arrangement, it may be argued, would effectively counterbalance each employer's monopsonistic powers, but it would hold in check any excessive misuse of monopolistic wage-fixing powers, since if wages and costs were set at uncompetitive levels in any one firm another employer with another group of workers could invade the market of the high-cost firm.

There are, however, some serious snags in these proposals. It is in fact much easier for employers to get together and make informal tacit agreements than it is for the workers concerned to do so, if for no other reason than simply because there are many fewer employers than there are workers to get together without any formal organisation. For this reason it would be difficult to ensure that a group of apparently competitive employers were not in fact exercising a monopsonistic power throughout the industry by means of a tacit informal agreement not to pay more than some agreed limited rate of pay. For this reason there may well be a number of cases in which the arrangement would not effectively restore equality of bargaining power.

In many cases it would be extremely difficult to define a single independent employer. There are in industry many degrees and forms of interlocking and overlapping of ownership and management. Some companies may be wholly owned by other companies. Some companies may be partially owned by other companies. Some companies with a widespread independent ownership in each case may nevertheless be controlled by boards the membership of which has a large common element. It would in fact be no easy matter to decide whether a group of companies in fact constituted effectively a single employer and thus justified the organisation of the workers of all the companies into a single monopolistic wage-bargaining group.

Moreover the proposal would do nothing to cope with those cases in which (e.g. because of the economies of scale) there must in effect be a single employer. In a natural monopoly like a national or regional railway network, whether nationalised or not, to say nothing of the public service of a local or national government, the principle of one-employer-one-union would make no contribution to the solution of the problem whether a wage claim impeded or promoted employment in the sector concerned.

There may well be some progress to be made on these lines. In Chapter IV and Appendix D we refer to the use of anti-monopoly anti-merger powers to promote competition among employing firms wherever that is compatible with efficient production; and we have emphasised the effect of any resulting competitive demand for labour in bidding up the wage rate. A combination of such action with the development of wage-bargaining by trade unions on a plant or a company level rather than nationally for a whole sector of the economy would help to promote employment without the sacrifice of wage-fixing units to counterbalance employers' monopsonistic powers. But, as we have seen, this solution has serious limitations.

4. General Limitation of Trade Union Powers

An alternative workable solution may be sought simply by seeking a legal background for trade union and similar pressure groups which gave them a moderate but not excessive amount of monopoly power. It has been argued that, if the existing powers of the trade unions are causing so great an upward thrust on money wage rates as to make it impossible to maintain full employment without a runaway inflationary explosion of costs and prices, the appropriate solution is to curb the powers of the trade unions without going so far as to deprive them of equality of bargaining power with the employers. Restoring a better balance of bargaining power between monopsonistic employers and monopolistic trade unions may be regarded as the philosophy lying behind the Employment Act of 1980.*

In this wicked world a pragmatic, second-best solution of this kind may be advocated; but it is in principle clearly inadequate and unsuitable. What we seek is some arrangement which will allow wage rates in each firm to be raised to, and be fixed at, levels which promote employment (Situation IV of Table I) without allowing them to be raised to monopolistic levels which seriously impede the promotion of employment (Situation III of Table I). But the powers which enable the former desirable objective to be attained are the same as the powers which can be used for the undesirable latter objective. There is no reason to believe that any single general set of legal rules (such as those in the Employment Act of 1980) could possibly give the correct answer in all cases. Initial bargaining conditions vary so much from case to case that in one sector very little legal power is needed to enable a very high monopolistic wage claim to be imposed (e.g. where a group of specialised persons can hold up a large range of economic activities simply by withdrawing their own labour), while in another sector very extensive powers are needed to gain a relatively small result. It is desirable, if possible, to find some alternative arrangement which will tailor the effect more directly to the conditions ruling in each particular case.

But while a revised set of universally recognised powers and immunities for all trade unions is bound to be to some extent defective in that it does not discriminate between different bargaining positions, it can be designed especially to curb those powers which are most likely to be used for the establishment of excessive monopolistic positions. Two such possibilities may be mentioned which, while they allow for the organisation of any group of workers to counterbalance the monopsonistic power of their own employer, do not impede competition from other outside groups who enjoy the same equivalent powers.

In the first place, as we have seen in Chapter V, before the passage of the Employment Act of 1980, there was in the UK a procedure of the following kind. If any employer in any sector of the economy was paying rates that were below the general trade union rates recognised in that sector, then the trade union or relevant associated group of employers

*See the discussion in Chapter V.

could set in motion a process which could result in compelling the offending employer to pay the rates that were generally recognised in that sector of the economy. It may be to the advantage of both the employers and the workers in the concerns paying the higher trade union rates to prevent the competition from outsiders at lower rates. But the exercise of this power may prevent an employer and a group of workers from carrying on an activity at rates of pay which are agreeable both to workers and employers; and it can thus prevent outsiders from breaking in to a restricted and protected preserve of a higher paid group. It is one thing for workers to be free to organize voluntary associations to present joint wage claims. It is quite another thing to endow them with legal powers to prevent others from competing with them if they so desire. The alternative for those others may be unemployment or being pushed out of the privileged circle into lower paid occupations.

In the second place, to operate a pre-entry closed shop should be unlawful. Freedom for a group of workers to associate in order to press jointly a claim to a given rate of pay is one thing. Freedom for that group of workers to insist that no other worker shall be employed in that occupation without their permission is a totally different and objectionable privilege. It means that a tight monopoly of a limited number of workers can preserve an exceptionally high rate of pay, preventing other less well paid workers from entering the occupation with the result, first, that unnecessary inequalities of earnings are preserved, the poor outsiders being disallowed from joining the rich insiders, and, second, that the supplies to the consumers of the services of the privileged group are unnecessarily restricted and charged at unnecessarily high prices.

Each individual should in general be free to offer his or her services in any occupation, though it may in some circumstances be right and proper that employment should be restricted to those who are properly qualified to carry out those services. Thus if a coal miner without proper training and skill would endanger the lives of his fellow workers, it is proper that the necessary training and skill should be a condition of employment. Or if the ordinary patient has no way of judging whether a medicine man is a quack, it is right and proper that certain qualifications should be demanded of the doctor. But in principle the restrictions on entry into any trade should not be handed over lock stock and barrel to a self-governing closed guild of those concerned. One has perhaps only to think of the present restrictive structure and practices of the legal profession to realise the disadvantages of such a system. The coal miner, the doctor, the lawyer, and the teacher would, of course, be the most influential because they would be the most knowledgeable persons in making representations and giving advice to any bodies which determined the necessary qualifications for their jobs. But it should not be a simple uncontrolled monopoly of those in the job to make the final decision.

This control of qualifications which may be needed in the social interest raises a number of difficult issues which it is not proposed to discuss at length in this book. In the first place, those concerned must decide how well qualified a practitioner must be. Is it better to have a large number of less well qualified doctors or university teachers or a smaller number of extremely well qualified persons? In the second place, if, as is argued above, there is to be otherwise effective free access to all jobs, there must be free access to training for the qualifications needed for those jobs. But if training is heavily subsidised (e.g. in universities) there may well need to be some limit to the numbers admitted for certain trainings. If so, who is to select among the candidates? And on what principle? This may well be an argument for no restrictions on the numbers of suitable candidates admitted for training, but for the training to be financed by loans to the trainees so that the ultimate net rewards for those who are finally qualified will correspond more nearly to the ultimate net excess of benefit over cost to society.

5. Increased Mobility of Labour

This competitive principle that persons should be free to move from less attractive, lower paid occupations to more attractive, better paid occupations is of the utmost importance. It is an important principle of freedom (permitting people to choose their own way of life); it is an important egalitarian principle (permitting the low-paid to share the advantages of the high-paid); and it is a principle of economic efficiency (permitting work to be done at jobs whose product is highly valued instead of at jobs whose product is lowly valued.) There remain some further ways of promoting this principle which we will merely note in this chapter.

In the first place, there are a number of labour restrictive practices besides closed shop arrangements which offend against the principle. Unnecessary apprenticeship requirements are an important case in point. In the process of economic development and change it is inevitable that the demands for some skills will rise and for others will fall. If one skill becomes relatively scarce and highly paid, it is desirable in the interests both of efficient productivity and of equality of reward that there should be no unnecessary obstacle to recruitment from all available sources. To rule that only youngsters after four years apprenticeship can be allowed gradually and in limited numbers to swell the supply available, even though many intelligent adults after a crash programme of a few months training could be made available, is to impede productivity and to protect inequality of rewards. Similar inefficiencies and inequalities can result from other unnecessary qualification requirements or from unnecessary demarcation rules which prevent some workers (whose jobs are in less demand) from doing work (for which there is an increased demand).

It is of the first importance that such unnecessary obstacles to flexibility and mobility should be removed; but it is not the intention of the present work to tackle this problem and to make any positive proposals on the subject beyond the following passing observations.

(1) The advocacy in this work of trade unions or other similar organisations as agents for setting *wage rates* at levels designed to promote employment must not, of course, be interpreted as an advocacy of the setting of other restrictive arrangements in such a way as to promote employment. Insistence on overmanning arrangements (two men to do the work of one) may well increase employment in the particular sector, if the demand for the product is sufficiently inelastic for the resulting rise in wage costs not to restrict very much the demand for the product. But such arrangements are in no way covered by the principle of setting the *wage rate* at a level which, given all the other surrounding conditions, will promote employment in that sector.

(2) Although the present work is not concerned with a discussion of the problems involved in relaxing restrictive practices in the labour market (one cannot cover every subject in every book), nevertheless the removal of such restrictive practices is very relevant for the cure of stagflation. The removal of restrictive practices in the labour market could be a most important way, possibly the most important single way, of raising output per head. And if, as has been suggested in Chapter II, the inflationary push of wage costs causes stagflation because of demands for rises in real wage rates which exceed the rises in output per head, measures which raise output per head could make a major contribution to the solution of the problems of stagflation.

(3) As is noted in Chapter IV and Appendix D, there exists a set of institutions, based on the Director General of Fair Trading, the Restrictive Practices Court, and the Monopolies and Mergers Commission, to prevent undesirable restrictive practices, a set of institutions from whose control restrictive practices in the labour market are exempt. There is, however, no easy solution to be found merely by cancelling this exemption, since that would be to throw out the baby with the bath water. As far as business practices are concerned, the Restrictive Practices Court disallows (except in the special circumstances described in Appendix D) any two or more businessmen getting together and agreeing that they will not sell their produce at any price lower than an agreed minimum. To apply this in the labour market would be to disallow any two or more workers getting together to agree not to sell their labour below a certain agreed minimum wage, that is to say, to disallow all wage-fixing by trade union action. The machinery for controlling restrictive practices in the labour market would need to be specially designed for that purpose.

Finally, in addition to the negative task of preventing undesirable restrictive practices in the labour market, there are a number of positive steps which can be taken to promote mobility from less attractive, low-paid jobs to more attractive, better paid jobs. Public or private agencies which serve to inform workers of available jobs and employers of available workers, and the public and private development of retraining facilities are examples of such action.

The reform of controls over housing provides another example. Existing arrangements in the market for housing can greatly impede geographical movement from one job to another. Both in private and public rented accommodation rent control together with legal or customary security of tenure for existing tenants can discourage movements, since those who are among the lucky ones to have a secure position at a low rent in one locality may well find themselves among the unlucky outsiders without the heritage of such accommodation if they move to a new locality. Some reform of private and public rented accommodation which does not divide the population in each region into lucky insiders with a privileged dwelling and unlucky outsiders without such a privilege, in addition to removing an important source of unjust and inefficient use of housing, would also incidentally improve both equality and efficiency by making it easier for people to move from low-paid to better paid jobs.* But it is not the purpose of the present work to examine these general problems of promoting mobility.

6.   Conclusion

Many of the measures discussed or merely noted in this chapter may well help to solve the problem of stagflation by enabling those who are outside any group which is maintaining an excessively high monopoly wage to exert pressure to be admitted to the charmed circle, and thus to bring down the over-protected wage and to reduce pressure in the under-protected occupations. But the basic question will still exist since wage-fixing powers will still remain without any assurance that they are being used in such ways as to promote employment in each sector. Can any institutions be devised which do preserve a decentralised system of wage-bargaining but nevertheless do also directly distinguish between wages which are set at levels that promote employment and wages which are set at levels that seriously impede that process? In Chapter VIII we will try to outline a decentralised form of institution appropriately designed for this purpose. But before we do so we will in Chapter VII consider in more detail the disadvantages of attempting to find the solution through a centralised incomes policy.

*See J.E. Meade, *The Intelligent Radical's Guide to Economic Policy* (London: Allen & Unwin, 1975), pp. 69–72.

CHAPTER VII

A Centralised Incomes Policy

In this chapter we will be considering the problems that arise if an attempt is made to restrain inflationary pressures by means of some centralised influence over, or control of, over-ambitious wage claims. Such centralised arrangements can take many different institutional forms and the institutions may be endowed with varied degrees of formal powers. At the one extreme they may be designed merely to give guidance to other wage-fixing bodies by the publication of reports on the general economic situation and its implications for what would constitute a reasonable non-inflationary form for wage settlements; we will refer to such bodies as 'centralised wage-guidance institutions'. At the other extreme the centralised institutions may be given formal powers to determine what shall be the actual rates of pay payable in the economy; we will refer to such bodies as 'centralised wage-fixing institutions'.

1. Centralised Wage Guidance

A centralised wage-guidance institution might consist of representatives of employers, employees, and the government. Its duty would be to survey and to report on the current economic situation in order to suggest what might be a reasonable non-inflationary rate of increase of money rates of pay in existing economic conditions. Its basic task would depend in one essential respect upon the principles which had been adopted for the operation of fiscal and monetary financial policies. In particular it would depend upon whether demand-management bodies were to be conducted on what in Chapter I we called 'Orthodox Keynesian' principles or on what we called 'New Keynesian' principles.

On Orthodox Keynesian principles financial policies for the management of demand would be conducted in such a way that total money expenditures would be raised to whatever level was needed to maintain real economic activity and employment at some predetermined full-employment level. The function of wage fixing in this case is to set rates of pay at levels that will restrain inflation by restraining the growth of money wage costs. The function of a centralised wage-guidance institution is then in essence straightforward. It must make some estimate of what it expects in present conditions to be the rate of increase of output per unit of labour for the economy as a whole. It must add some allowance for the extent to which money wage costs per unit of output may be allowed to rise. This allowance for cost inflation would presumably be a matter for governmental decision. It would be much higher during the early years of a transitional process from a situation of rapid inflation to one of low or zero inflation. To take a numerical example, if the current rate of money-cost inflation were 15 per cent per annum, the transitional figure for next year's money-cost inflation might be set at 10 per cent per annum. If the wage-guidance institution estimated that output per head might rise in the course of next year by, say, 2 per cent and if the government had set the transitional target for wage-cost inflation of 10 per cent for next year, then the recommended guideline or norm for increases in the rate of pay per unit of labour next year would be set at 12 per cent.

If, however, as is advocated in the present book, the financial policies for demand management are to be conducted on what we have called 'New Keynesian' lines, then the basic task of a centralised wage-guidance institution would be different. In this case the wage-guidance institution would have to start its survey on the assumption that financial policies for demand management were going to be so conducted as to cause a given rate of increase in the total money demand for the services of labour. This figure might be set at, say, 5 per cent per annum as the normal permanent level; but in the transition from a rapid inflation it might be set at, say, 15 per cent for next year. It would be the function of the centralised wage-guidance institution to accept this figure and, on the basis of the assumption that total money earnings will be 15 per cent greater next year, to consider the implications for the volume of employment.

For this purpose an estimate would have to be made of what level of employment next year might be regarded as the full-employment level, taking into account both probable changes in the total supply of labour and the current hidden or open volume of unemployment. A comparison of this estimate of next year's full employment with this year's actual employment would provide a figure of the percentage increase to the level of employment needed to establish next year's full employment. If the economy were this year suffering from a very heavy depression (with, say, an unemployment percentage of 12 per cent, whereas full-employment was judged to imply an unemployment percentage of only 4 per cent), it might be judged that the transition to full employment could not be made in a single year (involving in the above case an 8 per cent rise in employment in one year). Suppose it were judged that the target should be a 5 per cent rise in employment. In this case, given that demand-management policies were devised to increase total money earnings by 15 per cent, the guideline for the increase in money earnings per unit of labour should be a norm of 10 per cent.

Such would be the basic principles for setting guideline norms for increases in the general level of rates of pay. But that would not be the sole task for such guidance institutions. Real incomes depend not only upon rates of money pay but also upon the cost of living, the rate of income tax, and social benefits such as child benefits. Costs are influenced by the price of imported raw materials; and given the level of costs, prices are affected by profit mark-ups and by taxes. The centralised guidance institutions would serve a useful purpose by expanding their surveys and reports to explain what would be the implications of the guideline norms on real standards of living, given the probabilities of foreign economic developments, of future conditions affecting profit margins, and of various possibilities of governmental policies for taxation and public expenditure.

Guideline norms of the kind outlined above may well serve a useful purpose. Whatever other changes might be made in wage-fixing arrangements, a survey of this kind prepared by a responsible body representing the government and both sides of industry might well help to make clear the logic of the real factors which determine the standard of living and the relationship between wage costs and the price level. But this book, as has been explained in Chapters I and II, is based on the assumption that what has been defined as the full-employment level of employment is — or at least may well be — in excess of the non-explosive-inflation level of employment. In other words, we are assuming that if full employment is attained (and the ultimate guideline norms for wage increases are based on the assumption of full employment whether that be attained by Orthodox Keynesian or by New Keynesian policies) and if the present wage-fixing arrangements through uncontrolled monopoly-bargaining are continued, then a serious danger of explosive inflationary pressures will continue. We cannot easily assume that the mere announcement of a reasonable norm will be sufficient to dam the flood.

2. Centralised Wage-Fixing

If this is so and if a solution is to be found through a centralised incomes policy, we must consider the problems of a centralised institution which was concerned not merely with wage guidance but also with actual wage-fixing. We shall argue later that any acceptable system would require exceptions to the norm, that an average norm of, say, 5 per cent would have to be applied by allowing some to go above 5 per cent and requiring others to stay below 5 per cent, and that the need for any such centralised distinction between the sheep and the goats will greatly complicate matters. But the problems of enforcement would be difficult enough even if the need were simply to apply the same uniform norm of, say, 5 per cent to every rate of pay in every trade, occupation, and region without distinction. Some of the most obvious difficulties are enumerated under the following six headings.

(1) The authority in question would have to monitor not only a few

national settlements of basic rates of pay for different grades and occupational groups of workers. A great many wage settlements are made by bargains at the company, or firm, or shop-floor level. National rates often express only basic minimum rates which are topped up by a host of different and divergent local settlements. The scale of an effective policing of even a general uniform norm would thus be very large; and yet the incomes policy will almost certainly break down sooner or later if many settlements can in fact be made outside the norm to the great resentment of those who are effectively kept to the norm.

(2) A second major difficulty is due to the widespread use of piece rates or other forms of payment by result as contrasted with time rates of pay. The norm would have to be expressed as the permitted percentage rise in the rate of pay per hour of work. Piece rates are frequently set on the shop floor for small numbers of workers at a particular job and are subject to frequent changes as particular tasks vary. Moreover the earnings from an hour's work which result from a given piece rate may be difficult to assess, will vary from worker to worker (indeed, the possibility of such variation is part of the purpose of working to piece rates), will rise as the workers concerned learn by experience at a particular job, and will be frequently changed with job changes. It would be difficult to prevent the use of piece rates as an escape route from control in those cases where employers were willing to exceed the permitted norm — to the great resentment of workers on time rates who could be more easily policed.

(3) The existence of overtime rates or special rates for working at unsocial hours might also be a source of trouble in so far as it were possible to increase average earnings by an increase in the proportion of work that was paid at the higher rates.

(4) It would similarly be necessary to ensure that bonus payments of various kinds were brought into account in computing changes in the average rate of pay.

(5) The institution of a norm of, say, 5 per cent would apply to the rate of pay for each given class of work. It could not preclude a worker who was genuinely promoted from a lower paid grade of work to a higher paid job. Acquisition of skills and of experience and movement to posts of greater responsibility or irksomeness would have to be legitimately rewarded with the normal movement to a higher scale of pay; and in such cases a rise in pay above the norm would be legitimate. Similarly many jobs, particularly in the salaried and professional grades, are paid on scales according to which the rate of pay rises automatically with the age or length of service of the worker. Problems would arise to ensure that nominal and otherwise bogus promotions of workers from one grade to a higher grade had not been made, and that the introduction or revision

of rising scales of pay had not been arranged, simply as means of making illegitimate increases of pay above the norm.

(6) Finally, there are many fringe benefits by which an employer can reward employees outside the regular pay packet, such as holidays, pension rights, rights to redundancy pay, sick pay, free meals, loans on favourable terms, and various amenities. Serious problems would arise in determining how far improvements in such benefits could or should be accounted for in computations of the rate of increase in rates of pay.

Thus in a developed industrial economy with so many points at which pay is determined, with so many different structures of pay, with part-time and full-time workers, with piece rates and other systems of payment by results, with various bonuses and fringe benefits, with special rates for overtime work or work at unsocial hours, and with the possibilities of movements of labour from one grade or occupation to another as well as between industries and regions, the scale and complexity of monitoring even a single uniform norm would be immense. But effective enforcement involves not only monitoring the behaviour of the various pay packets, but also the imposition of sufficient penalties on those who break the norm to ensure that by and large the norm is respected. Clearly bureaucratic surveillance of private enterprise would ultimately be required on a very extensive scale.

3.   The Adjustment of Relativities

These problems would be compounded by the fact that a single norm could not be applied without exception to all the sectors of the economy. If a single uniform norm were in fact successfully enforced year after year, it would mean that relativities between rates of pay in the various sectors of the economy were frozen for ever on whatever happened to be the position ruling at the initiation of the scheme. The initial situation might well be full of anomalies particularly since the scheme would be likely to be introduced during a period of serious stagflation. If relations were then frozen at some particular point of time and the process of transition to higher levels of employment were put in motion, it is virtually certain that a situation would soon arise in which there were scarcities of labour and bottlenecks in some sectors while heavy unemployment still continued in other sectors. Quite apart from such initial maladjustments, the process of future economic development and change would be bound to mean that adjustments would become necessary to meet variations in the need for labour in different sectors.

In Chapter VI we have given reasons for the view that in a society in which the individual is given freedom of choice of job, adjustments of relative rates of pay should in fact constitute an important element in the mechanism for the deployment of labour. As was argued in that chapter, there is much to be said for not making large abrupt changes; but moderation in the rate of change in relativities must not imply rigidly fixed relativities.

This means that if a centralised wage-fixing institution announces a norm which represents what the increase in rates of pay should be on the average for the economy as a whole, then in some sectors where there is an exceptional shortage of labour increases in rates of pay above the norm should be permitted. Some mechanism has to be devised to determine the cases in which such exceptions should be permitted and by how much in each case the norm should be exceeded.

Such a mechanism would probably have to take a form in which the employers and employed in a particular sector took the initiative and made a case to the centralised wage-fixing institution for a rise in pay of a given amount in view of a serious shortage of labour in that sector. But that, alas, is only the beginning of the trouble. If the norm represents what the average increase should be over the whole economy some settlements must be kept below the norm when other settlements are allowed to go above the norm. It is possible that some settlements in sectors in which there is still heavy unemployment will in fact voluntarily be made at below-norm levels in order to promote employment. But it is a basic assumption of this book that one cannot rely on that outcome. For a successful application of the centrally fixed norm some procedure would have to be devised for compelling below-norm settlements in some sectors as well as for permitting above-norm settlements in other sectors.

It is not possible to envisage a system in which the officials of the centralised wage-fixing institution should take the initiative in picking and choosing those particular settlements which in its view should be damped down. The only conceivable procedure would be for the centralised wage-fixing institution to announce as a norm not what it considered to be the appropriate *average* rise for the economy as a whole, but what it considered to be the *minimum* rise which should be automatically allowed in all cases. Thus if it considered that 5 per cent represented the desirable average figure, it might announce 2 per cent as a minimum norm permissible automatically in all cases. All rises above 2 per cent would need the authorisation of the centralised wage-fixing institution. Such a system would mean that the initiative would remain in the hands of the employers and the employed in the various sectors. But it would, of course, add greatly to the work of the central institution, since the number of cases in which above-norm increases had to be examined and authorised would be greatly increased.*

4. An Intermediate System

The system of centralised wage guidance outlined in Section 1 contained no element of compulsion whereas the system of centralised wage-fixing outlined in Sections 3 and 4 went to the other extreme and assumed that wage increases above those permitted by some central authority would in all cases be outlawed. It is possible to envisage systems which fall somewhere in between these two extremes.

Thus a norm determined more or less on the principles discussed in Section 1 for the determinations of a voluntary guideline might be transformed into an annual basic pay award. This basic increase in pay (e.g. an increase of 5 per cent for a particular year) could by law be automatically incorporated into all contracts of employment so that, unless the employers or the employees in any sector took further action, every one's rate of pay would automatically rise by 5 per cent.

There could then be some flexibility for subsequent upward and/or downward adjustments of individual rates of pay around this automatic basic upward lift of 5 per cent. Such flexibility could at one extreme take the form of completely free bargaining, in which case employers and employees would be free to settle any collective bargain as at present – with the ultimate threat of industrial action by lock-out or strike – so as to readjust the rate of pay in an upward or downward direction from the new basic award. At the other extreme any divergence from the basic award might require the sanction of some tribunal, arbitration court, or pay commission. Or there could be an intermediate arrangement whereby any divergence from the basic award which was agreed by both employers and employed was permissible, while any dispute about any such divergence had to be taken to a tribunal, arbitration court, or pay commission; and this could be combined with various degrees of sanction or lack of sanction against a party which did not accept any resulting decision of the arbitral body. There are many variations possible around the main theme which is the replacement of the completely voluntary guideline norm of Section 1 by a basic award which is automatically incorporated into all contracts of employment.

The system of wage fixing in Australia is a particular instance of such a system. A variation of the system, tailored to suit UK conditions has

*A most illuminating account of the many administrative and similar problems encountered in the operation of a centralised incomes policy is to be found in the following report by the Pay Board under the chairmanship of Sir Frank Figgures: 'Pay Board. Experience of Operating a Statutory Incomes Policy. July 1974', issued by the Department of Employment.

been proposed by Professor Sir Henry Phelps Brown.* He suggests that a national pay award might be made annually by a central arbitral body after hearing evidence from representatives of employers and employed, from the government, and from other independent experts. The central arbitral body would, however, be completely independent of the government, its members having the standing of judges of the High Court. The government could give evidence – for example, if it so wished, about intended monetary and fiscal policies designed to keep the total money demand for goods and services on a steady 5 per cent per annum growth path – and the central arbitral body would no doubt pay much attention to such evidence. But it alone would be responsible for the final decision about the appropriate level for the basic pay award in the light of all the evidence which it received from all quarters.

The terms of its pay award would automatically become implied terms of the contracts of employment of all employees so that, if for example the national award was for a 5 per cent increase of pay, all employees would automatically receive a 5 per cent rise under their existing individual contracts of employment.

This would not, however, in any way rule out the possibility of subsequent collective bargaining between employers and employees for increases or decreases of rates of pay above or below the new rates resulting from the national award. The representatives of employees who considered that they had a case for a rise in excess of the national award could bargain with their employers for such a rise; and employers who considered that they could not afford to pay the national award could bargain with their employees for a reduction of the rise.

In the case of disputes which could not be settled by agreement the parties would be under an obligation to take the dispute to the arbitral body, subject to penalties if they took industrial action without having submitted the dispute to arbitration. But they would be under no obligation to accept the decisions of the arbitral body and would be free, as at present, to take industrial action after hearing the award of the arbitral body – a procedure which amounts in fact, in Sir Henry Phelps Brown's words, to a system of compulsory conciliation rather than of compulsory arbitration.

There are three important differences between the Phelps Brown proposals and the proposals made in the present book.

First, the 'wage-guidance' norm proposed in the present book is replaced by a 'wage-fixing' national award which is applied automatically to all employees. Subsequent negotiations for increases of pay above the award would almost certainly be more frequent and more successful than those for downward adjustments. The 'wage-fixing' award would be

*Professor Sir Henry Phelps Brown, 'Incomes policy: a modest proposal', Unservile State Papers No. 30, Poland Street Publications, London, 1981.

likely to represent a minimum rather than an average rise in pay, a matter which the central arbitral body would no doubt take into account.

Second, it is an essential feature of the Phelps Brown proposals that the arbitral body should not be subject to any direct official instructions, since, it is argued, such independence would be an essential condition for its acceptance by the trade unions. In this book we have argued the necessity of a system in which the wage-fixing institutions, whatever their character, should be required to place great emphasis on the promotion of employment in each individual sector of the economy. It is a thesis of the present book that one must find a system which is both generally acceptable and at the same time puts emphasis, as a matter of policy, on the fixing of wage rates as instruments for the promotion of employment in the various sectors of the economy. This is without doubt politically very difficult. Indeed perhaps it will remain for ever politically impossible, which may mean that there exists no effective solution for the problem of stagflation.

Third, the Phelps Brown proposals impose an obligation on the parties to a dispute to take the dispute to arbitration but do not impose any penalties against subsequent industrial action taken in opposition to an arbitral award, whereas — to anticipate the analysis of the following chapter — the proposals in this book cover also penalties for industrial action taken in opposition to an arbitral award, once more on the political assumption of a general consensus of opinion in favour of such a system. Once again this may be a necessary condition for an effective solution of the problem of stagflation, but one that presents great, if not insurmountable, political difficulty.

5.　Conclusions

A fully centralised wage-fixing system may possibly have a role to play as a temporary measure to reverse an explosive inflationary situation. But it is difficult to conceive it as a permanently acceptable and workable system in a free society; for there is a very serious dilemma. On the one hand, for the reasons given above, if an attempt is made to construct a permanent system of this kind, which really covered all sectors, the degree of centralised bureaucratic interference with the conduct of free-enterprise business arrangements and with voluntary agreements between employers and employed would almost certainly become unbearable. On the other hand, if intervention is confined to a limited number of the main structural settlements, the number and extent of anomalies that will arise from uncovered settlements (such as arise from local wage bargains, piece rates, fringe benefits, etc.) will increase progressively. Resentment will grow on the part of those who are effectively kept back. Such resentments may also well arise as a result of the procedures for exceptional treatment of those who are covered. If, whether justifiably or not, it is thought that one powerful body obtained exceptionally lenient treatment on political grounds because of its strong bargaining power rather than on the merits of its case, the willingness of other groups to accept the system would be greatly weakened.

A guideline norm or a basic wage award may have a useful role to play. But one must find some decentralised and flexible but effective method for obtaining, around this norm or basic award, variations which are designed to promote employment in each sector of the economy. In Chapter VIII we will consider the possibility of finding such a solution through the development of arbitration procedures.

CHAPTER VIII

Not-Quite-Compulsory Arbitration

We are left with the search for some decentralised system for fixing rates of pay in the various sectors of the economy which will promote employment in each sector. In Chapter VI we mentioned certain ways in which, without depriving trade unions and other bodies of their legitimate role in setting rates of pay for the job, the decentralised forces of competition might be given a greater influence than they have at present in the determination of those rates. But, as we argued at the end of that chapter, that cannot be the final answer to the problem of choosing in each sector that rate of pay which will promote employment in that sector.

In Chapter VII we gave reasons for the view that an acceptable solution to the problem cannot be found through any centralised system of setting the rates of pay to be observed in each sector of the economy.

1.   The Promotion of Employment through Arbitration

We search therefore for a free, decentralised method for fixing rates of pay, but one that is nevertheless subject to some degree of social control in the final choice of rates of pay so as to put more emphasis on the promotion of employment in the sector concerned than would otherwise be the case. Perhaps the most hopeful, civilised approach to the problem is to continue with the existing system of bargaining between workers and employers but to replace the ultimate appeal to the strike weapon with an ultimate appeal to some external impartial arbitral body or pay commission which in making its award will put great emphasis on the promotion of employment.

It is encouraging to note that the desirability on social grounds for some ultimate appeal to outside arbitration was the view of those ancient protagonists of the trade union movement, Sidney and Beatrice Webb, who in 1902 after a general discussion of the functions of the trade unions continued with their analysis as follows:*

> So far democracy may be expected to look on complacently at the fixing, by mutual agreement between the directors of industry and the manual workers, of special rates for wages for special classes. But

*Sidney and Beatrice Webb, *Industrial Democracy,* 2nd ed (London: Longman Green, 1902), pp. 813–15.

this use of the Method of Collective Bargaining for the advantage of particular sections — this 'freedom of contract' between capitalists and wage-earners — will become increasingly subject to the fundamental condition that the business of the community must not be interfered with. When in the course of bargaining there ensues a deadlock — when the workmen strike or the employers lock out — many other interests are affected than those of the parties concerned. We may accordingly expect that, whenever an industrial dispute reaches a certain magnitude, a democratic state will, in the interests of the community as a whole, not scruple to intervene, and settle the points at issue by an authoritative fiat. The growing impatience with industrial dislocation will, in fact, where Collective Bargaining breaks down, lead to its supersession by some form of compulsory arbitration.

Moreover, it is clear that they were aware of the need for the arbitral body to seek a balance between supply and demand for labour in each particular sector of the economy, since they argued that the employers would have to rest their case against a wage claim on the grounds that 'equally competent recruits could be obtained in sufficient numbers without the particular "rent of ability" demanded by the trade union over and above the national minimum'.

The following is an outline of a system of what may perhaps be called 'not-quite-compulsory arbitration'. Consider a state of affairs in which there is no authoritarian setting of any compulsory wage norms by the central government, and in which there is a simple return to uncontrolled monopoly bargaining — but with one basic modification. Any group of workers and employers would be free to settle by voluntary agreement any rate of pay or other terms of employment which they chose. But in the case of an unsettled dispute between them, either party to the dispute, employers or employed, could take the issue to a permanently established national arbitration court or pay commission. In determining its award it would be the statutory duty of the arbitral body to lay stress on the promotion of employment in the sector under review; that is to say, it would have to determine whether or not the rate of pay that was in dispute would be likely to impede or to encourage employment in the sector of the economy under examination, taking into account the knowledge that fiscal and monetary policies would be so designed as to cause a predetermined steady rate of growth in the total money demand for labour (of, say, 5 per cent per annum) and having regard to the probable development of rates of pay in other comparable employments.

It would not be unlawful for either side to the dispute to take industrial action, for example, by way of strike or lock-out, even against the terms of such an award. But in the case of such industrial action taken in opposition to the terms of such an award the party concerned would be penalised in certain ways that would result in a significant reduction in its bargaining powers. We will consider later the possible nature of such penalties, the basic idea being simply to make it more difficult and costly to enforce a demand in opposition to an arbitral award, leaving existing bargaining powers untrammelled in other cases.

Such a system of arbitration would in two respects not be compulsory: first, it would operate only if at least one of the parties to the dispute wished it to operate, though it might be wise to give the government also the power to take any major unsettled dispute to the arbitration tribunal; but, second, it would not be illegal to refuse to accept an arbitral award, though the bargaining powers of any party that did take industrial action in such a case would be impaired. Such a system one may perhaps properly call a system of 'not-quite-compulsory arbitration', though it would be very nearly compulsory if the government could and did take most unsettled disputes to arbitration and if the impairment of the bargaining powers of any party that failed to accept the award were sufficiently severe.

This system would to the greatest possible extent leave the fixing of rates of pay to uncontrolled agreements between employers and workers. Only in the case of a dispute would the system be applied and then only in such a way as to weaken the bargaining strength of any party that opposed an arbitral award which would be designed to promote employment in the sector concerned.

2.   The Need for a Single Permanent Arbitral Body

The arbitral body or pay commission would be a permanent institution which covered rates of pay in all sectors of the economy. The system must be clearly distinguished from the spasmodic institution of *ad hoc* arbitral bodies which have so often been employed in the past as a method of granting without loss of face an inflationary award to a particular group in order to ward off a particular threatened strike. The pay commission would be a permanent tribunal set up with a statutory duty to reject wage increases which, against the background of the restrained monetary and budgetary policies, impaired prospects of employment and to grant claims which did not impair employment prospects; and the grant of the award would strengthen the bargaining power of the party in whose favour the award was given.

The same national institution would have to cover all sectors of the economy. We have argued in Chapter III that in determining appropriate rates of pay attention would have to be paid to the longer-term prospects of the need for labour in various sectors of the economy, and that for this purpose attention would have to be paid to the comparability of rates of pay in various sectors of the economy in so far as they were effective in attracting labour into one sector or another. In order to avoid a competitive inflationary leap-frogging of rates of pay it is of the greatest importance that the same body should bear the ultimate responsibility for recommendations about rates of pay in all the sectors between which comparisons may be made. If one body copes with doctors, another with civil servants, and yet another with the armed forces, a pay explosion will be very probable.* Human nature being what it is, each body is likely to give the benefit of the doubt in favour of the group for which it is responsible; and it is only necessary for one body to think that the candlestickmakers should have the edge on the butchers and bakers and for another body to think that the butchers and bakers should have the edge on the candlestickmakers, for the keeping-up-with-the-Joneses syndrome to lead to a pay explosion (see Chapter II).

But if a single body is to be ultimately responsible for the whole range of pay settlements, it is greatly to be desired that the vast majority of disputes should be settled by bargaining without reference to the pay commission in order to avoid the danger of the system breaking down by being overloaded with work. Moreover settlements between employers and employed are complicated matters which normally involve many considerations other than one or two simple rates of pay. The parties to the bargain will naturally be in a better position to take account of all the relevant background considerations and detailed conditions than will any outside arbitral body. There is a possible modification of the proposed arbitration procedure which should greatly encourage the outside settlement of disputes.† It might be ruled that, if and when an appeal to the arbitration court for a settlement was made by either party, there should ensue a period of, say, thirty days during which the parties would be free to continue to negotiate for an agreed settlement. If at the end of the thirty-day period no agreed settlement had been reached, the arbitration court would make an award. But the court's power would be restricted to making its award either in favour of the last offer made by the employers or in favour of the last claim presented by the employees; it would

---

*It is particularly important that the same body should cover all professions. The difficulties in such cases are particularly severe for two reasons (see Chapter VI); first, the need to take into account and to compare qualifications which in the social interest may be set for admission to a particular profession; and, second, the relatively long period needed for training for a profession, and thus the relatively long period before rates of pay can have any effect in attracting more or fewer persons to the numbers available for employment.

†The following ingenious suggestion was made to me by Mr George P. Shultz who experimented with the idea when he was Secretary of Labor in the US Administration. The idea is contained in S. Stevens, 'Is compulsory arbitration compatible with bargaining?', *Industrial Relations,* February 1966; and it is discussed in J. T. Addison and W. S. Siebert, *The Market for Labor* (Santa Monica, Calif.: Goodyear, 1979) and in A. Rees *The Economics of Work and Pay* (New York: Harper and Row, 1979). I am indebted to P. Dolton and J. G. Treble of the University of Hull for these references and for comments on the proposal.

not have the right to propose any modification of detail in either case. After hearing each side make its case for its own latest offer or claim it would have to choose between the two existing proposals on the basis of the one which was most likely to promote employment in the sector concerned. Each side would have to take care not to pitch its claim or offer too wide of what it thought the pay commission was likely to regard as the rate best suited to promote employment. Such an arrangement would, therefore, give the maximum incentive to the parties concerned to moderate their claims and offers and thus to be in a position to reach agreement without reference to the pay commission; and they would be doing so with all their detailed knowledge of the background conditions.

3.   Avoidance of Abrupt Changes

Up to this point it has been assumed that the sole criterion for the pay commission in judging between the employer's offer and the employees' claim would be the promotion of employment in the sector concerned. But in Chapter VI we gave reasons for the view that this criterion should be modified to the extent necessary to avoid excessively large and abrupt changes in rates of pay. An element of gradualism in the adjustment of rates of pay could readily be introduced into the system. To take a numerical example, suppose that there were a general guideline for a rise of the rate of pay of 4 per cent on the average for the economy as a whole (see Chapter VII). Then it might be ruled that the pay commission should not grant against an employer's wishes any rise in the rate of pay above, say, 7 per cent or against the employee's wishes any rise in the rate of pay below, say, 1 per cent.* It would, of course, be possible for employer and employees to agree on a rise greater than 7 per cent or less than 1 per cent if they so wished. The arrangement would simply mean that no employer could be forced to grant a rise above 7 per cent unless he so desired (e.g. to attract workers to his business) and that no group of employees could be forced to accept a rise of less than 1 per cent unless they so desired (e.g. to protect their jobs from redundancy).

We have stressed in Chapter I the need for transitional arrangements as the passage is made from an initial position of high employment and rapid inflation to one of full employment and only a moderate controlled

---

*The formal method of doing this for a pay commission that was confined to a choice between the employer's latest offer and the employees' latest claim would be to scale any employees' excess claim down to the level of 7 per cent or to the employer's offer, whichever was the higher, or to scale up any employer's deficient offer to a level of 1 per cent or to the employees' claim, whichever was the lower. It would choose between the employer's latest offer and the employees' latest claim after having made any such adjustment.

rate of inflation. The arrangements mentioned in the previous paragraph could readily be devised for this purpose. Thus in a transitional year the guideline for the rise in the average rate of pay for the economy as a whole might have been set at 10 per cent; and in this case the pay commission might be instructed not to impose any increase in pay on an unwilling employer of more than, say, 14 per cent, and not to impose any increase in pay on an unwilling set of employees of less than 6 per cent. As the transition took place and as the guideline for the average rates of pay increase was reduced, so the upper and lower limits set for the pay commission's awards could be reduced *pari passa*.

4. Two Possible Variations on the Scheme

In the preceding paragraphs one particular possible scheme has been described in some detail. There are, however, a number of possible variations on the general theme of using arbitration procedures for settling rates of pay in the interests of avoiding inflation and promoting employment. For the purpose of illustration two possible variations are outlined below.

Variation I. In this case a guiding norm of, say, 4 per cent would be set together with an upper limit of, say, 7 per cent and a lower limit of 1 per cent, as suggested in the previous case.* Any employer who wished to resist a claim which he considered to exceed the upper limit of 7 per cent could refer the claim to the pay commission whose sole job would be to determine the fact whether the claim did or did not exceed the 7 per cent limit. If it were judged to be in excess, the employees would be invited to scale their claim down to 7 per cent. Industrial action to support their original claim would not, however, be unlawful; but in this case it would carry with it a serious curtailment of their legal bargaining powers, which would remain undiminished in the case of any claim that had not been judged to exceed the 7 per cent limit.

Similarly, any body of employees who wished to resist an employer's offer below the 1 per cent limit could obtain a ruling that the offer was below 1 per cent; and if it were found to be so, sanctions would be applied to the employer to obtain a scaling up of the offer to the 1 per cent limit.

This variation of the scheme has the advantage that the task of the pay commission would be confined to judging how much a given claim or offer would in fact raise the cost of a unit of labour, a task which would be onerous enough in view of the factors discussed in Chapter VII. But it is a crude mechanism which, while it might serve to damp down an

---

*As described above, higher figures for the guiding norm and for the upper and lower limits could be applied during the transitional period.

excessive inflationary or deflationary movement of wage costs, would not in itself pay attention to the need to promote employment in each of the various sectors of the economy. Any scheme which did so would, of necessity, impose on the pay commission the additional and much more difficult task of assessing future market conditions for the supply and demand for labour in the particular sector under review.

Variation II. In this case there would in general be very severe restrictions on the legal monopolistic bargaining powers of the trade unions and similar organisations, restrictions which alone could leave them at the mercy of the employers. But in return any group of employees whose claim was resisted by the employers could take the claim to the pay commission whose duty would be to judge whether the claim was either (1) one that did not exceed the lower limit of a ruling guiding norm or (2) one that went beyond the lower limit but nevertheless did not threaten to impede the promotion of employment in that sector of the economy over a reasonably foreseeable future. If either of these two conditions was satisfied, the pay commission would give an award in favour of the claim, which would be enforced on the employers.

This is the most radical scheme. If and when the full confidence of the employees and trade unions could be gained in the constitution and working of a pay commission, it could be the best solution. It would simply replace the exceptional legal powers, with which the trade unions are at present endowed for bargaining through the threat and actual use of industrial action, by the award of an outside impartial body; and something of this kind one must hope will ultimately be recognised to be the civilised way of replacing costly conflict by the rule of reason, while at the same time ensuring that employees did not suffer as a result of lack of bargaining power.

5.   The Need for General Acceptance

In any case, whatever particular form of scheme were chosen, radical reform of institutional arrangements for the fixing of rates of pay of the kind discussed in this chapter would be possible only if it were widely accepted as desirable by the general body of workers and trade unionists. It could not be imposed by authoritative fiat on a generally hostile working population. The argument of this book is based on the thesis that the present disruptive system is to the great disadvantage of workers and trade unionists and that an alternative system of the kind outlined in this chapter would be to the great advantage of the vast majority of citizens, including the workers and trade unionists. No such alternative system could be made to work unless there were wide acceptance of it. The problems of operating such a system are, therefore, discussed only on the assumption that it has attained widespread popular acceptance.

All the schemes discussed in this chapter rely on the possibility of taking steps to weaken the bargaining powers either of employers or of the employed in any action taken against an arbitral award. There remains, therefore, a final and perhaps decisive question. By how much and by what methods would the parties' bargaining powers be affected? Or, in other words, what penalties or sanctions would be imposed on any party that opposed an award?

We are assuming that the case for relying on impartial arbitral awards rather than on the present disruptive use of monopolistic bargaining strength is generally accepted. But this does not mean that one can totally ignore the problem of sanctions against those few who from time to time may be moved to oppose such awards. There is widespread agreement that robbery is wrong: that does not mean that there should be no penalties against robbers.

6. The Problem of Sanctions

What then are the penalties which, given a favourable climate of opinion, might be imposed? One must distinguish between penalties that would be suitable to curb the opposition to an award on the part of the employer and those suitable in the case of opposition by employees.

As far as employers are concerned, it would be possible simply to make it unlawful for the employer to employ anyone except on the terms of the award.* This is an extreme penalty since it means that the employer must accept the award or close down his business; and one could add for good measure that if he closed down his business his employees would be eligible for redundancy payments. The design of effective penalties for the recusant employer presents little difficulty.

The design of sanctions against recusant workers and trade unionists is a much more difficult matter. It is above all necessary to avoid penalties that rest in the end on the imprisonment of strikers as criminals or as being in contempt of court. There are, however, a number of possibilities which do not involve any such consequences.

First, all supplementary benefits could be paid only in the form of a loan to those who were on strike in opposition to an arbitral award. It must be remembered that with the introduction of universal child benefits these financial supports for children will be paid in all cases; they would not cease because a parent goes on strike against an award.

---

*As described in Chapter V, Section 7 this procedure has in the past been adopted as the method by which an employer could be legally required to pay to his workers the generally recognised trade union rates of pay in the sector concerned. Those provisions of the law have been abolished; but there is no reason why the procedure should not be adopted for the present purpose.

What would still be at stake is any additional supplementary benefit which, in the absence of other means, is at present paid in support of a striker's wife and family, including the payment of rent. Such payments might be paid only in the form of a loan made available to the striker at the current rate of interest and repayable by deductions like PAYE at the source from his future earnings.

Second, under present PAYE tax arrangements when earnings fall in the course of the year the wage earner will normally have a right to receive refunds in respect of some of the tax deducted from his previous earnings. It would be possible to rule that such tax refunds should be postponed so long as a person was on strike against an award.

Third, it would be possible to rule that any worker who went on strike against an award should be treated as having thereby terminated his contract of employment. This would have a double effect. It would mean that if his employer refused to re-engage him at the end of the strike he would in no circumstances have any right to claim that he was unfairly dismissed. It would also mean that, even if he were re-engaged, the continuity of his employment with that employer would have been broken.

There are at present a number of rights which mature for a worker the longer he remains in the continuous employment of one employer. The most important of these is his right to a redundancy payment if he is later dismissed because his employer no longer has work for him to do. The size of the redundancy payment to which he is entitled depends among other things upon the length of time for which he has been in continuous employment with his employer. Absence from work because of a trade dispute does not at present break the continuity of employment for the purpose of assessment of the right to redundancy payment. But if striking against an award were treated as a termination by the striker of his contract of employment, the continuity of his employment would be broken and his accumulated right to redundancy payment thereby lost.

The strike might, of course, ultimately be settled on terms which restored to the strikers their lost accumulated rights to redundancy payments. But such payments are financed in part not by the individual employer but out of a central fund. If, for the purposes of making claims on the central fund, strikers against an award lost their accumulated rights, and if a feasible method for enforcing the central recording of the loss of such rights could be devised, full restoration of redundancy rights would impose an extra cost on the employer, and to this extent the strikers' expectations of obtaining a net increase in reward from the employer would be diminished.

Fourth, as described in Chapter V certain actions taken by an individual in contemplation or furtherance of a trade dispute enjoy some far-reaching legal immunities which prevent those whose interests are hurt as a result of the action from suing the striker for compensation in respect of the damages which they have suffered. It could be ruled that these immunities did not apply in the case of industrial action being taken in opposition to an arbitral award. This would mean that an individual striker could be sued to pay for damage done to others, for example, through inducing others to break their contracts or by interference with their trade or business. It could be ruled that the payment of such damages would be made subsequently by deduction at source, as in the case of PAYE, from future earnings.

Fifth, at present the funds of a trade union as such are immune from all such actions for damages. In the case of industrial action in opposition to an award this immunity could be removed if the strike had the official support of the trade union. This would mean effectively that the strikers in such circumstances could not expect any strike pay from their union, since this would mean that the strikers had had the official support of the union whose funds would then be at risk for any damages caused by the strike.

Finally, it could be ruled that expulsion from a trade union because a member had refused to take industrial action in opposition to an award was unreasonable in terms of the Employment Act of 1980 and would as a result make the union liable to pay compensation to the expelled member, as explained in Chapter V.

These sanctions may sound more formidable than they would in fact prove to be. In present circumstances by far the greater part of the finance of strikes comes directly or indirectly out of the strikers' own personal resources. Supplementary benefit, tax repayments, and strike pay make up a strictly limited part of the total finance of strikers;* and it is uncertain how far the risk of claims for damages against individual workers or of the loss of accumulated redundancy claims would be taken seriously into consideration. It is, however, assumed that strikes taken in defiance of an award would be generally unpopular and considered to be unjustified; and in such conditions the whole package of measures against such strikes might well have a serious deterrent effect.

7.   Conclusions

The schemes discussed in this chapter all rest upon either side to a dispute being able to take the matter to a pay commission whose basic function would be to consider the effect of the proposals on the prospects of employment in the sector concerned, with a consequent reduction in the bargaining power of any party to the dispute which took industrial action in opposition to an award by the pay commission. The proposal could work only if there were general agreement that the system was preferable to the present disruptive, inefficient, and inflationary arrangements.

*See John Gennard, *Financing Strikers* (London: Macmillan, 1977).

A radical change is essential; but not-quite-compulsory arbitration would in fact be much less radical than would an effective centralised incomes policy. Unlike a centralised incomes policy, not-quite-compulsory arbitration would leave collective bargaining between independent employers and employees as the basic mechanism with nothing to prevent the application of any bargain freely struck between the two sides. Where agreement could not be reached, the trade union officials and the employers' representatives would still play their central roles, but in the preparation of the cases to be put to the pay commission instead of in preparation for the unarmed guerilla warfare of industrial action. The rule of reason would replace the exercise of muscle power.

CHAPTER IX

Labour Co-operatives, Labour–Capital Partnerships, and Profit-Sharing Schemes

One radical reform of our institutions which has been advocated as a way of coping with stagflation is the replacement of our capital–entrepreneurial firms by labour co-operatives. It is proposed to get rid of the problems of the wage explosion by getting rid of wages.

1. The Case for Competitive Labour Co-operatives

In its simplest unadulterated form the labour co-operative is a productive firm in which the workers themselves own and manage the business. The funds needed for the purchase of the capital equipment and for the finance of the working capital are raised by borrowing at fixed interest in the capital market. The workers purchase the necessary materials, put the necessary sums aside to meet the depreciation of the capital equipment, and pay the interest on the capital funds which they have borrowed. They produce the product and sell it. The excess of their receipts from the sale of the product over their outgoings on (1) inputs of raw materials, (2) tax payments, (3) depreciation allowance for the maintenance of their real capital equipment, and (4) interest on borrowed capital may be called their 'earned surplus'.* This earned surplus is then distributed equally among the workers and takes the place of their wages under the capitalist-entrepreneurial system. In fact the workers instead of the capitalists have become the risk-bearing entrepreneurs.

This system could be combined with the monetary–budgetary policies which we have already noted in Chapter I as being devised to keep the

---

*The excess of receipts from the sale of the product over outgoings on (1) inputs of raw materials, (2) tax payments, and (3) depreciation allowance for the maintenance of the fixed capital equipment we will call the 'net value added' of an enterprise. Thus, as we have defined it, a concern's 'earned surplus' is its 'net value added' less the payment of interest on borrowed capital. Two warnings should be issued. First, the 'net value added' is reckoned 'net' after deduction of any taxes which are levied directly on sales or other operations of the enterprise. Second, 'value added' as defined for the Value Added Tax (VAT) is reckoned after deduction not of depreciation allowances on fixed capital but of any sums actually spent on such capital goods whether these outgoings be for replacement, maintenance, or addition to the capital stock. This is really an unfortunate misuse of the term 'value added'.

total money demand for the country's output of goods and services on a steady 5 per cent per annum growth path. As a result the total earned surplus for the country's workers as a whole would grow steadily in money terms. Against this background the workers in each individual co-operative would receive whatever they could earn. There would no longer be a situation in which an explosive inflation was threatened by workers pressing for a rise in money wages that represented a rise in real standards which exceeded the rise in productivity. They would, as the entrepreneurs, take in the form of the earned surplus whatever their productive efforts achieved.

This advantage of a system of labour co-operatives depends upon their operating in a system of competitive markets. The monopolistic upward pressure on wage rates through a trade union organisation representing all the paid workers in a particular trade would have evaporated. But it could, of course, be replaced by a similar 'trade union' or 'guild' of all the co-operative workers in a particular trade which imposed a set of minimum prices at which the products of members of the guild should be sold; and by exerting an upward pressure on the selling price of their products, in place of the upward pressure on the wage rate, the 'guilds' could attempt to achieve increases in their earned surpluses which in total exceeded the increase in the community's productivity. Such a generalised system would lead to a threat of an explosive price inflation similar to that which is described in Chapter II for a capitalist-entrepreneurial system.

And similarly a process of leap-frogging between the monopolistic 'guilds' could also lead to an explosive inflation. If the guild of candle-stickmakers attempted to set a selling price for candlesticks which gave candlestickmakers an earned surplus per head that was 5 per cent higher than the earned surplus per head of butchers and bakers, and if at the same time the guilds of butchers and bakers attempted to set selling prices for meat and bread which gave their members an earned surplus per head that was at least as high as that enjoyed by the candlestick-makers, there would result an upward explosive inflation of the prices of candlesticks, meat, and bread. The leap-frogging of the prices of the products would merely replace the leap-frogging of wage rates, which is described in Chapter II.

A basic condition for a successful fight against stagflation by the replacement of capitalist-entrepreneurial firms with labour co-operatives is that the policies devised for the prevention or regulation of business restrictive practices and the growth of monopoly which are discussed in Chapter IV and Appendix D should be retained and applied in the case of production by labour co-operatives as they are in the case of capitalist-entrepreneurial firms. There is nothing to be gained in the fight against stagflation if an excessive upward pressure on wage rates due to monopolistic trade unions of wage earners is simply replaced by an excessive upward pressure on prices due to monopolistic guilds of labour co-operators.

But does not this imply that the substitution of labour co-operatives for capitalist-entrepreneurial firms is advocated merely as a disguised form of trade union bashing? If the advantage of labour co-operatives rests upon not allowing monopolistic guilds to replace monopolistic trade unions, would one not achieve the same result in the fight against explosive price inflation simply by outlawing trade union pressures on wage rates?

In fact the two cases are not the same; and *competitive* labour co-operatives could achieve the main justifiable result of *monopolistic* trade unions. As was argued in Chapter IV, the basic economic justification of trade union organisation is to offset the monopsonistic powers of employers by a better balance of bargaining powers between a small number of employers and a large number of workers. With labour co-operatives this particular problem disappears. The workers are the employers. What would be a monopsonistic profit for capitalist-entrepreneurial employers automatically becomes part of the earnings per head of the labour co-operators. This argument for the monopolistic organisation of workers disappears; and the rest of this chapter is written on the assumption that it is not replaced by monopolistic action of organised guilds of labour co-operators.

2. Labour Co-operatives and the Scale of Production

There are, however, categories of workers for whom the organisation of labour co-operatives would be impossible or inappropriate and for whom the problems of wage-fixing would necessarily continue. The most obvious case is that of governmental civil servants. It is clearly impossible in the case of the armed forces or other governmental servants for such work to be organised by a set of labour co-operatives offering their 'products' of defence or administrative services in competition with each other to a single centralised employer; nor would such an organisation be possible in the case of the services of local government. At present the public services of the central and local governmental authorities (including health and education services, but excluding the nationalised industries) account for no less than 20 per cent of the total number of persons employed in the country.

It is also questionable how far the labour-co-operative solution would be appropriate in the case of those industries in which for reasons of technology the individual firm or productive co-operative must be conducted on a very large scale. In those cases (such as the railways) in which because of economies of large scale there is room in the market for only one or at the most for a very few separate productive units, there is bound to be a considerable degree of monopolistic power in the hands of whatever body is in charge of the productive decisions. By producing and selling more the individual enterprise will inevitably affect the market and cause an appreciable reduction in the selling price; by restricting its output and sales it could raise the selling price of its product. For this reason in the extreme cases of monopolistic power due to economies of scale the government properly intervenes either by price control or by nationalisation. For example, the railway system of the UK is nationalised and those in charge of it are not instructed or motivated to set output and prices at levels which will maximise any available monopoly profit, but are instructed to relate prices to costs − with or without state subsidisation for social purposes − on some economic principles other than the maximisation of monopoly profit. If the railways had been left in private ownership, it is virtually certain that for similar reasons the state would have intervened by the regulation of the prices charged for transport by rail, with or without subsidisation for certain social purposes.

Consider then the situation that would arise if the railways were handed over to the railway workers for their ownership and management. It is clear that the state would need to intervene in the regulation of transport charges (with the same case for or against the subsidisation of certain services on social grounds) in order to control the railway workers' monopolistic maximisation of the earned surplus per head, just as it would have needed to intervene in the case of the maximisation of monopoly profit if the railways had been left in the ownership and management of capitalist entrepreneurs. Indeed, for reasons which are discussed below, the need for such anti-monopoly control of transport charges would in one respect be more essential if the railways were run by a labour co-operative than would be the case if they were being run by private capitalist entrepreneurs.

Labour co-operatives are designed to get rid of the conflict between 'them' and 'us', between 'owners or bosses' on the one hand and 'workers' on the other hand. It is for this reason that their institution may be advocated as a means of coping with the problems of explosive inflationary wage pressures. There no longer exists the possibility of pushing 'our' wages up in order to capture some of 'their' profits.

In the case of a small co-operative there is also an improvement in the direct economic incentives. If there are only ten members of a co-operative anything that one member does (such as relaxing his insistence on some restrictive demarcation rule) to increase revenue from sales or to reduce costs will bring one-tenth of the increase in total earned surplus into his own pocket instead of into the pockets of some capitalist-entrepreneurial owners. For this reason productivity may well be improved, with the result that the gap between productivity and aspirations for increased earnings may be reduced, a gap which we argued in Chapter II constituted a major factor in causing stagflation.

In a large-scale labour co-operative these advantages evaporate. If there are 100,000 workers in the concern, a single worker will enjoy only 1/100,000th part of any increase in the concern's total earned surplus which may be caused by his own efforts. Even in this case, of course, there may be a greater incentive to make efforts on behalf of the concern, from which there may be a smaller sense of alienation than in the case of a concern which is owned and managed by an outside group of persons. But however the managers are appointed and controlled, with a workforce of 100,000 to be organised and managed, there is almost certain to grow up some sense of tension between 'them – the bosses' and 'us – the workers at the bench'.

Much more important, however, is the alienation between 'us the workers' and 'them the government' which will arise as soon as the mono-polistic powers of a giant labour co-operative have to be controlled. The earned surplus of the workers will be restricted by the governmental control of the co-operative's selling prices or will be maintained by govern-mental subsidies paid for social reasons. The workers in the co-operative will have an incentive to strike or take other industrial action against the government and its price-subsidy policies instead of against a set of private capitalist owners and their profits – a development which one already senses in the case of the nationalised industries such as coal and steel.

We stated above that the need to control monopolistic action would in one respect be more necessary with a large-scale labour co-operative than with a capitalist-entrepreneurial concern. The reason is as follows. In the latter case any pure monopoly profit accrues to the given owners of the equity capital invested in the concern. There will be an incentive to maximise this total monopoly profit. In the case of a labour co-operative the monopoly profit will be part of the earned surplus. But the existing members of the co-operative will desire to maximise not the total earned surplus, but the earned surplus per member, with the result that the existing members will be willing to expand output by admitting new members only so long as its monopoly profit is thereby increased at least in proportion to the increase in the size of its membership. It will thus have a more restrictive bias.

A simple numerical example may be useful to illustrate the difference. We assume in columns (a), (b), and (c) of Table II that there is a concern which, with a given amount of fixed capital, financed at a fixed interest payment of £50 per annum, can produce an output that will sell at £300 if 100 men are employed and a larger output that will sell for £302 if 101 men are employed. If the wage of a man in the rest of competitive industry were £1, then with a capitalist-entrepreneurial system the wage bill would rise from £100 to £101 (column d) and the monopoly profit from £150 to £151 (column e) if the extra man is employed. With the labour co-operative the total earned surplus, which would include any

Table II

Number of Workers	Value of Output	Debt Interest	Capitalist-Entrepreneurial Concern		Labour Co-operative	
			Wage Bill	Monopoly Profit (e) = (b) − (c) − (d)	Earned Surplus (f) = (b) − (c)	Earnings per member (g) = (f) ÷ (a)
(a)	(b)	(c)	(d)			
100	300	50	100	150	250	2.5
101	302	50	101	151	252	2.495

element of monopoly profit, would rise from £250 to £252 (column f) but the earnings per head would fall from £2.5 to £2.494 (column g). The expansion would take place with the capitalist-entrepreneurial arrangements but not with the labour co-operative.

3.   The Implications of the Egalitarian Principle

The same numerical example may be used to examine the implications of a most important feature of the organisation of labour co-operatives. The extra restrictive propensity of a labour co-operative, illustrated in Table II, is due to the fact that it is assumed to be organised on the egalitarian principle that all members should receive an equal share of the earned surplus. We are not concerned for the moment with the question whether the skilled and the unskilled members of a co-operative should receive the same reward. Differentials due to differences of ability, skill, training, age, etc., are discussed in Appendix E. The egalitarian principle which is illustrated in Table II is simply that all members of the same grade of skill, etc., should receive the same reward and that there should not be two workers of the same skill, etc., working together at the same bench but receiving different shares in the co-operative's total earned surplus. The easiest way to examine the implications of this egalitarian principle is to assume for the time being, as is implicitly done in Table II, that there is only one homogeneous grade of labour in the whole workforce.

If the egalitarian principle were set aside, the extra restrictive propensity of a labour co-operative would disappear. In terms of the numerical example given above the admission of one new member will add £2 to the co-operative's total revenue from the sale of its products. The outside competitive wage rate is assumed to be £1. Any outside worker would gain from admission to membership if he were given a share in the earned surplus greater than £1. The existing members would gain from his admission if they granted him a share less than £2, since in that case there would remain some part of the additional revenue to be added to their existing shares. Thus everyone would gain if a new member were admitted with a share in the earned surplus which was, for example, equal to one half of the share allotted to the existing members.*

The egalitarian principle could equally well be broken if the existing members took on additional workers at a fixed wage rate. In the above example, they would have an incentive to do so at any wage less than £2, while outside workers might be attracted at any wage greater than £1. But in this case the labour-co-operative principle would be essentially abandoned. The existing members would take the place of the capitalist entrepreneurs and the tension between 'them' and 'us' would reappear. It is an open question how far this same conflict between 'them' and 'us' (e.g. between the new members with a half share and the old members with a whole share in the earned surplus) would reappear in the case of a true, but inegalitarian, labour co-operative.

Is then the egalitarian principle to be regarded as a fundamental feature of the labour co-operative? The problem is presented above in terms of the ownership by the lucky existing members of a property right in a monopoly profit that is protected by economies of large-scale production. But this is not the only possible case. A group of enterprising workers may have set up a small co-operative at very considerable risks to themselves to exploit a new idea, whether it be a new design of product or a new process of production. They make a success of the business and wish to expand. Is it wrong that the initial members who are responsible for the initial enterprise and risk-bearing which has led to the firm's success should be paid more than any members subsequently admitted to expand the scale of the business? However this question may be answered, it remains of basic importance. As will be argued later many of the improvements which one may hope to gain from the development of labour co-operatives and of other forms of labour participation in industrial affairs rest upon a willingness to breach the egalitarian principle. In particular, it will be argued, the efficacy of labour co-operatives in the fight against stagflation will be much affected by the question whether or not the egalitarian principle must be observed.

A labour co-operative which had a monopolistic position in the market for its product would thus tend to be less restrictive if it were organised in a way that did not insist on the egalitarian principle. It would, however, in any case be at least as restrictive as a similarly monopolistic capitalist-entrepreneurial concern; it would never wish to expand to such a point as to reduce the total monopoly profit available for distribution among its members. There would thus always be at least as strong a case for the regulation of its prices or for some form of governmental control as there would be in the case of a similar concern organised on capitalist-

---

*In this case an existing member's share of the earned surplus of £252 would rise to £2.5075 (approx) and the new member would enjoy a share of £1.2537 (approx) instead of a wage of £1.

entrepreneurial lines; and, as we have seen, in such conditions industrial
action to force the government to raise its prices might simply replace
industrial action to compel a rise in the wage rate.

4. Labour Co-operatives and Capital Intensity

There is another category of concerns for which the labour-co-operative
type of organisation is inappropriate, namely, the concern whose production technology is necessarily very capital-intensive. In many cases
concerns which are very capital-intensive in their technical processes of
production are also concerns in which there are economies of large-scale
production. The two categories of concerns often overlap. But there
may well be firms which are inevitably very capital-intensive in their
techniques of production even though their economies of scale relative
to the total market for the product are not sufficiently marked to run
into serious problems of monopoly power. In these cases also, however,
orthodox labour co-operatives are probably to be ruled out because of
the problem of risk-bearing.

Consider a capitalist-entrepreneurial concern which was so capital-
intensive in its technology that the amount that it would have to earn
on its production to pay the market rate of interest on the large amount
of capital employed was 9 times as great as the amount that it would have
to earn to pay the market rate of wages to the small labour force that it
needed to employ. In equilibrium £90 out of each £100 of the net sales
of its net product (i.e. of its 'net value added' as defined in the footnote
on page 119), is used to pay interest and dividends on its capital and
£10 to pay its wage bill. If its net value added fell unexpectedly by 5 per
cent from £100 to £95, its dividends would fall from £90 to £85 or by
5.5 per cent. Suppose, however, that it had been a labour co-operative
that had borrowed the necessary capital at a fixed interest, which imposed
on it the necessity of paying the £90 in interest whatever its good or
bad fortune. An unexpected fall of 5 per cent in its net value added from
£100 to £95 would cause its earned surplus to fall by 50 per cent from
£10 to £5. The reward per worker would be halved.

In the case of a labour-intensive product the boot would be on the
other leg. If £90 out of the £100 went to wages and only £10 to dividends, then in the case of a capitalist-entrepreneurial organisation the
5 per cent fall in its value added would cut the dividends in half from
£10 to £5; and in the case of the labour co-operative the earned surplus
would be cut by 5.5 per cent from £90 to £85.

There is in fact very good reason why capital should bear risk rather
than labour. Broadly speaking a man can at any one time work only at
one job — or at least at a very limited number of jobs — whereas he can
invest his total capital in small sums in various shares in many different

concerns. With his work all his eggs are in one basket; with his capital he can have one egg in each basket. In the capitalist-entrepreneurial regime workers in any case run the risk of losing their jobs and having to face, if not unemployment, then the cost of movement to other and perhaps less attractive jobs; but they do not bear the whole of the risk of a fall in the concern's net value added; the owners of the capital at least share the risk and face a fall, if not a total loss, of their profits. In the labour co-operative the risk is much more highly concentrated on the workers. If the concern goes bankrupt those who have lent their capital will face loss with the workers; but otherwise the workers face the whole of any upward or downward fluctuations. These considerations weigh in general against labour-co-operative and in favour of capital-entrepreneurial enterprises. Other arguments for labour co-operatives may turn the balance of advantage in their favour in the case of labour-intensive concerns; but the risks to workers who are committed to a highly capital-intensive co-operative would be intolerable.

5. Competitive Labour Co-operatives as a Cure for Stagflation

If we rule out the application of labour-co-operative organisation to the services of government servants, of large-scale monopolistic concerns, and of capital-intensive concerns, we are left with the sectors of the economy in which fairly small-scale, reasonably labour-intensive technologies are feasible. Would the organisation of labour co-operatives remove the problems of stagflation from these sectors of the economy? For the reasons given above we must assume that conditions for competition between the co-operatives are assured. In these circumstances, if financial policies were successfully implemented to maintain total money expenditures on the products of such concerns on a steady growth path of, say, 5 per cent per annum, the threat of an explosive inflation of money prices would be removed. The members of the individual labour co-operatives would have to accept whatever earned surplus they were able to achieve by their own productive efforts.

But the cure of stagflation requires the avoidance of unemployment as well as the avoidance of price inflation. Whether or not a regime of such small-scale, labour-intensive, competitive labour co-operatives, combined with restrained financial policies to maintain the total level of money expenditures on a steady growth path, would ensure the maintenance of full employment requires further discussion; and the answer, as we shall see, depends in large measure upon the question whether the egalitarian principle must be observed by the labour co-operatives. It will in fact probably prove more difficult in a world of small-scale labour-intensive competitive concerns to ensure full employment if the concerns are organised on egalitarian labour co-operative principles than if they are organised either on inegalitarian labour co-operative principles or on capitalist-entrepreneurial principles. The point can be made clear by the following simplified contrast between the different institutional arrangements.

Consider then the position of an economy at any one time composed of a number of such independent productive concerns, each with its given equipment of fixed capital and land. Suppose it to be faced at any one time by a given level of total money expenditure on the products of the economy, a level that is being kept on a steady 5 per cent per annum growth path by means of financial policies of the kind described in Chapter I. Each concern is charging a certain price for its product, is producing a certain output, and is employing a certain number of workers. Assume, however, that there remains a substantial volume of unemployed labour.

Suppose first of all that these concerns are all run on capitalist-entrepreneurial principles. Each will have employed labour up to the point at which what it can add to its net revenue from the sale of additional output no longer exceeds what it must add to its wage bill to hire the labour needed to produce that additional output. A rise in the money demand for the products of industry relative to the wage rate will thus give an incentive to expand employment in each concern. Thus if the money wage rate is not raised, the steady 5 per cent per annum growth in the total money demand for the products of industry will lead to the steady absorption of the unemployed workers by the existing firms. When full employment is reached, further expansion in the demand for the products of industry and so in the demand for labour will permit a corresponding steady rise in money wage rates without any threat to the maintenance of full employment.

Suppose, however, that the concerns are all run as egalitarian labour co-operatives, so that the incentive for any one co-operative to take on more partners does not depend in any way upon a wage that is demanded by new partners. In expanding the partnership there are two advantages and two disadvantages to a growth of the number of partners. Income per head will be raised in so far as the expansion of output brings any increasing returns to pure scale and in so far as the fixed debt on fixed capital can be spread over more partners; income per head will be reduced in so far as there are diminishing returns to the application of more labour to a given amount of fixed capital and in so far as increased output in conditions of imperfect competition leads to a reduction in selling price. But once the optimum size of partnership is attained by the balance of these factors there is no outside wage mechanism available to mop up any remaining unemployment.

Indeed as the money demand for the products of the co-operatives was steadily expanded, the existing co-operatives might well have an incentive to contract rather than to expand output and employment.

With a given amount of fixed capital, financed at the cost of the payment of a fixed amount of money interest, the incentive of an egalitarian co-operative will depend upon the relation between (1) the level of earnings per head (which is what the existing members must be prepared to pay out to any new member) and (2) the additional revenue that will result from the sale of the additional net output due to the work of the additional member (what is called the marginal revenue product of a new member). If (1) is less than (2), then the expansion of the membership will contribute an additional earned surplus which can be used to raise the earnings per head for all members. If (1) is greater than (2), then the new member can be paid as much as the old members only if the earnings per head is reduced all round sufficiently to make up for the deficiency of the marginal revenue product of the new member.

Suppose then that the money demand for the products of the co-operatives is raised by 10 per cent. If outputs are not increased the prices of the products will rise by some 10 per cent. In this case the marginal revenue product of a new member (what he could add to the co-operative's revenue by the sale of his additional output) will also probably be raised by some 10 per cent. But the earned surplus, and so the earnings per head of the existing members, are likely to be raised by more than 10 per cent. The net earned surplus would be raised by 10 per cent if, when the total revenue rose by 10 per cent, the cost of the debt interest also rose by 10 per cent. But if the revenue rises by 10 per cent and the fixed money debt cost does not rise, the net surplus of revenue over debt cost will rise by more than 10 per cent. Thus as a result of a 10 per cent rise in selling prices the existing earnings per head are likely to rise in a greater proportion than the marginal revenue product of a new member; and the incentive for the existing partners will be to reduce rather than to expand their membership.

Of course, the membership of the existing co-operatives would not be actually reduced except by the departure of existing partners as they reached retiring age, unless the rules of the partnership somehow permitted the unwilling dismissal of existing partners. But there would be no incentives for the existing concerns to expand and to mop up any existing pool of unemployed workers.

This contrast between an egalitarian labour co-operative and a capitalist-entrepreneurial concern is of such basic importance that it may be worthwhile illustrating it with a numerical example. The first half of the example given in Table III simply repeats the example already given in Table II with two changes. We now assume that the debt interest is £100 instead of £50 and that the wage rate is £2 instead of £1. With these changes the monopoly profit of the example in Table II disappears because we assume higher capital and wage costs. We are now dealing with a competitive equilibrium. In these conditions, as can be seen from the first half of Table III, both types of organisation will be in equilibrium and will be

Table III

Number of Workers	Value of Output	Debt Interest	Capitalist-Entrepreneurial Firm		Egalitarian Labour Co-operative	
			Wage Bill	Excess Profit (e) = (b) − (c) − (d)	Earned Surplus (f) = (b) − (c)	Earnings per member (g) = (f) ÷ (a)
(a)	(b)	(c)	(d)			

Case (i) Price of Output £1   Wage Rate £2

100	300	100	200	0	200	2
101	302	100	202	0	202	2

Case (ii) Price of Output £1.1   Wage Rate £2

100	330	100	200	30	230	2.3
101	332.2	100	202	30.2	232.2	2.299

indifferent between the employment of 100 or of 101 workers. The capitalist-entrepreneurial firm will just cover its costs with 100 or 101 workers; it will be indifferent between the two levels of employment because the 101st worker will add £2 to the value of output (£302 − £300) but will also add a wage rate of £2 to the cost. The egalitarian labour co-operative will achieve an earnings per head equal to £2 whether it admits 100 or 101 members, because the 101st member will add £2 to the value of output which is just equal to the share of £2 in the earned surplus that will be allotted to him.

In the second half of Table III we assume that the selling price of the product has risen by 10 per cent from £1 to £1.1. The capitalist-entre-preneurial firm will now make a net profit. But − and this is the important point − it will now have a definite incentive to increase its employment from 100 to 101 men, since its net profit will now be larger with 101 men than with 100 men (i.e. £30.2 instead of £30). This is so because the 101st man now adds £2.2 to the value of the output while his wage is still only £2. In the case of the egalitarian labour co-operative the earnings per member will, of course, be raised. But − and this is the important point − earnings per member will now be greater with only 100 members (namely, £2.3) than with 101 members (namely, £2.299). By taking on the 101st member the co-operative will, like the capitalist-entrepreneurial firm, now add £2.2 to the value of its sales. But on the egalitarian prin-ciple it will have to grant to the additional member a share equal to the new higher rate of share (about £2.3) instead of the old share worth £2. There would thus be a smaller addition to the total earned surplus than the additional outgoings to the new member.

Up to this point the argument has been concerned with the willingness of existing firms to take on more labour to employ with a given amount of fixed capital when the money demand for their products expands. In the case of the capitalist-entrepreneurial system there will be such an incentive if the money wage rate does not rise; in the case of the egalitarian co-operatives the existing money earnings per head will rise and this will remove the incentive for expansion.

Thus the immediate short-run incentives for expansion of existing firms will unquestionably be less in the case of the egalitarian co-operatives than in the capitalist-entrepreneurial case. But longer-term expansion can come about by an increased incentive to invest in additional plant and machinery and thus to expand employment, first, by the additional employment needed to produce the new machines and, second, by the additional workers needed to operate them. Both the egalitarian co-operative and the capitalist-entrepreneurial concern will have an incentive to increase its investment in plant and machinery if the debt interest that it would incur in order to raise the funds needed to purchase the new equipment is less than what would be added to the net value of the revenue from the sale of the additional product due to the operation of the machine (what may be called the money marginal revenue product of the machine). If the rate of interest at which money could be borrowed were the same and if the money cost of a machine were unchanged, then in both cases an increase in the demand for the products of a firm would give an incentive for expansion through new investment in plant and machinery, by raising the money marginal revenue product of a new machine without raising the money debt interest payable on the machine. But if the machines were themselves produced by egalitarian labour co-operatives, the outcome would be less expansionary than in the capitalist-entrepreneurial case. For when the demand for new machines increased, capitalist-entrepreneurial firms that produced machines would themselves take on more labour and supply more machines to the machine-using industries if the money wage rate in the machine-producing firms was not raised. But in these same conditions egalitarian labour co-operatives that produced machines would tend to raise the price charged for machines rather than expand their membership and produce more machines for the reasons which have already been discussed in connection with Table III. And if the price of a machine is raised *pari passu* with the price at which its product can be sold, then, with any given rate of interest, the machine-using co-operatives will have no incentive to invest in additional machinery.

6. The Crucial Role of New Co-operatives

There remains a third form of expansion which may serve to mop up any existing pool of unemployed workers, namely, the setting up of new firms. An increase in the money demand for the products of industry will make capitalist-entrepreneurial concerns more profitable and will raise the earnings per head in egalitarian labour co-operatives. In both cases there will be an increase in the opportunities and incentives for starting up new competing firms. This will be true of labour co-operatives as well as of capitalist-entrepreneurial concerns. Indeed effective expansion of employment must rely on the unemployed workers with their zero earnings and relatively low unemployment pay having an incentive to get together and to set up new competing co-operatives which are prepared if necessary to undercut the existing co-operatives (with their high earnings per head) and to accept a somewhat lower earnings per head.*

Expansion to mop up any pool of existing unemployed thus relies much more upon the ease of setting up new firms in the case of egalitarian labour co-operatives than it does in the case of capitalist-entrepreneurial concerns, since in the latter case the individual concerns will also have an incentive to expand. Indeed in the egalitarian labour-co-operative economy unemployment could be reduced only by the low-income unemployed setting up new co-operatives to compete with the high-income employed. But the setting up of new concerns requires investment in new fixed capital. It would take time even if the problems of finance of the capital on fixed-interest terms by the inexperienced concerns could be overcome. With the capitalist-entrepreneurial system the restraint of money wage rates would be equally effective in promoting the establishment of new concerns. But above all it would in addition have an immediate and direct effect in promoting the expansion of existing concerns. In the case of labour co-operatives this incentive could exist only by the abandonment of the egalitarian principle, that is to say, only if such co-operatives were prepared either (1) to hire labour at lower fixed rates of pay in addition to the continued employment of the profit-sharing partners at a higher earnings per head or (2) to admit new partners on profit-sharing terms that were less advantageous to the newly admitted partners than to the existing partners. The egalitarian labour co-operative economy has no such incentive to employ unemployed workers; unlike the capitalist-entrepreneurial system it must rely for

---

*Even in this case the scales are weighted against expansion in an egalitarian labour-co-operative system. The setting up of new concerns involves the installation of new plant and machinery. If the new machinery is produced by egalitarian labour co-operatives then, for the reasons given in connection with Table III, the new demand for machines for the setting up of new co-operatives may not lead to the immediate production of more machines, but merely to the new machine-using co-operatives acquiring some of the existing output of machinery which would otherwise have gone to replace machinery in the existing machine-using co-operatives. This does not mean that there will be no increase in employment, since the new co-operatives will be prepared to accept a lower earnings per head and thus to employ more workers per machine than the existing co-operatives. But that will be a slow and clumsy way of expanding employment.

its expansion on ease of entry for new competing co-operatives; and this is its basic weakness as a proposed universal remedy for the disease of stagflation.

7. The Case for Inegalitarian Labour—Capital Partnerships

The unadulterated egalitarian labour co-operative is not the only form of organisation in which the wage rate can be replaced by an earned share in the income produced by a productive concern. As we have seen, the abandonment of the egalitarian principle would itself remove some of the excessively restrictive features of such co-operatives. The possible scope for their useful organisation would be greatly increased if some means would also be found by which those who provided the capital that was invested in the concern shared the risks of the venture with the workers.

The possibilities may be illustrated by outlining in a 'pure' form the organisation of what one may call an Inegalitarian Labour—Capital Partnership, in which the concern's income, with its risks, is shared between the workers and the owners of the capital funds but without adherence to the strict egalitarian principles which would inhibit its expansion.

In such a partnership there would be no fixed payments of interest or rent. Both those who had provided the capital funds and those who were providing the labour in the enterprise would own shares. These would represent shares in the 'net value added' of the enterprise (that is to say, in the excess of the receipts of the enterprise from the sale of its products over (1) the cost of its inputs of raw materials, (2) an allowance for the depreciation in the real value of its fixed capital equipment, and (3) any taxes to which the concern was liable, as indicated in the footnote on page 119). Each share would give to its holder, whether a capitalist or a worker, the same *pro rata* claim on the net value added and the same *pro rata* voting power in the direction of the enterprise, for example, in the appointment of a board of directors and managers at a shareholders' meeting.

But the shares would be of two kinds.

Capital shares would be lasting shares once the funds had been put into the enterprise; the funds themselves could not be withdrawn but the shares could be bought and sold, for example, on the Stock Exchange.

Work shares would give voting rights and a *pro rata* claim on the net value added only so long as the worker made himself available for work in the enterprise. No worker could be dismissed against his will once he was admitted to membership, but so long as he was a member he would in principle be under an obligation to do any job in the partnership which the management might require him to do. He would be free to leave at any time, in which case he would surrender his work shares.

The management of the partnership would be free to issue new capital shares provided it could do so at a price which, in its opinion, would finance an addition to the partnership's real assets sufficient to produce so great an addition to the concern's net value added that the net result would be a rise in the ratio of net value added to the new total number of shares outstanding, whether in the form of capital shares or work shares. In other words, new capital would be raised only if the terms were both attractive to the new subscribers and held out the prospect of increasing the income of every existing partner, whether capitalist or worker.

Similarly, the management of the partnership would be free to employ a new worker provided that the worker would be willing to join the partnership in return for an issue of additional work shares such that the addition to the net value added of the concern due to the additional work done was so great that the net result would be a rise in the ratio of net value added to the new total number of shares, whether capital shares or work shares. Conversely, any worker who retired or otherwise withdrew and thus gave up his work shares would not be replaced on the old terms if the resulting loss of net value added was so small relative to the reduction in the number of work shares that the net result was a rise in the ratio of net value added to the total number of remaining shares outstanding, whether capital shares or work shares. In other words, decisions to increase or decrease the size of the workforce would be taken only if they held out the prospect of advantage to all shareholders, whether capitalist or worker.

As compared with the egalitarian labour co-operative, the inegalitarian capital–labour partnership has two outstanding advantages. The abandonment of the egalitarian principle would remove the excessive restrictive tendencies of the egalitarian co-operative and would thus, as we have seen, make it a more effective system for attaining and preserving full employment. The introduction of capitalists as well as workers as equity shareholders would improve greatly the problems of risk-bearing and would enable the system to cover capital-intensive processes which would otherwise be ruled out. In both these basic respects it would be a more effective means of combating stagflation.

8. Conflicts of Interest in Labour–Capital Partnerships

A great advantage of the labour co-operative is that it removes the conflict between labour and capitalist entrepreneurs in the management of the concern and, as we have argued, it is the removal of the tension between 'them' and 'us' which does away with the need for the monopolistic upward pressure on wages by trade unions in order to obtain a larger share of the profits of the enterprise.

The full capital—labour partnership could also remove the conflicts of interests between capital and labour in any partnership since, as we have shown, decisions would be taken only if they were to the advantage of all holders of shares, whether capital shares or work shares. But in some cases it would be rather difficult to achieve this result. A number of things which will cost the partnership money (e.g. canteen facilities and many other fringe benefits) will be to the advantage of workers holding work shares but not to the advantage of those holding capital shares, though the cost will fall on both groups. Possibly an even more important case of a conflict of interest of this kind would arise in any decision to reduce hours of work or to increase the length of annual holidays for the workers, thereby taking an increase in real income out in the form of leisure. Holders of capital shares would also sacrifice the return on their shares without enjoying any increase of leisure.

There is another very important way in which in a full capital—labour partnership the conflict between labour and capital might be more difficult to resolve. In this chapter we have confined our attention to the case in which all workers were of the same grade of skill, etc. In Appendix E we discuss some of the problems which arise when there are differences between skills, etc. One problem which arises in the setting of differentials is particularly likely, in the absence of special rules, to lead to conflict between the interests of labour and capital in a full capital—labour partnership. It is questionable whether when a new partner was recruited he could be issued with a number of work shares which then remained unchanged during the whole of his working life in the partnership. If differentials in payment to different grades of workers exist, the problem of payment on promotion from one job to another will arise. Problems of promotion could give rise to a direct conflict of interest between the capitalist and the worker partners. Promotions which involved the issue of additional work shares would automatically reduce the amount of any given net value added which was available for payment on capital shares. Thus a policy of easy and widespread upgrading of the workforce could be a means for redistributing the income of the partnership from the capitalists to the workers. In principle it is not impossible to devise rules which mean that promotion of an individual partner with an increased issue of shares should take place only when it was to the advantage of all existing share-holders — or at least only when it was not to the disadvantage of any other existing shareholders. This would imply that such an increased issue of work shares should be made only if (1) such promotion was judged to be needed to retain the services of the worker in the partnership and (2) the loss of net value added which would result from his leaving the partner-ship would be greater than (or at least not less than) his increased rate of earnings on his work shares.

The application to such matters as hours of work, holidays, fringe benefits, and promotion of the principle that no decision should be to the disadvantage of either type of shareholder could be ensured by ruling that such decisions had to receive the agreement of both capital share-holders and work shareholders separately. But this inevitably implies some tension between workers and capitalists and, in the last resort, it might lead to industrial action by the holders of work shares to enforce the agreement of the holders of capital shares.

9. Conclusions

From this analysis it is perhaps possible to deduce a number of important conclusions.

First, the organisation of labour co-operatives or capital–labour partner-ships is not appropriate for some forms of economic activity; in particular it would be inappropriate in the case of civil servants or of workers em-ployed in industries for which, because of economies of large-scale or other factors leading to serious problems of monopoly, state regulation of prices or nationalisation is inevitable.

Second, the formation of labour co-operatives or of capital–labour partnerships in the remaining competitive market industries may help with the cure of the evils of stagflation. But these advantages will be lost unless rules against restrictive practices are effectively applied, in-cluding rules against the formation of monopolistic guilds of workers.

Third, in the case of industries whose technology is highly capital-intensive labour co-operatives are to be ruled out on grounds of the excessive risks to be borne by the workers, though capital–labour partner-ships would still be acceptable.

Fourth, if the egalitarian principle is maintained in labour co-operatives it is essential, in the interests of achieving and maintaining full employ-ment, that it should be easy for unemployed workers to set up new co-operatives in competition with existing co-operatives, though the design of the necessary capital-market institutions to finance such new concerns will not be simple.

Fifth, the egalitarian principle is, however, likely to be abandoned. An unsuccessful labour co-operative is unlikely to survive. If, on the other hand, it is successful, there will be very strong market forces to break the egalitarian principle since (for the reasons explained above) there will then exist a very strong incentive for the existing members to take on new members if, but only if, the egalitarian principle is broken; and at the same time there will be strong incentives for outsiders to become insiders even on less advantageous terms than the existing insiders.

Sixth, there will almost certainly in such cases be outsiders who would prefer a job at a fixed wage rather than a job at an earned share which was subject to variations according to the fortunes of the concern. As a result a successful labour co-operative is likely to be transformed into an inegalitarian concern with the 'owners' earning more than the 'wage hands'.

Seventh, in the case of a capital—labour partnership there may well be outside owners of capital who would prefer to lend to the concern at a fixed rate of interest rather than on an equity basis and on terms which were attractive to the existing holders of shares in the partnership. There would be a strong incentive for the existing shareholders to admit some capitalists on a fixed interest basis just as there may well be an incentive to take on some workers on a fixed wage basis, as noted in the preceding paragraph.

Eighth, in the present chapter we have examined these problems only in the case of two 'pure' types — the unadulterated labour co-operative and the unadulterated capital—labour partnership. But there may well be adulterated forms of profit-sharing in which the workers were all employed at a notionally fixed wage and the capital all raised at a notionally fixed rate of interest, but in which any profit or loss which results after the deduction of these fixed returns is shared in some predetermined ratio between capital and labour — a ratio which may not correspond to the division of the notionally fixed payments between capital and labour. If such a division of profit or loss does correspond to the division of the fixed payments, the concern is like a capital—labour partnership. If the profit or loss falls mainly on the owners of the capital, it moves in the direction of a capitalist-entrepreneurial enterprise. If it falls mainly on the workers, it moves in the direction of a labour co-operative. Pure forms are not essential and different institutional combinations can be sought for different enterprises in order to find that compromise which gives the best balance of the relative merits and demerits of the different forms.

Ninth, the analysis of labour—capital partnerships suggests the importance of combining participation in profits with participation in management. Participation in profits without participation in management will invite workers, whether justifiably or not, to blame low gains from profits on bad management; and participation in management without participation in profits will tempt workers to press for benefits without due regard for their effect on the concern's future prosperity.

The final moral to be drawn is probably: that labour co-operatives and/or capital—labour partnerships and/or profit-sharing schemes do not provide a full answer to the problems of stagflation; but that different forms of such institutions may help to relax the tension between 'them, the capitalists' and the 'us, the workers' and thus help to make the problems of stagflation more tractable; and that for that reason, wherever appropriate, experiments in such varied forms of labour participation in management and ownership are greatly to be encouraged.

CHAPTER X

Fiscal Devices for the Control of Inflation

Many proposals have been made for the design of tax/subsidy arrangements to provide an incentive to refrain from raising money prices or money costs. There is a great range of possibilities. In this chapter we will examine two examples of such schemes. Our purpose is to enquire whether they are likely to act as efficient instruments in reducing the rate of price inflation and thus to be welcomed as supplements to, or even complete substitutes for, the other proposals discussed in Chapters VI, VII, VIII and IX. Some tax schemes may, of course, lead to unemployment by reducing the total level of spending power and so the demand for goods and services or by raising costs of production in any given conditions of total money expenditures on goods and services. Since the whole purpose of this work is to consider ways of combining full employment with reasonable price stability we will throughout this chapter neglect any possibility of tax/subsidy schemes restraining wage-cost inflation by the creation of unemployment; we will consider their effects upon (1) wage-fixing and (2) profit mark-ups in conditions of full employment and will assess their usefulness as anti-inflation devices in conditions of full employment.

1. A Great Variety of Devices

(1) Some schemes are designed to operate on wage rates by, for example, imposing a tax on increases in wage rates above a certain norm. Other schemes are designed to operate on selling prices, that is, on profit margins as well as wage costs, for example, by imposing a tax on excessive increases in the value added (i.e. on profits plus wages) per unit of output. It is argued that schemes will be politically more acceptable and indeed more relevant for the discouragement of inflation if they are designed to curb excessive profit margins as well as excessive wage costs.

(2) Some schemes rely solely on a tax on inflationary increases of price or wage above some permitted norm, while other schemes are designed also to subsidise those whose increases are below the stated norm. Since the aim of these schemes is to curb general inflation it would seem desirable to encourage by subsidy those who are more moderate than the norm as well as to tax those who go above the norm.

(3) If a tax-cum-subsidy scheme is adopted, it is possible to aim to set the rate of tax/subsidy at a level which causes the average rate of wage or price rise to conform to the norm. In other words, it is possible to aim at a scheme which is self-balancing in revenue, the rate of tax/subsidy being such as to cause the revenue from those who go above the norm to finance exactly the expenditure on subsidies for those below the norm. In some schemes it is suggested that this result could automatically be achieved by allotting to each firm or economic agent concerned licenses to raise their wage or price by the permitted norm and then to allow trade in these licenses, so that those who had sufficient motive to exceed their permitted norm could buy in the market the right to do so from those who, given the price offered for the surrender of their licenses, were prepared to remain below the norm.

(4) Proposals have also been made for schemes of a quite different kind, namely, for a tax on any increase in an individual taxpayer's income from one year to the next over and above a given norm. Thus suppose that the norm were set at 5 per cent and the rate of tax on excess incomes at 50 per cent. If Mr Smith's income this year were 9 per cent greater than last year he would be liable to an extra payment of tax equal to 2 per cent of his income.

A scheme of this kind, (4), may conceivably have a role to play as a temporary once-for-all shock to help put a stop to a rampant inflation, since it would reduce the gain to be achieved by obtaining any given rise in pay above the norm. But it is doubtful how useful such a scheme would be.

In the first place, it could conceivably lead to an even greater pressure for increases in rates of pay above the norm, since, with a tax on excess rises of 50 per cent, a rise of 8 per cent instead of only 4 per cent above the norm would now be needed to obtain the previous net advantage of a 4 per cent excess above the norm. Secondly, the scheme could not distinguish between increases in income due to the inflation of the rate of pay for a given job and increases in income due to greater effort, promotion, or movement to a better paid job. As more than a very temporary measure it could for this reason have a severely deleterious effect on individual incentives. Thirdly, a tax on increases in income is not the same as a tax on high incomes, and a scheme which resulted in a special tax on improvements in the position of a low-paid worker with no similar tax on the steady income of a millionaire could be open to criticism on distributional grounds.

It is impossible to examine all possible schemes. In this chapter and in Appendix C we will consider two possible schemes, which are rather less open to these criticisms. These are chosen partly on the basis of their inherent merits, partly on grounds of administrative feasibility, and partly because they provide good illustrations of the various considerations which arise with schemes of this kind.

2.   A Scheme for Control of Price Inflation

With the first scheme (Scheme A) a tax is imposed on the excess of this year's over last year's level of a firm's value added per unit of output (i.e. on its profit plus wages per unit of output). The firm would, however, be allowed tax-free a certain 'norm' rise in its value added per unit of output, and any taxable excess of value added per unit of output would be weighted by the firm's total output. The firm would receive a corresponding subsidy if its value added per unit of output were kept below the 'norm'.

This would correspond to a control not of a firm's selling price, but of that part of its selling price which it had added to the cost of any raw materials or similar inputs into its productive process which it had bought from outside sources. Since for a closed economy as a whole one firm's input is another firm's output, this would imply a control over the general level of selling prices for the economy as a whole. But it would still leave uncontrolled any price changes due to the costs of imported raw materials into the country's productive processes.

In such a scheme the amount of tax or subsidy payable or receivable in year t could be expressed by

$$T_t^* \left(\frac{\overline{VA}_t}{Q_t} - \eta_{t-1} \frac{\overline{VA}_{t-1}}{Q_{t-1}} \right) Q_t = T_t^* \left(\overline{VA}_t - \eta_{t-1} \overline{VA}_{t-1} \frac{Q_t}{Q_{t-1}} \right) \qquad (1)$$

where T_t^* is the current rate of tax/subsidy in year t, $\overline{VA}_t$ is the total value added (i.e. wages plus profits) of year t, Q_t is the total output of year t, and η_{t-1} (which we will call the expansion factor) measures one plus the permitted tax-free 'norm' rate of increase of $\overline{VA}/Q$.

The application of this scheme would involve each firm or employing agent in calculating the firm's total value added each year, $\overline{VA}$, and an index of the firm's output Q_t/Q_{t-1}. It should be administratively feasible to base the calculation of $\overline{VA}$ upon the total of profits (including all relevant forms of return on the firm's capital) plus wages as assessed for income tax and/or corporation tax, though this raises all the well-known questions about the true meaning of profits when one allows for the requirements of inflation accounting, about the proper definition and treatment of capital gains, and about the treatment of fringe benefits.

The problems of the output index Q_t/Q_{t-1} would, however, be quite novel and exceedingly difficult to manage in the case of a firm producing a wide range of different products of different qualities. It would be essential to devise some short cut. One possibility would be to assume that output per head was growing from year to year at some stated rate. One could thus assume $Q_t/Q_{t-1} = \lambda L_t/L_{t-1}$ where $\lambda - 1$ measured the assumed rate of growth of output per head. We will call λ the productivity growth factor. The tax/subsidy formula would then become

$$T_t^* \left(\overline{VA}_t - \lambda \eta_{t-1} \; \overline{VA}_{t-1} \; \frac{L_t}{L_{t-1}} \right) \tag{2}$$

which involves increasing the expansion factor from η_{t-1} to $\lambda \eta_{t-1}$ to allow for the assumed rate of growth of output per head and using an index of labour employed L_t/L_{t-1} instead of an index of output Q_t/Q_{t-1}.

The formula in equation (2) would in one respect be preferable to that in equation (1) quite apart from any improvement of administrative feasibility. The productivity growth factor λ would be common to all firms and would be based on the general level of productivity growth for the economy as a whole. In equation (2) the limit would be set on value added per unit of labour employed instead of being set on value added per unit of output as in equation (1). As a result equation (2) would give an incentive to sectors of the economy in which productivity was growing more rapidly to lower their selling prices relative to the prices charged in sectors with less rapid productivity growth.

Such a result may well be considered wholly desirable in those cases in which increases in output per head occur in a costless fashion, simply by a bright and costless new idea. But where exceptional increases in output per head are the result of exceptional expenditures of one kind or another, either on new capital investment or on special payments to workers for new effort or disturbance of existing arrangements, the equation (2) formula would have disincentive effects by taxing any resulting increases in value added per head.

In the case of increases in value added per head which result from increased expenditures on resources other than direct labour employed (for example, an increased capital investment), there is a possible modification of the equation (2) formula which would remove this disincentive effect.

Thus suppose a firm were to increase its output per unit of labour by means of a large investment in capital equipment. Equation (1) would not imply any disincentive to such investment since the tax-free base would be raised in proportion to the increase in output which it had caused. But equation (2) would work as a disincentive since the tax-free base would be raised only by the additional employment of labour and not by the additional use of capital.

The administrative difficulties in making a direct allowance for additions to the use of capital as well as for the additional use of labour would be extremely formidable. One way out of the difficulty would be to use for value added not total profits plus wages, but what may be called 'net sales', which is the base for the so-called Value Added Tax

(VAT). This is the difference between the value of a firm's sales of goods and services and the value of its purchases of goods and services other than the wages paid to its own labour force. This amounts to wages plus true profits minus any net investment in new capital goods or plus any net disinvestment of the existing stock of capital goods.

The use of 'net sales' instead of true 'value added' would remove any tax/subsidy disincentive or incentive to investment, provided that the tax/subsidy rate was expected to remain unchanged. This can be seen from the numerical example given in Table IV. We consider a firm which employs a constant labour force and would have had a constant value added of 100 a year if it had not invested 10 in year 1 (column a). This investment, given a yield on capital of 10 per cent, raises true value added to 101 from year 2 onwards (column b). The firm's net sales (column c) are its true value added less expenditure on new capital goods (i.e. columns b minus a). Assuming an expansion factor of unity, its tax/subsidy base is the rise or fall in its net sales (column d). If one assumes a constant rate of tax, T^*, of 50 per cent (column e), then column f gives its cash flow. Instead of the constant 100 which it could have received if it had not undertaken the investment, it now 'saves' 5 in year 1. This invested at 10 per cent should give it 100.5 in year 2; but it receives only 95.5, thus 'saving' another 5. From year 3 onwards it receives 101 instead of 100, representing a yield of 10 per cent on the combined savings of 10 of years 1 and 2. This can be compared with column c which shows the cash flow which would have occurred in the absence of the scheme. The only difference is that the firm would have saved the whole 10 in year 1 instead of 5 in year 1 and 5 in year 2, but the rate of yield of 10 per cent is not affected.

This example shows that the use of net sales as the tax/subsidy base leaves the rate of yield on the investment unaffected by the scheme, provided that the tax/subsidy rate is unchanged. But if, for example, the rate of tax had been expected to fall from 50 per cent to zero between years 1 and 2, the cash flow would have been 100, 95, 101, 101, ... giving a net yield of 20 per cent on the savings of 5; and conversely if the rate had been expected to rise. However, in spite of this it would seem

Table IV

Year	Invest-ment	True Value Added	Net Sales	Tax/Subsidy Base	Tax/Subsidy Rate	Net Cash Flow
	(a)	(b)	(c)	(d)	(e)	(f)
0	0	100	100	0	0.5	100
1	10	100	90	− 10	0.5	$90 + 0.5 \times 10 =$ 95
2	0	101	101	+ 11	0.5	$101 − 0.5 \times 11 =$ 95.5
3	0	101	101	0	0.5	101
4	0	101	101	0	0.5	101

wise to use for an equation (2) type of scheme 'net sales' rather than 'true value added' for the tax/subsidy base. This would give relative ease of administration and would remove disincentives to invest except in those cases in which substantial increases in T^* were expected.

3.   Administrative Problems of a Price-Control Scheme

If the calculation of the labour-employed index for equation (2) made no distinction between different types, grades, and skills of workers, it could be based simply upon a count of the total man-hours worked in an employer's firm each year. Such a count would involve some, but presumably not insuperable, administrative problems for the employer; and there would remain the further and more formidable problem of the enforcement of the scheme which would require the tax authorities to check the employer's returns of total man-hours worked.

But if differences in types, grades, and skills were neglected in this way, an employer would have an incentive to substitute low-wage labour for high-wage labour, since any such substitution would reduce his actual wage bill without reducing the wage bill which was used as the tax-free norm for the permitted selling price of his output, thus giving a bonus to the permitted tax-free expansion of his profits. While a tax on high-paid labour and a subsidy to low-paid labour would be very acceptable on distributional grounds, it would involve an inefficient distortion against highly skilled modern techniques.

To avoid this effect it would be necessary to weight the man-hours worked by various categories of labour according to their relative wage rates or some other simpler broad classification in order to calculate a final index of man-hours worked.

This would present a formidable, if not impossible, administrative task for employers and enforcement problem for the authorities; and even if it were feasible, it would invite tax avoidance by artificial increases in the index L_t/L_{t-1}, through the artificial promotion and upgrading of workers from a lower to a higher category. It would be impossible to prohibit all such upgradings, since those which resulted from true increases of training, experience, and responsibility could not be properly disallowed.

This suggests that an equation (2) type of scheme based upon returns of 'net sales' as defined for VAT purposes and returns of unweighted man-hours worked for the employment index could probably be made to work and that the possibility would have to be accepted that this would act as a tax disincentive against any arrangement for raising output per head which involved higher rates of pay per head.

Some further administrative problems would still remain. When the scheme was started in year 1, each firm or employing agent would start with a norm based on its value added in year 0. But some employing agents might have done exceptionally well in year 0 and would thus be favoured, while others might (e.g. because of a strike) have an exceptionally low $\overline{VA}$ for year 0. Consideration would have to be given to the problem of a fair adjustment of the starting base.

A somewhat similar problem would arise for a new firm or employing agent çoming into existence. It might be sufficient to allow a first year free of restriction and to base the second year's norm on the first year's performance. But this might impose a very heavy penalty on a new firm in a line of activity where the first two or three years were likely to yield exceptionally low returns.

The question arises whether the scheme could or should cover all employing agents. The scheme would not be appropriate for central and local government services. Should self-employed persons be included? Could they be expected to report their own man-hours worked? Should a producer of agricultural products whose value added is liable to extreme fluctuations due to variations in crop yields be included? Could small businesses (e.g. small retail shops) cope with the requirements of the scheme? And if some sectors were not covered, how far could the scheme be avoided by movement from the covered to the uncovered sectors (e.g. by a large concern splitting into a number of small subsidiary concerns or a corporate body turning into a partnership)?

There are thus a number of serious administrative problems. It may be that they could be faced; but the scheme is sufficiently complicated for it to be worth adoption only if it had great and sure merit as a permanent institution. We turn accordingly to an examination of the basic merits of a scheme of the kind described by equation (2) above.

4.   A Self-Balancing Scheme

There is one possible effect of fiscal schemes of the kind examined in this chapter which we intend to rule out. Such a scheme might impose a net tax burden on profits, and the fact that post-tax available profits were reduced in this way might lead to a reduction in the rate of wage inflation because the squeeze on profits caused employers to resist wage claims more strictly and workers to press wage claims less persistently than they would have done if available post-tax profit had been more plentiful. But any such dampening effect on inflation of a net tax on profits could be achieved as effectively and much more simply by a rise in the rate of an existing tax on profits.

In order to isolate this possible indirect effect on the schemes upon inflation we shall in this chapter examine the schemes on the assumption that they are imposed in a form which is self-balancing in so far as public revenue and expenditure is concerned. This would automatically be the case if the schemes took the form of limiting by license the right of each employing agent to a specified value added total each year, but allowing such employing agents to trade these licenses between each other. An alternative device would be for the authorities to impose a fixed tax/ subsidy rate T_t^* at a level which they considered likely to result in tax payments on inflations above the chosen norm being equal to subsidy claims in respect of inflations below the norm. This second self-balancing tax subsidy method would be difficult to apply. It could in fact be operated only by a process of trial and error, lowering T^* and/or raising η if tax revenue exceeded subsidy payments, and *vice versa*.

In this connection it should be realised that T_t^* does not represent the net tax cost to an employer in raising his $\overline{VA}_t$ this year. It can be seen from equation (2) that if he raises his $\overline{VA}_t$ this year an employer will raise his tax-free permitted base next year which will be equal to

$$\lambda \eta_t \ \overline{VA}_t \frac{L_{t+1}}{L_t}$$

Thus the net tax cost of a rise in $\overline{VA}$ this year is T_t^* less the present value of the rise in next year's tax-free base; and this last element will depend upon expectations about next year's tax/subsidy rate, T_{t+1}^*, and next year's expansion factor, $\lambda \eta_t$. The effect of a given rise in T_t^* on the incentive to avoid rises in this year's prices is thus a complicated one and will affect the trial-and-error response to a change in T_t^* of the balance between this year's tax revenue and subsidy payments.

But in spite of the difficulties involved in attempting to keep the tax—subsidy—revenue balance it is probable that this system would have to be adopted rather than a self-balancing market in licenses to inflate. There are three reasons for holding this view.

First, it would be difficult if not impossible for any employing agent to calculate until after the event the extent to which he had exceeded or fallen below his permitted licensed norm. Such a calculation would depend upon a calculation of his value added (profit plus wages) or his net sales for the year and upon a calculation of his index of man-hours employed during the year. It could easily be that most employers had on balance inadvertently considerably exceeded their total licensed norm. Demand for licenses would exceed supply and, unless additional licenses were provided at a penalty price, the price of licenses would be bid up to infinity. A tax/subsidy regime would operate on the basis of a *post hoc* calculation of the net outcome for each employer on the basis of a tax rate announced in advance.

Second, it would be desirable that, in order for employers to plan their employment, output, and sales policies for the year and for the orderly determination of wage bargains by employers and employed, the tax/subsidy rate of charge on divergences from the norm should be known in advance at the beginning of the fiscal year.

Third, as will be shown later, the effects of the scheme are necessarily uncertain. A given restriction on inflation ($\lambda\eta$ sufficiently low) could well drive up the market price of licenses in a self-clearing market for licenses to levels that were unexpected and quite unacceptably high. To fix the tax/subsidy rate in advance might mean that tax revenue unexpectedly exceeded subsidy payments; but it would not have involved an unacceptably high rate of tax.

On the basis of these assumptions we proceed to examine the effects of Scheme A as described in equation (2) above.*

5.   The Efficacy of a Scheme for Control of Price Inflation

There are two possible ways in which a scheme of this kind might moderate increases in price. First, it might induce a reduction in the profit margin which is added on to wage and other variable costs. Second, it might induce a reduction in the rate of rise of money wages and so a reduction in the rate of rise of the wage costs to which the profit margin is added. These two effects may, of course, interact.

Scheme A may well induce a reduction in the profit margin. A reduction in the profit margin charged by any firm will, of course, represent a reduction in value added per unit of output. In any given conditions of demand and any given wage cost this will be rewarded by the avoidance of a tax or the gain of a subsidy, as can be seen from equation (1). There will, therefore, be an inducement to charge a lower profit margin than would otherwise be the case.

This may in turn moderate future wage claims. The introduction of the scheme may cause the immediate price rise to be less than would otherwise have been the case because of the reduced profit margin. This reduction in the rate of inflation may cause wage earners to reduce their expectation of future inflation and thereby induce them to settle for a lower rate of increase in the money wage rate than would otherwise have been the case. It is also possible that, even apart from the actual experience of any such reduction in the inflation rate, the mere introduction of the scheme together with the official propaganda for it might moderate wage claims through the expectation that the scheme would successfully reduce the rate of inflation. Moreover, the reduction in the profit margin by reducing the available fund of profit from which wage increases could be financed might in itself stiffen employers' resistance to wage claims

*See Appendix C, Section III for a formal analysis of the conclusions of this examination.

and lessen the employees' pressure for a wage claim; and we will consider this possibility at greater length in Section 7 below.

There are, however, three possible snags to this favourable outcome.

First, it is very uncertain how far the cutting of the profit margin will itself moderate wage claims given, as we are assuming, that full employment is maintained.

Second, in spite of any moderating effect of the cut in the profit margin on real wage claims, it is possible that at full employment, there remains some quart-out-of-a-pint-pot inflation; that is to say, it remains possible that wage earners will continue to attempt to get annual wage increases which, after allowing for a rise sufficient to offset any expected inflation of the cost of living, are sufficient to ensure a rise in the real standard of living which outstrips the rise in real output per head. In this case, while the imposition of the scheme may delay somewhat the process of explosive inflation which we described in Chapter II, it cannot prevent its re-emergence.

Third, in order that the scheme should exercise a lasting moderating effect upon inflation the tax/subsidy rate on rises in value added per unit of output and the consequential cut in the profit margin may well have to be permanent. For if the tax/subsidy rate is reduced to zero, the incentive to cut the profit margin will disappear. But a restoration of the profit margin will cause prices to rise more quickly in the year in question, and this increase in the rate of inflation may restore the expectation of future inflation and will also remove any additional moderating effect on wage claims of the reduced fund of profits available for the finance of such claims.

On the other hand, the permanent continuation of a tax/subsidy rate imposed at the level needed to cope adequately with the existing inflationary problem may well involve so large a cut in profit margins for the purpose of tax avoidance that profits become insufficient to give needed incentives for investment and innovation.*

6. A Scheme for the Control of Wage Inflation

In an economy in which prices are basically formed by a profit mark-up on variable costs of which labour costs are the principal component, fiscal schemes for the control of inflation stand to succeed or fail according as they do or do not succeed in moderating money wage claims.

---

*As shown in Appendix A an inflation of wage costs may cut profits to an unacceptably low level because of a delay in applying a constant profit margin to rising wage costs. A reduction of the profit mark-up due to the introduction of a scheme during a rampant inflation would represent an intensification of this process of profit erosion.

It is for this reason that we have chosen for Scheme B a scheme that is similar to Scheme A in other respects but which places the tax/subsidy rate not on excesses or deficiencies of value added per unit of output above a given norm but upon excesses or deficiencies of money wages per unit of output above or below a certain norm.*

Scheme B can accordingly be represented by a tax or subsidy equal to

$$T_t^* \left(\frac{\overline{WL}_t}{Q_t} - \eta_{t-1} \frac{\overline{WL}_{t-1}}{Q_{t-1}} \right) Q_t$$

$$= T_t^* \left(\overline{WL}_t - \eta_{t-1} \overline{WL}_{t-1} \frac{Q_t}{Q_{t-1}} \right)$$

$$= T_t^* \left(\overline{WL}_t - \lambda \eta_{t-1} \overline{WL}_{t-1} \frac{L_t}{L_{t-1}} \right) \tag{3}$$

where $\overline{WL}_t$ measures the total wage bill paid in year t.

This scheme would raise many of the same administrative problems as did Scheme A, but would be somewhat simpler in that it would not require the assessment of total value added (which raises problems connected with the measurement of true profits or of net sales) but only of the total wage bill. The problem in connection with the proper measure of the firm's employment index L_t/L_{t-1} (including the discouragement of those increases in output per head which involved higher rates of pay) would however remain, as would the problem of wage increases given in the undeclared and untaxed form of fringe benefits.

Since with Scheme B the tax is confined to increases in wage payments and is not affected by increases in selling prices as such, there would (unlike the case of Scheme A) be no incentive for producers to cut their profit mark-ups. Indeed unless the scheme for some reason or another led to a reduction in the wage settlements that would otherwise have taken place in full employment and at the existing expected rates of price inflation, it would in fact intensify rather than damp down the future rate of price inflation. The cost to the producer of employing more labour would be the wage cost plus any net tax payable on the employment of the additional workers. If the permitted norm had been set as high as the wage rate increase which would in any case have taken place, there would be no tax on the employment of additional labour; but in that case the scheme would simply have no effect. But suppose that in an attempt to discourage excess wage increases the permitted norm

*For political acceptability it might well be necessary to impose some form of limitation on profits or dividend payments to accompany a scheme in which the tax on excess payment applied only to earnings.

had been set lower than the wage rate increase that would otherwise have taken place. If in these circumstances there were no direct effect on the wage settlements that would have taken place in the absence of the scheme, there would be a net tax levied on the wages paid to workers. The producers would have every incentive to apply their profit mark-ups to the labour cost, including the tax cost as well as the wage cost. The price inflationary forces would be intensified instead of being damped down.

In the case of Scheme B this is indeed the crux of the matter. Would the existence of the scheme for some reason or another moderate the wage settlements even in the absence of any indirect effects through a rise in unemployment or a reduction of past inflation or of expected inflation? Would it for some reason or another cause employers to be more resistant to, and wage earners to be less insistent on, increased wage payments?

This question, which is crucial for Scheme B, is also of great importance for Scheme A. As we have seen, Scheme A by inducing a cut in profit margins may have a direct effect on inflation and so on the expectation of inflation, which will in turn have an *indirect* beneficial effect on future wage claims. But this gain will be achieved only by a cut in profit margins which may itself have undesirable disincentive effects on investment and enterprise, and in any case will only postpone the resurgence of an explosive inflation if, at full employment, there remains any quart-out-of-a-pint-pot attempts to obtain real wage increases which are out of line with productivity increases. In the case of Scheme A as well as Scheme B a basic question is whether and, if so, how far the existence of the tax/subsidy scheme, with its stick/carrot effect, will lead *directly* to a moderation of money wage settlements.

7.   The Direct Effect of the Schemes on Money Wage Settlements

The answer depends in a critical manner on the institutional arrangements for wage-bargaining and the financial policies adopted for demand management. The scope of a wage bargain and its resulting wage settlement can range from one which refers only to a single firm, through those which cover a single industry or region or other composite sectors of the economy, up to a national arrangement covering the whole of the economic system.

Consider at the one extreme a national wage bargain between the CBI and the TUC (each having effective powers to put the bargain universally into effect) which set for each individual employer the rate of pay at which he could hire whatever number of workers he chose to employ. Suppose further that the financial authorities were carrying out, and known to be carrying out, an effective Orthodox Keynesian demand-management policy which would expand total money expenditures on the products of labour to whatever extent was necessary to maintain full employment. There would in such circumstances be little reason to expect the introduction of either Scheme A or Scheme B to increase the resistance of the employers as an organised bargaining group to a given money wage claim.

The individual employers as producers of products would remain in competition with each other. On the basis of any wage rate that was fixed they would each of them mark up their selling prices in the way which they regarded as best in their interests to maintain their share of the market in competition with their rivals. But in their collectively organised setting of a single wage structure for all employers, each individual producer would know (1) that each of his rivals would be faced with the same increase in wage cost and (2) that the total volume of goods sold would not be allowed to fall off as a result of the universal rise in wage costs. To concede an additional 1 per cent rise in money wage rates would result in a 1 per cent rise in all money wage costs, in all marked-up prices, and in all money incomes. Each individual producer's money profits might be expected to be raised by the same 1 per cent; and real profits would remain unchanged by the rise in the wage rate since the general level of prices and so of the cost of living would also have risen by 1 per cent. The introduction of Scheme A might well have caused each producer to have cut his real profit margin, but the effect on this real profit margin of a universally applied 1 per cent increase in the wage rate would be negligible, just as it would be in these same conditions under Scheme B or in the absence of any scheme.

At the other extreme consider the case of company-by-company wage bargains. Each employer negotiates with a different independent union the wage rate at which he can employ as many workers as he chooses to employ. If he concedes an extra 1 per cent wage rise, this will not apply to his competitors. His money profit will be hit in the absence of any scheme and also with Schemes A and B; and since the prices and costs of all the other producers will be unaffected the fall in his money profit may be taken as a measure of the fall in his real profit. He will, therefore, in all cases have an incentive to resist the additional wage claim. But there is reason to believe that, for rather different reasons in the two cases, his resistance to the wage claim will be greater with the existence of Scheme A or Scheme B than it would be in the absence of either scheme.

With Scheme A the reduction in his profit due to a given wage concession will be broadly the same as in the absence of any scheme, namely, equal to the wage increase on the number of workers in his employment. But as we have already shown, under Scheme A he will have had good reason to cut his profit margin and his total profits. Thus a given absolute reduction of profit will represent a bigger proportionate reduction; he is likely to take a more serious view of a given loss of profit if his profits are already low than if his profit is high. Moreover, it is possible that his employees will press their claim less persistently if they realise that the employer's profit is low than if they see a large sum of profit out of which the wage claim might be financed. There is, therefore, some reason to believe that in these conditions the existence of Scheme A may well lead directly to lower wage settlements.

In the case of Scheme B the reason for such a result is more straightforward. If an individual employer concedes a rise in the wage rate which does not apply to any of his competitors or in any other sector of the economy, his money profit and so his real profit will be reduced by the increased wage bill plus the increased tax (or the reduced subsidy) payable on the increased wage bill. He obviously stands to lose more from a conceded wage increase under Scheme B than he would in the absence of the scheme, and his resistance to a wage claim may be *pro tanto* increased.

In the real world most wage settlements are likely to fall somewhere between these two extremes. In the case of a wage settlement covering all the competing producers in a single sector of the economy (for example, the whole of one industry) each producer will lose from a collectively conceded wage claim less than he would have lost if he alone had made the concession, since his competitors will have to meet the increased wage cost as well as himself. But he will lose something, because he cannot assume that the total demand for the products of the industry will rise *pari passu* with an increase of wage which is confined to that industry. This will be true even if by Orthodox Keynesian policies the effective demand for the combined real outputs of all industries is maintained unchanged; it will be even more marked if New Keynesian policies are in operation so that it is only the money demand for all products which is maintained. And in these cases for the reasons given above the producers in the industry in question are likely to resist the claim rather more strongly if either of the schemes is in existence than they would in the absence of either scheme; with Scheme A the consequential loss of profit will represent a larger proportionate loss and with Scheme B it will have added to it an increased tax liability.

Both schemes are thus likely to exercise some direct moderating influence on wage settlements, depending upon (1) the type of scheme, (2) the rate of tax, (3) the scope of coverage of collective wage settlements, and (4) the type of demand-management policies adopted by the financial authorities. But the degree of direct moderating effect on wage settlements remains doubtful and there would seem to be no way of deciding *a priori* how effective any scheme would be in this respect.

8.   Conclusions

A scheme for the control of inflation of selling prices (Scheme A) designed to tax increases in value added per unit of output which exceeded a stated norm and to subsidise the extent to which such increases were below the norm might be feasible in spite of formidable difficulties and costs of operation and of enforcement. There is, however, doubt how far such a scheme would discourage wage-push inflation without too great an erosion of profit margins.

An alternative type of scheme for the control of wage inflation (Scheme B) designed to tax increases in rates of pay which exceeded a stated norm and to subsidise the extent to which such increases were below the norm might also be feasible, subject to similar problems of operation and enforcement. Such a scheme would be effective only in so far as the added cost to employers of granting a pay increase strengthened their relative bargaining power in resisting wage claims.

Neither scheme could avoid price changes due to changes in the cost of imports or in rates of indirect tax imposed for fiscal reasons. The scope of the scheme might have to be limited, and in particular it would not readily apply to civil servants and similar public employees.

It remains doubtful whether the advantages to be expected from either type of scheme are worth the severe problems connected with their introduction and continued operation.

CHAPTER XI

Summary of Conclusions: The Way Ahead

The UK economy is at present suffering from mass unemployment of labour and from under-used capital equipment. At the same time there are a thousand and one useful things which these unused resources of men and machines might produce — goods and services for the underprivileged at home and abroad, improvements in public services and amenities, the renewal and improvement of capital equipment for future industrial production, a general rise in standards of personal consumption, and so on and so on. To one who took up the study of economics in the 1930s because he thought that the phenomenon of mass unemployment — of poverty in the midst of potential plenty — was both foolish and wicked and who had the unspeakable good fortune of falling under the intellectual guidance of Keynes, the present situation provides an intolerable return to wasteful folly, a folly which one had mistakenly thought to have been put aside for ever after the Second World War.

But there is a fundamental difference between the Great Slump of the 1930s and the Great Stagflation of the 1970s. During the 1930s mass unemployment was accompanied by a general deflation of money prices and costs. Though it may now seem incredible, money wage rates were actually falling during the Great Slump of the 1930s. In those circumstances Keynesian proposals for the stimulation of economic activity by policies designed to increase the demand for goods and services — public works programmes, tax reductions and increased social benefits with the consequential increased purchasing power of the individuals concerned, easier monetary policies, and reduced interest rates so as to make private capital developments and house building less expensive — carried no serious inflationary threat. On the contrary, increased expenditures on goods and services were desirable both to stimulate real output and employment and also to put a stop to price deflation.

The present position is in this respect totally different. Mass unemployment is combined with an horrifically rapid inflation of money wages and money prices. This presents a tragic dilemma. If Keynesian policies are adopted to stimulate the demand for goods and services, idle resources will be put to useful work once more; but this will carry with it the threat of an explosive and perhaps runaway inflation of money wages and prices, as unemployment and fear for loss of jobs cease to hold back the upward pressure of over-ambitious wage claims. To avoid such inflationary pressures and indeed to reduce the rate of inflation of money wages and prices, the opposite policy of restraining money expenditures could be adopted, so that the existence of mass unemployment and competing idle resources kept down the rise in money wages and prices; and putting on one side the mumbo-jumbo talk about monetarism, this is what the present government in the UK has been doing. The choice between restriction of demand to fight inflation and expansion of demand to fight unemployment is an important ingredient in the present unfortunate polarisation of British politics between extremists on the right and on the left. But the dilemma cannot just be brushed aside. The threat of an explosive inflation is a very real one. It is essential to find some set of agreed economic and financial policies and institutions which would enable a high and steadily expanding effective demand for goods and services to be combined with no more than a moderate and steady upward pressure of money wages and prices.

This problem of stagflation is in one sense much less basic than many others; nuclear weapons, the world population explosion, the extreme differences in income and wealth between the developed and undeveloped countries, a prospective energy shortage, possible pollutions of the environment – all these present 'real' problems which cannot be cured simply by a change of attitudes and institutions. The cure of stagflation, on the other hand, is by contrast a matter which depends solely upon the design of better institutions for financial and wage policies together with the changes in attitudes needed for their general understanding and acceptance. Everyone could be better off at no 'real' cost.

The present depression of output and employment in the UK is frequently ascribed to the world recession or to the oil crisis or to some other set of external and inevitable events. There is, of course, an element of truth in this; but it is by no means the whole of the truth. There is a frightening tendency for a relapse of attitudes back to the old-fashioned view that booms and slumps are acts of God which have to be accepted, and that during a depression one must simply wait patiently for better times. But the present world recession is in fact due primarily to the unwillingness of the main developed countries of the world to adopt Keynesian expansionary policies because of their fear of inflation; and it is just not true that the present government in the UK is restricting money expenditures in order to save energy; it is doing so in order to fight inflation. It is of the first importance that the national governments of the main free-enterprise developed countries should find some way of maintaining Keynesian full employment without a threat of rapid and explosive inflation of money costs and prices.

To find such a cure is important not only for its own sake, that is to say, for the avoidance of the wastes of unemployment and idle resources; it is important also as a *sine qua non* for tackling many of the other basic 'real' problems which confront us. One example must suffice. The rich industrialised countries could make a major contribution to the wealth and development of the poor underdeveloped countries of the world if they imported freely and bought in large quantities all the goods which such countries learnt to produce. But the free import of competing products from the poorer countries by the richer countries is politically extremely difficult, if not impossible, so long as there is heavy unemployment in the importing countries. To admit free imports is infinitely easier if there is no lack of alternative jobs for those whose present jobs are threatened by cheap imports from abroad.

How then can we hope to find a set of policies and institutions which will successfully maintain full employment without a rapid inflation of money prices and costs?

One line of approach, which we call the Orthodox Keynesian approach, is to adopt measures for the expansion of money expenditures on goods and services to the extent necessary to provide a market for all the products of a fully employed economy. If this is found to cause a rapid inflation of money wages and costs, then some general centralised incomes policy has to be devised to prevent money rates of pay from rising more rapidly than in line with some moderate 'norm'. If money wage costs and, with constant profit mark-ups, money selling prices can be stabilised in this way, then Keynesian demand-management policies which expand the level of money expenditures will expand the *volume* of goods and services purchased rather than the *prices* at which they are bought. In other words monetary and fiscal policies should be designed so as to control the amount of goods and services that will be demanded, and an incomes policy should be designed so as to control the money prices at which they will be sold.

An alternative line of approach, which we call the New Keynesian approach, is to design a set of monetary and budgetary policies to keep total *money* expenditures on goods and services on a steady, moderate upward growth path, and against this background of a steady growth in the money demand for the products of labour to design a set of wage-fixing institutions which will promote the *volume* of employment in each firm or other employing agency. This involves raising the wage rate whereever there is a shortage of labour and a need to attract more labour to the firm in question, and to restrain any rise in wages wherever there are already workers available who can be taken into additional employment. With a steady increase of, say, 5 per cent per annum in the total money demand for the products of labour, the average wage rate would be steadily bid up as each typical employer sought to find the labour needed to satisfy the increased demand for his products.

The theme of the present work is to advocate the New Keynesian approach to the cure of stagflation and to analyse the problems involved in carrying out any such set of policies. A main reason for preferring the New Keynesian to the Orthodox Keynesian approach is the fact that the latter approach implies a centralised incomes policy with the danger of an inefficient and unacceptable regime of bureaucratic control, whereas the former can be based more easily on a less centralised and more flexible system of wage fixing. (See Chapters VII and VIII.)

The analysis of the problems involved in New Keynesianism falls naturally into two parts: first, the design of financial policies (that is to say of monetary, budgetary, and foreign exchange policies), for the purpose of keeping the level of total money expenditures on UK products on a steady growth path; and, second, the design of wage-fixing arrangements which against the background of this steady growth in the total demand for the products of labour will promote employment throughout the economy.

The study has, therefore, naturally fallen into two parts which, while they differ substantially in the detailed questions and technical problems that they cover, are nevertheless very closely connected. For it is a main thesis of the work that, on the one hand, there is little to be gained by designing wage-fixing arrangements to promote employment unless this is against a background of a sustained steady expansion in the demand for the products of labour, and that, on the other hand, it would be pointless and possibly catastrophic to restrict the expansion of total money expenditures to a very moderate rate unless wage-fixing arrangements were moulded appropriately to match this moderate growth in the total money demand for labour.

A subsequent volume, entitled 'Demand Management', will be concerned with the problems involved in designing financial policies to keep total money demand for the products of labour on a steady growth path. The present volume on 'Wage-Fixing' has simply assumed that there are effective demand-management policies which are successfully providing a steady rate of growth in the total demand for labour; and it has been devoted to an examination of possible wage-fixing arrangements that would promote employment in these circumstances.

The analysis in the present volume has been based on one other fundamental assumption. If adjustments of money wage rates are made primarily to promote employment, their use as weapons for a planned redistribution of income must be extremely limited. It has been argued in this volume that fiscal and similar measures are in fact much more effective than wage-fixing as instruments for achieving a socially desirable redistribution of income and wealth. It has accordingly been assumed throughout that wage-fixing for the promotion of employment takes place against a battery of other measures for promoting a socially desirable distribution of income and wealth.

The analysis of the wage-fixing problems in this volume has led to the conclusion that the solution is most likely to be found by a combination of four different lines of approach.

In Chapter IX we argued that in appropriate conditions the development of labour co-operatives, labour–capital partnerships, or profit-sharing schemes could help to solve the problem of stagflation in so far as it implied that pay would be received as a share of the concern's revenue from sales rather than being set in advance independently as a cost of production. But it was shown that the contribution to the cure of stagflation through this means would be limited: it would have no contribution to make in the setting of rates of pay for the large range of civil servants, members of the defence forces, and similar public employments; it would not help in the cure of stagflation in the case of large-scale monopolies, including the main nationalised industries: it could be effective only where competition between the co-operative concerns was active and where the setting up of new competing co-operative concerns was relatively easy; and in capital-intensive industries it would need to take the form of partnerships that included the owners of capital as well as the workers. Nevertheless in the case of small-scale private competitive sectors of the economy it could make a significant contribution to the cure of stagflation, quite apart from any other advantages to be gained from the extension of the general principle of participation in decision making.

In Chapter IV we argued that the cure was not to be found by crude and extreme trade union bashing to restore competition between individual workers in the labour market, but that institutional wage-fixing through trade unions or some other form of organised body was an essential feature of the modern free-enterprise economy. However, in Chapter VI it was argued that competitive forces have nevertheless an extremely important role to play. Some of the existing immunities of labour monopolies described in Chapter V should be modified in so far as they are such as to protect one group of high-paid workers from competition of the other less privileged workers. In particular, pre-entry closed shop arrangements which prevent an outsider from joining the ranks of a privileged group should be banned, and a whole range of measures that would enable low-paid workers to move into high-paid occupations, industries, or localities should be encouraged. Such measures are desirable in themselves in so far as they lead to a more efficient use of labour and to an equalising tendency between the high-paid and the low-paid, but they will also help to curb excessive inflationary upward pressures on wage rates by the previously highly protected groups.

The co-operative partnership principle and the permissible forces of competition cannot be relied upon adequately to restrain the upward inflationary pressures from wage claims. There is a real dilemma here. Trade unions must be left with substantial monopolistic powers if they are effectively to fulfil their wage-fixing functions; but such powers can be used to excess. Something more is found to be needed. In Chapter VII reason was given for the belief that attempts to find the solution through a centralised, authoritarian setting of rates of pay were doomed to failure, but that a central body which issued a guideline 'norm' of the rate of pay increases that could in general be paid without involving undue inflation or unemployment or which determined a similar basic pay award would serve a useful purpose.

Finally in Chapter VIII we argued in favour of the development of some system for the settlement of disputes between employers and employed about rates of pay by reference to an independent arbitral body or pay commission, the awards of such a body being based primarily upon the principle of setting rates of pay for the promotion of employment in the concerns under examination. A number of variations of the provisions in any such arbitral system were discussed in Chapter VII. But the general principles remained unchanged, namely: that any bargain freely struck between employers and employed would be permitted; that any unresolved dispute about rates of pay could be taken by either party to arbitration; that (subject to limitations on the abruptness of rates of change of pay) the arbitral body's award should be designed primarily to promote employment in the sector of the economy under examination; and that industrial action taken in opposition to the terms of an award should not be illegal but would be accompanied by penalties that would reduce the bargaining power of the party that took such action. The hope would be that the knowledge by both parties that they could get the effective support of such an award would induce them in general to seek agreement on wage claims that were likely to conform to the employment-promotion criterion of the arbitral body.

It is not maintained that a solution on these lines is a certainty. On the contrary, the problem is politically an extremely difficult one. Whether or not a solution can be found on these lines depends not merely on the construction of suitable institutions (important and necessary though that is) but above all on a change of attitude on the part of the great body of people, employers, and employed, who are concerned. The matter cannot be put right simply by legislation; the general acceptance by the great majority of trade unionists and others of the idea that this would provide a much more sensible way of conducting affairs is an essential condition for its success. It could not possibly be imposed from above on an unreceptive population.

But what is maintained in this volume is that, if it were accepted, it would in fact greatly improve the welfare of the vast majority of the population, whether trade unionists or others. It could eliminate the wastes of loss of output due to industrial action, but much more importantly the wastes of loss of output due to mass unemployment, without the threat of explosive price inflation. From such a base the other 'real' problems of society could be confidently tackled.

APPENDIX A

The Inflationary Implications of Orthodox Keynesian Demand Management for Full Employment Combined with Wage Settlements Designed to Achieve an Over-Ambitious Real Wage

I

This appendix describes a simple model in which wage rates are fixed not so as to promote employment, but so as to attain a certain real standard of living which is in some sense over-ambitious, given the real productivity of labour and given the profit mark-up used in setting selling prices and so in determining the cost of living. Given any level of wage and other costs, the price level can be reduced by a reduction of the profit margin. For this reason it is important for the control of inflation as well as for other reasons that the profit margin should not exceed the level needed to enable depreciation and interest costs on capital to be met and to provide a sufficient stimulus for risky productive enterprise. As will be made clear in this appendix, an inflation of money wage costs can in certain conditions eat into profits and profit margins. But this is not a desirable method of control over profit margins. It is arbitrary in its effect and there is no built-in restraint to ensure that profits are not so far eroded as to fail to cover capital costs and to give any incentive for new investment and economic expansion.

As we have argued in Chapter I it is essential for a successful economy that excess monopolistic profit margins should be restrained by other measures, namely, the promotion of competition and deliberate price control or nationalisation where significant monopoly in production is inevitable. In this appendix we assume that excess monopolistic profit margins are held in check by such measures and accordingly take as acceptable the ruling profit margin.

In the models in this appendix we abstract from many important aspects of reality in order to isolate for examination in its simplest form the feedback relationships from a money wage settlement, leading to wage costs, leading to selling prices sufficiently high to cover costs including capital costs, leading to a rise in the cost of living, leading to a reduction of the real value of the money wages, leading to an increased money wage claim, and so on round the inflationary spiral.

For this purpose we make the following assumptions:

(1) that there are annual settlements of money wage rates in every sector of the economy;

(2) that once a year shortly after each wage settlement the employers fix selling prices for their products by adding a single fixed proportionate rate of mark-up on the wage cost per unit of output resulting from the recent wage settlement, this profit mark-up being held in check by measures to promote competition and to control excess monopoly profits;

(3) that output per worker is growing at an underlying constant rate;

(4) that the volume of employment is constant, for example that any dynamic effects on employment of changes in wage rates, prices, profits, costs, etc., are successfully offset by Orthodox Keynesian demand-management policies which ensure a level of effective demand sufficient to maintain full employment.

It is the purpose of this appendix to show how over-ambitious wage settlements reflecting claims for real wage rates which are in some way or another out of line with the available real output per head in such circumstances lead to inflationary developments. But over-ambitious wage claims may take many forms within the framework of the wage-fixing institutions described above; and a main purpose of the models developed in this appendix is to distinguish between (1) those forms of over-ambitious wage claim that will result in high, but constant, rates of price inflation and (2) those much more dangerous forms which will cause an explosive-inflationary situation in which, although the initial rate of inflation may be low, the rate of price inflation will rise continuously to ever higher levels.

Since the present purpose is thus to consider in its simplest form the feedback relationships between wages, costs, prices, and wages, we neglect taxes and foreign trade, we assume variable costs to be made up wholly of labour costs, and we neglect any difference between wage rates and earnings. Of course, these neglected features are of importance; but they do not alter the basic underlying inflationary implications of the wage-fixing institutions described above.

Thus an improvement in the international terms of trade (which is equivalent to a once-for-all rise in output per head) or a shift of demand from goods on which the profit mark-up is high to goods on which it is low (which is equivalent to a once-for-all reduction in the average mark-up of prices) will reduce the current rate of inflation. A change in the level of activity (e.g. from running the economy at a 10 per cent to running it at a 5 per cent unemployment percentage) may have a similar effect in two ways: first, by spreading overhead labour costs over a larger output it may represent an increase in output per head; and, second, by increasing the national tax base and by reducing the cost of unemployment relief, it may enable the rates of tax to be reduced so that a given improvement in real post-tax wages can be achieved by a smaller rise in the pre-tax wage. These are all changes that will reduce the current rate of inflation; but if the underlying relationships are of an explosive kind, the inflationary situation will sooner or later reproduce itself.

The factors mentioned in the preceding paragraph will help to postpone the evil day; but some of them (e.g. a deterioration in the terms of trade or a shift of demand from labour-intensive to capital-intensive products) may work in reverse and speed up the evil day. There are other factors also which may have this effect. Thus if there is any underlying 'Phillips-curve' effect (if, that is to say, real wage demands become more ambitious when there is a brisk demand for labour), a once-for-all decrease in the un-employment percentage will stoke up the inflation; and its effect may not be merely a once-for-all rise in the rate of inflation. If the effect of a fall in unemployment is to raise not only the level but also the rate of increase of the workers' real wage claims, then it will cause not merely a once-for-all increase in the rate of inflation, but an actual rise in the rate of explosion of the rate of inflation.

More important probably is the problem of expectations. One may start with the assumptions (1) that the money wage demands at each settlement merely represent a claim for a real wage at the current cost of living, and make no attempt to anticipate the fall below this target level that will occur before the next wage settlement as a result of the future inflation of the cost of living and (2) that with a certain delay after each annual wage settlement employers revise their price lists with the given conven-tional mark-up on the new wage costs, regardless of any loss of profit during the delay period in which goods produced at the new and higher wages will have been sold at the old unrevised and lower prices. At high levels of inflation these assumptions become increasingly unreal. At some point wage earners in setting wage claims will try to compensate for the future rise in prices during the currency of the settlement or — what has a similar effect — will revise the settlements more and more frequently (e.g. once a quarter instead of once a year) in order to catch up on the rapid inflation of the cost of living. Similarly producers will set prices at levels above the conventional mark-up or will revise their price lists more promptly after each wage settlement in order to compensate for, or to avoid, losses made during periods of sale of high-cost goods at low-cost prices.

All such attempts will, of course, stoke up the inflationary forces; and it is a main feature of the models in this appendix to examine the impli-cations of such attempts by employees and employers to avoid losses due to inflation.

II

The following Table V may be useful in classifying the notation used in the following models. We reckon time in units of a year. Time $t = 1980$

Table V

Time	$t-1$	$t-1+\gamma$	t	$t+\gamma$	$t+1$	$t+1+\gamma$	$t+2$
W	W_{t-1}		W_t		W_{t+1}		
P		P_{t-1}		P_t		P_{t+1}	
L				L^*			
Q				$Q_t = Q_0 e^{lt}$			

represents the beginning of 1980 (i.e. 1 January 1980) and year t is the year running from t to $t+1$. γ is a fraction of a year. We assume that Orthodox Keynesian demand-management policies are keeping employment continuously at a given full-employment level L^*. Output per head (Q/L) and, with a constant labour force (L^*), total output (Q) are assumed to grow at a constant exponential rate l, so that $Q_t = Q_0 e^{lt}$ represents the rate of output at any moment of time t.

The wage rate W is adjusted only once a year at the beginning of the year (i.e. just before dawn on 1 January) and stays constant till the beginning of the following year. Thus W_t represents the wage rate which rules throughout the year t. The selling price of output is also adjusted only once a year. It is obtained by a fixed mark-up of $(\mu - 1)$ on the labour cost of a unit of output which ruled after the wage adjustment made on 1 January. But there is a delay of a fraction of a year γ between the wage adjustment and the consequential price mark-up. We use the convention that P_t represents the new price settled during year t and which rules therefore from time $t+\gamma$ till time $t+1+\gamma$. We will call μ 'the mark-up factor'. Thus if selling prices were set at labour costs plus 20 per cent, μ would equal 1.2.

The price mark-up equation is therefore represented by

$$P_t = \mu \, \frac{W_t L^*}{Q_t} \tag{1}$$

If we write π_t for P_{t+1}/P_t, ω_t for W_{t+1}/W_t, and $\lambda \equiv e^l$ for Q_{t+1}/Q_t, we can deduce from (1) that

$$\pi_t = \frac{\omega_t}{\lambda} \qquad (2)$$

We will call π_t 'the price-inflation factor', representing one plus the rate of price inflation between time and $t + \gamma$ and $t + 1 + \gamma$. Similarly ω_t is 'the wage-rate-inflation factor' representing one plus the rate of inflation of the wage rate between time t and time $t + 1$. It is to be observed that with our notation if one is interested in the inflation between time t and time $t + 1$, wage inflation is measured by ω_t but selling price inflation by π_{t-1}, which highlights the fact that selling prices are determined with a lag by a mark-up on earlier wage costs. We will call λ 'the productivity factor' since with L^* constant it represents the ratio of output per head at time $t + 1$ to output per head at time t. We assume λ to be constant.

Thus equation (2) states that the price rise between $t + \gamma$ and $t + 1 + \gamma$ will depend upon the wage-cost rise between t and $t + 1$, which in turn will be equal to the wage-rate rise discounted by the rise in labour productivity.

While Q_t represents the rate of output at any moment of time t, we will use the term $\bar{Q}_t$ for the amount of output produced during the year t, so that

$$\bar{Q}_t = \int_t^{t+1} Q_0 e^{lt} = Q_t \frac{e^l - 1}{l} = Q_t \frac{\lambda - 1}{l} \qquad (3)$$

The multiplier $(\lambda - 1)/l$ is in fact little different from unity. Thus if $\lambda - 1 = .02$, $l = .01980263$ and $(\lambda - 1)/l = 1.00997$.

We will use the term $\bar{\theta}_t$ to represent the proportion of the national product which accrues to labour during the year t. The money wage per worker during year t is W_t and for a fraction of the year γ the cost of living is P_{t-1} (i.e. what it was at the beginning of year t) and for the remainder of the year is P_t (i.e. what it will still be at the beginning of year $t + 1$). Thus the real wage earned per worker during the year is

$$W_t \left(\frac{\gamma}{P_{t-1}} + \frac{1-\gamma}{P_t} \right)$$

With L^* workers and a total output $\bar{Q}_t$ we have

$$\bar{\theta}_t = \frac{W_t L^*}{\bar{Q}_t P_t}$$

Using equation (2) we obtain

$$\bar{\theta}_t = \bar{\theta}(\gamma \pi_{t-1} + 1 - \gamma) = \bar{\theta}\left(\gamma \frac{\omega_{t-1}}{\lambda} + 1 - \gamma \right) \qquad (4)$$

where $\bar{\theta} \equiv W_t L^* / \bar{Q}_t P_t$ measures what the wage share $\bar{\theta}_t$ would be if the whole of the product of year t were sold at the price P_t, that is, if the delay γ between the setting of the wage rate at W_t and the mark-up of the selling price were negligible. From equations (1) and (3) it can be seen that

$$\bar{\theta} \equiv \frac{W_t L^*}{\bar{Q}_t P_t} = \frac{l}{\mu(\lambda - 1)} \tag{5}$$

which is a constant depending solely on the mark-up factor, μ, and the productivity factor, λ.*

Thus $\bar{\theta}$ represents the wage share if there is no delay in marking up selling prices. But from equation (4) it can be seen that, even if γ were not negligible, $\bar{\theta}$ could still represent the share that could accrue to wages if $\pi_{t-1} = \omega_{t-1}/\lambda = 1$, that is if the rise in the money wage rate merely matched the rise in labour productivity so that there was no cost inflation capable of eating into profits; thus $\bar{\theta}$ may be regarded as the 'normal', that is, non-inflationary, value of the wage share that would result from given levels of the mark-up factor and of the productivity factor.

It may be observed from equation (4) that with $\gamma = 0$, $\bar{\theta}_t = \bar{\theta}$ but with $\gamma = 1$, $\bar{\theta}_t = \bar{\theta} \, \omega_{t-1}/\lambda$. In other words if producers mark up their selling prices on wage costs with no delay ($\gamma = 0$), the wage inflation cannot eat into the profit share. But if the producers delay the whole year until the next wage round ($\gamma = 1$), then the wage claim will eat into the profit share and will raise the wage share by a factor depending upon the excess of the wage-rate inflation factor over the labour productivity factor.

Equations (2) and (4) thus determine the price inflation factor and the share of output between wages and profits in terms of the wage inflation factor, ω. It remains, therefore, to consider the factors which determine the money wage rate.

The purpose of this appendix is to examine the inflationary implications of the setting of money wage rates which represent a claim for a certain real wage, given the maintenance of employment at the constant full-employment level L^* by means of effective demand-management policies.

The resulting money wage claim we will represent by the equation:

$$\begin{aligned} W_t &= \bar{R}_t^e \{ \gamma P_{t-1} + (1 - \gamma) P_t^e \} \\ &= \bar{R}_t^e P_{t-1} \{ \gamma + (1 - \gamma) \pi_{t-1}^e \} \end{aligned} \tag{6}$$

*From equation (1) it can be seen that $1/\mu$ represents what the wage share would be at the beginning of year t if the selling price were immediately marked up to P_t. But since the money wage rate and the money selling price are then fixed for the whole year, the year's increase in productivity accrues to profits, so that the share of wages over the whole year t is slightly less than $1/\mu$. With a profit mark up of 20 per cent ($\mu = 1.20$) and a productivity growth of 2 per cent per annum ($\lambda = 1.02$), we would have $1/\mu = 0.83$ and $\bar{\theta} = 0.825$.

$\bar{R}_t$ represents the real wage rate which the wage-earner receives during year t, and $\bar{R}_t^e$ represents the real wage rate which he expects to receive or plans to receive during year t, when he sets the money wage at W_t at the beginning of year t. Selling prices will remain constant at the level P_{t-1} for a fraction γ of the coming year but will rise to P_t for the remainder of the year. If P_t^e represents what the wage-earners expect to be the new and higher price level, so that π_{t-1}^e represents what they expect the inflation factor π_{t-1} to be, equation (6) measures the money wage rate W_t which must be set at time t if the wage-earner is to expect to receive a real wage of $\bar{R}_t^e$ in the course of the year. Given the existing price level P_{t-1} there are thus three factors which will determine the money wage rate W_t, namely: the real wage demanded $\bar{R}_t^e$, the speed with which prices are marked up γ, and the expected price-inflation factor π_t^e.

III

We will start by considering a set of cases, which we will call the A-Cases, in which the aim of the wage claim at time t is to obtain a real wage during year t which represents a multiple, ρ, of the real wage enjoyed at the time of the new wage settlement. This can be represented by:

$$\bar{R}_t^e = \rho \, \frac{W_{t-1}}{P_{t-1}} \tag{7}$$

since the current real wage is W_{t-1}/P_{t-1}. We will call ρ 'the real-wage-aspiration factor'. Eliminating $\bar{R}_t^e$ between equations (6) and (7) we obtain

$$\omega_t = \rho\{\gamma + (1-\gamma)\pi_t^e\} \tag{8}$$

and from equation (2)

$$\pi_t = \phi\{\gamma + (1-\gamma)\pi_t^e\} \tag{9}$$

where $\phi \equiv \rho/\lambda$ or the ratio of the real-wage-aspiration factor to the labour-productivity factor. We will call ϕ 'the excess-real-wage-aspiration factor'.

There is an alternative way of considering this wage claim. Instead of considering $\bar{R}_t^e$, the real wage income at which the wage-earners aim, we could consider

$$\bar{\theta}_t^e = \frac{\bar{R}_t^e L^*}{\bar{Q}_t} \tag{10}$$

namely, the proportion of the national product of year t which the wage-earners seek to obtain.* In the A-Cases equations (10), (7) and (5) give

$$\bar{\theta}_t^e = \rho \, \frac{W_{t-1}}{P_{t-1}} \cdot \frac{L^*}{\lambda \bar{Q}_{t-1}} = \frac{\rho}{\lambda} \, \bar{\theta} \tag{11}$$

so that in these cases $\phi = \rho/\lambda = \bar{\theta}^e/\bar{\theta}$. A claim for a given rise in real wage income for the year t can, given the prospect of the total national product for year t, always be represented as a claim for a given share in year t's real income, whether the wage-earners are in fact thinking primarily of their real standard of living or of the relation of their share to the profit share in the national product.

Equations (9) and (4) will give solutions in the A-Cases for the price inflation factor π_t and the wage share $\bar{\theta}_t$ in terms of the delay γ and the expected price inflation factor π_t^e. In Table VI we display nine possible cases. We make three possible assumptions about π_t^e, namely: first, that wage-earners neglect any possible erosion of their wage claims through future inflation, which is the same as assuming $\pi_t^e = 1$; second, that wage-earners fully understand how the system works and have rational expectations about future inflation so that $\pi_t^e = \pi_t$; and, third, that wage-earners have a simple form of adaptive expectations and assume simply that this year's inflation rate will be the same as last year's, so that $\pi_t^e = \pi_{t-1}$. For each of these three assumptions about the expectation of inflation we make three possible assumptions about the value of γ, namely: first, that $0 < \gamma < 1$ which is the general case; second, that producers in order to avoid any erosion of their profit margins through inflation reduce the delay γ to a negligible value, so that $\gamma = 0$, an event which may well occur if wage inflation becomes very marked and producers experience an ever more serious threat of profit erosion; and, third, that producers are extremely slow and remain very slow in marking up their selling prices, so that $\gamma = 1$. These nine cases are numbered A(i) to A(ix) in Table VI.

We start with Cases A(i), (ii), and (iii) which arise if wage-earners disregard the possibility of future inflation, that is, $\pi_t^e = 1$. From equations (9) and (4) we see that in all these cases

$$\pi_t = \phi \tag{12}$$

and

$$\bar{\theta}_t = \begin{cases} \text{(i)} & \bar{\theta}(\gamma\phi + 1 - \gamma) \\ \text{(ii)} & \bar{\theta} \\ \text{(iii)} & \bar{\theta}\phi \end{cases} \tag{13}$$

---

*The divergence between $\bar{\theta}_t^e$ and $\bar{\theta}$ corresponds to the conflict between the claims of wages and of profits described by R.E. Rowthorn in 'Conflict, Inflation, and Money', *Cambridge Journal of Economics*, vol. 1, September 1977, pp. 215–39.

Table VI

A-Cases	$0 < \gamma < 1$	$\gamma = 0$	$\gamma = 1$
$\pi_t^e = 1$	(i) $\pi_t = \phi$ $\bar{\theta}_t = \bar{\theta}(\gamma\phi + 1 - \gamma)$	(ii) $\pi_t = \phi$ $\bar{\theta}_t = \bar{\theta}$	(iii) $\pi_t = \phi$ $\bar{\theta}_t = \bar{\theta}\phi$
$\pi_t^e = \pi_t$	(iv) (a) If $(1-\gamma)\phi < 1$ $$\pi_t = \frac{\gamma\phi}{1 - (1-\gamma)\phi}$$ $$\bar{\theta}_t = \bar{\theta}\left\{1 + \frac{\gamma(\phi-1)}{1-(1-\gamma)\phi}\right\}$$ (b) If $(1-\gamma)\phi > 1$, π_t immediately explodes to infinity and $\bar{\theta}_t$ is meaningless	(v) π_t immediately explodes to infinity and $\bar{\theta}_t$ is meaningless	(vi) $\pi_t = \phi$ $\bar{\theta}_t = \bar{\theta}\phi$
$\pi_t^e = \pi_{t-1}$	(vii) $\pi_t = \frac{\gamma\phi}{1-(1-\gamma)\phi} + \left\{\pi_0 - \frac{\gamma\phi}{1-(1-\gamma)\phi}\right\} \times$ $\{(1-\gamma)\phi\}^t$ $\bar{\theta}_t = \bar{\theta}\{\gamma\pi_{t-1} + (1-\gamma)\}$	(viii) $\pi_t = \phi^t\pi_0$ $\bar{\theta}_t = \bar{\theta}$	(ix) $\pi_t = \phi$ $\bar{\theta}_t = \bar{\theta}\phi$

according as (i) $0 < \gamma < 1$, (ii) $\gamma = 0$, or (iii) $\gamma = 1$. The inflation factor will remain constant and equal to the excess-real-wage-aspiration factor. The wage share will also remain unchanged from period to period ranging from a value of $\bar{\theta}$ if $\gamma = 0$ to an upper value of $\bar{\theta}\phi$ as $\gamma \to 1$.

It is convenient next to consider cases A(vi) and (ix) which are the two remaining cases in which $\gamma = 1$. If $\gamma = 1$, this means that the wage-earners will not make any allowance for future inflation in their wage claim not simply because they have forgotten to do so ($\pi_t^e = 1$), but because there will be no inflation during the year ($\gamma = 1$). The result is that the outcome is the same as in Case A(iii). In Cases (i), (iii), (vi), and (ix), therefore, the inflation factor will be constant at ϕ and in Cases (iii), (vi), and (ix) the wage share will be constant at $\theta\phi$.

We turn next to Cases A(iv) and (v) which are the remaining cases with rational expectations. If one writes $\pi_t^e = \pi_t$ in equation (9) and assumes that $(1 = \gamma)\phi < 1$, one obtains for Case A(iv)

$$\pi_t = \frac{\gamma\phi}{1 - (1 - \gamma)\phi} \tag{14}$$

and from equation (4)

$$\bar{\theta}_t = \bar{\theta} \left\{ 1 + \frac{\gamma(\phi - 1)}{1 - (1 - \gamma)\phi} \right\} \tag{15}$$

so that once again the inflation factor and the wage share are constant from period to period.

This expression for $\bar{\theta}_t$ draws one's attention to a paradoxical feature of this particular case. $\partial\bar{\theta}_t/\partial\gamma$ derived from equation (15) is < 1, which means that a *reduction* in the employers' delay period γ will *increase* the proportion of the national product actually going to wages. A natural reaction of employers to avoid a decrease in the proportion going to profit would be to reduce the delay period of sales of high-cost products at low-cost prices. But with $\phi > 1$ and starting with $(1 - \gamma)\phi < 1$, as γ is reduced, so $(1 - \gamma)\phi \to 1$; and thus from (14) $\pi_t \to \infty$. In fact (with $\pi_t^e = \pi_t$) the resulting increase of the money wage during the shortened delay period is so great that it outweighs the restoration of the conventional profit proportion $\bar{\theta}$ during the lengthened remainder of the year.

The values of π_t and $\bar{\theta}_t$ in equations (14) and (15) depend critically upon the value of $(1 - \gamma)\phi$. Suppose that γ becomes smaller and smaller. It can be seen that from equation (14) that as $(1 - \gamma)\phi \to 1$, so $\pi_t \to \infty$. Case A(v) with $\gamma = 0$ is merely an extreme instance of a situation in which there would be an immediate infinite explosion of the rate of inflation. With rational expectations wage earners are taking *effective* measures to obtain a share which is greater than $\bar{\theta}$ (from equation (11) $\bar{\theta}_t^e = \phi\bar{\theta}$) while, by reducing γ to zero, producers are taking *effective* measures to keep $\bar{\theta}_t = \bar{\theta}$. An irresistible force has met an immovable object and the price level goes up in a big bang. In such conditions the actual value of the wage share $\bar{\theta}_t$ is meaningless.

With Cases A(vii) and (viii) we turn to the more probable assumption of adaptive expectations by wage-earners with $\pi_t^e = \pi_{t-1}$. Substituting this value of π_t^e in equation (9) and solving the resulting difference equations gives:

$$\pi_t = \frac{\gamma\phi}{1-(1-\gamma)\phi} + \left\{\pi_0 - \frac{\gamma\phi}{1-(1-\gamma)\phi}\right\} \{(1-\gamma)\phi\}^t$$

$$= \{(1-\gamma)\phi\}^t \pi_0 + \{[(1-\gamma)\phi]^t - 1\} \frac{\gamma\phi}{(1-\gamma)\phi - 1} \quad (16)$$

From the first formulation for π_t in equation (16) it can be seen that if $(1-\gamma)\phi < 1$, then π_t approaches gradually the rational expectations value given in equation (14). From the second formulation of π_t in equation (15) it can be seen that if $(1-\gamma)\phi > 1$, then π_t rises indefinitely without limit; and if $\gamma = 0$, giving the greatest possible value of $(1-\gamma)\phi$, then $\pi_t = \phi^t \pi_0$, so that the inflation factor is itself multiplied by ϕ from one period to the next.

IV

We turn now to the Class B variations of the model. For the Class A variations we assumed that the wage earners' claims at the beginning of the year were aimed simply at obtaining an increase $(\rho - 1)$ in whatever real wage they were in fact enjoying at the time of the settlement. Now in the Class B cases we go further and assume that the wage earners have a real wage target, $\bar{R}_t^e$ which grows continuously through time at an annualised rate of $(\rho - 1)$. At the beginning of each year in the wage settlement they claim a money wage rate which is designed to bring their wage up to the current level of the real wage target.* In this case if $\rho > \lambda$, the target real wage will over time rise continuously relatively to real output per head, and the target will become more and more out of line with what is feasible in reality.

We can express this real wage target by

---

*This is the basic feature of the wage-fixing equation used by the Cambridge Economic Policy Group. See Francis Cripps and Wynne Godley, 'A formal analysis of the Cambridge Economic Policy Group Model', *Economica*, November 1976, vol. 43, pp. 335–48; and Ken Coutts, Roger Tarling, and Frank Wilkinson, 'Wage bargaining and the inflation process', *Cambridge Economic Policy Group Review, 1976*, Chapter 2.

$$\bar{R}_t^e = \bar{R}_0^e \rho^t \tag{17}$$

so that from equation (6)

$$W_t = \bar{R}_0^e \rho^t P_{t-1} \{\gamma + (1-\gamma)\pi_{t-1}^e\} \tag{18}$$

and substituting for P_{t-1} from equation (1) and using equations (3) and (5) we obtain

$$\omega_{t-1} = \frac{\bar{\theta}_1^e}{\bar{\theta}} \frac{\rho^{t-1}}{\lambda^{t-2}} \{\gamma + (1-\gamma)\pi_{t-1}^e\} \tag{19}$$

where $\bar{\theta}_1^e = \bar{R}_1^e L^*/\bar{Q}_1$, or the proportion of the national product of year 1 which the wage-earners are attempting to gain when they fix a wage W_1 at the beginning of year 1 with the intention of obtaining a real wage income of $\bar{R}_1^e$ during the coming year.

Using equation (2) we then obtain

$$\pi_t = \frac{\bar{\theta}_1^e}{\bar{\theta}} \phi^t \{\gamma + (1-\gamma)\pi_t^e\} \tag{20}$$

where $\phi = \rho/\lambda$ as before.

Since the real wage claim $\bar{R}_t^e$ is growing by the real-wage-aspiration factor ρ and the national product $\bar{Q}_t$ is growing only by the productivity factor λ, the wage-share claim $\bar{\theta}_t^e$ will be growing by the factor $\phi = \rho/\lambda > 1$. Thus as we move forward in time $\bar{\theta}_t^e$ will be continually rising and as we move backwards in time continually falling. It is convenient to choose a time scale such that, at $t = 1$, $\bar{\theta}_1^e/\bar{\theta} = 1$, in which case

$$\pi_t = \phi^t \{\gamma + (1-\gamma)\pi_t^e\} \tag{21}$$

where

$$\phi^t = \frac{\bar{\theta}_{t+1}^e}{\bar{\theta}}$$

Using equations (21) and (4) we can now analyse the nine B-Cases which correspond to the nine A-Cases discussed in Section III. These nine B-Cases are displayed in Table VII. It is to be observed that in all nine cases there results an explosive inflation factor which increases without limit as time passes, a result which is to be expected from the fact that in all these cases the real claim of the wage-earners on the national product grows continually more and more out of line with the national product itself.

Table VII

B-Cases	$0 < \gamma < 1$	$\gamma = 0$	$\gamma = 1$
$\pi_t^e = 1$	(i) $\pi_t = \phi^t$ $\bar{\theta}_t = \bar{\theta}\{\gamma\phi^{t-1} + 1 - \gamma\}$	(ii) $\pi_t = \phi^t$ $\bar{\theta}_t = \bar{\theta}$	(iii) $\pi_t = \phi^t$ $\bar{\theta}_t = \bar{\theta}\phi^{t-1}$
$\pi_t^e = \pi_{t-1}$	(iv) (a) With $(1-\gamma)\phi^t < 1$ $\pi_t = \dfrac{\gamma\phi^t}{1 - (1-\gamma)\phi^t}$ $\bar{\theta}_t = \bar{\theta}\left\{1 + \dfrac{\gamma(\phi^t - 1)}{1 + (1-\gamma)\phi^t}\right\}$ (b) With $(1-\gamma)\phi^t > 1$, π_t explodes immediately to infinity and $\bar{\theta}_t$ becomes meaningless	(v) π_t explodes immediately to infinity and $\bar{\theta}_t$ is meaningless	(vi) $\pi_t = \phi^t$ $\bar{\theta}_t = \bar{\theta}\phi^{t-1}$
$\pi_t^e = \pi_t$	(vii) $\pi_t = (1-\gamma)^t\,\phi^{t(t+1)/2}\,\pi_0 +$ $+ \gamma\{\phi^t + (1-\gamma)\phi^{t+t-1} +$ $+ (1-\gamma)^2\phi^{t+t-1+t-2} + \ldots$ $+ (1-\gamma)^{t-1}\phi^{t(t+1)/2}\}$ $\bar{\theta}_t = \bar{\theta}\{\gamma\pi_{t-1} + 1 - \gamma\}$	(viii) $\pi_t = \phi^{t(t+1)/2}\,\pi_0$ $\bar{\theta}_t = \bar{\theta}$	(ix) $\pi_t = \phi^t$ $\bar{\theta}_t = \bar{\theta}\phi^{t-1}$

We start with Cases B(i), (ii), and (iii) with $\pi_t^e = 1$ in which cases

$$\pi_t = \phi^t \tag{22}$$

and

$$\bar{\theta}_t = \begin{cases} \text{(i)} & \bar{\theta}\{\gamma\phi^{t-1} + (1-\gamma)\} \\ \text{(ii)} & \bar{\theta} \\ \text{(iii)} & \bar{\theta}\phi^{t-1} \end{cases} \tag{23}$$

Cases B(iv) and (ix) are also cases in which the wage-earners as in Case B(iii) need to take no account of future inflation and in which their claims are not eroded by future inflation because of the delay on the part of the producers in marking up their selling prices ($\gamma = 1$). The results are the same as in Case B(iii).

In Cases B(iv) and (v) with the rational expectations assumption of $\pi_t^e = \pi_t$, we obtain from equations (20) and (4), so long as $(1-\gamma)\phi^t < 1$,

$$\pi_t = \frac{\gamma\phi^t}{1-(1-\gamma)\phi^t} \tag{24}$$

and

$$\bar{\theta}_t = \bar{\theta}\left\{1 + \frac{\gamma\phi^{t-1}}{1-(1-\gamma)\phi^{t-1}}\right\} \tag{25}$$

But even if $(1-\gamma)\phi$ is < 1, as time passes $(1-\gamma)\phi^t$ will come to exceed unity.

If, as in Case B(v) with $\gamma = 0$, $(1-\gamma)\phi > 1$, or if with $(1-\gamma)\phi < 1$ sufficient time has passed to raise $(1-\gamma)\phi^t$ above unity, then π_t will explode immediately to infinity and $\bar{\theta}_t$ will become meaningless.

With the assumption of adaptive expectations in Cases B(vii) and (viii) we obtain from equation (20) the result

$$\begin{aligned}
\pi_t = {} & (1-\gamma)\phi^{t(t+1)/2}\pi_0 + \\
& + \gamma\{\phi^t + (1-\gamma)\phi^{t+t-1} + (1-\gamma)^2\phi^{t+t-1+t-2} + \cdots \\
& + (1-\gamma)^{t-1}\phi^{t(t+1)/2}\}
\end{aligned} \tag{26}$$

which, with $\gamma = 0$, gives for Case B(viii)

$$\pi_t = \phi^{t(t+1)/2}\pi_0 \tag{27}$$

and

$$\bar{\theta}_t = \bar{\theta} \tag{28}$$

In these cases there is a very rapid explosion of the price inflation factor.

The term $\phi^{t(t+1)/2}$ is due to the combined effect of two explosive forces: first, to the fact that the real claim on the national product is growing more rapidly than the national product itself and is thus continually raising the rate of inflation; and second, to the fact that wage-earners are raising the money wage claim not merely to obtain an ever-increasing real wage but also to offset last year's ever-rising rate of price inflation.

V

The various models which have been described in Sections III and IV give very different results both for the rates of inflation and for the proportion of the national product going to wages. The best way of displaying these differences may be by means of a numerical example. In Table VIII we assume $\rho = 1.05$, $\lambda = 1.02$, $\mu = 1.2$, and $\gamma = $ either 0.25 or zero. With these values $1/\mu = .83$ and $l/(\lambda - 1) = .99013136$ so that $\overline{\theta} = l/\mu(\lambda - 1) = .82510947$; and $\phi = \rho/\lambda = 1.0294118$. We examine the case for $\pi_t^e = 1$, π_t, or π_{t-1}. In the relevant cases of explosive inflation we assume $\pi_0 = 1$, that is, that we start from a zero rate of price inflation.

In the A-Cases it is only the two last cases A(v) and A(viii) which inevitably lead to explosive situations with no upper limit to the inflation rate, though A(vii) would also do so if $(1 - \gamma)\phi > 1$, that is, if $\gamma < (\phi - 1)/\phi = 0.0286$. The adaptive expectations of A(viii) are more probable in the real world than the rational expectations of A(v), in which case the attempt of wage-earners rationally to foresee the actual rate of inflation combined with the immediate price-fixing by employers to prevent any reduction of realised profit margins would mean an immediate breakdown of the system.

But the case illustrated in A(viii) is not unrealistic. It rests on the reasonable assumptions: (1) that wage-earners attempt each year merely to raise whatever is their existing real standard at a rate somewhat higher than the rate of increase of output per worker, (2) that they learn by experience to attempt to forestall the erosion of their real claims through inflation and allow each year for a rate of inflation equal to that which they have just experienced, and (3) that employers learn to adjust their prices promptly to changes in money costs in order to avoid inflationary losses. In so far as the employers succeed in the immediate adjustment of prices, the wage-earners fail to achieve any extra proportion of the national product; but the rate of price inflation explodes without upper limit, reaching – in our numerical example – 34 per cent per annum by the tenth year and 79 per cent by the twentieth year.

The B-Cases lead either to an early complete explosion and breakdown of the whole system or else to a continuous rise in the rate of inflation without upper limit. In the former cases, B(iv) and B(v), it is meaningless to ask what will be the effect on the distribution of income between wages

Table VIII

$\gamma=$		1		0.25				1		0			
$\pi_t^e=$		1		π_t		π_{t-1}		1		π_t		π_{t-1}	
		A(i)		**A(iv)**		**A(vii)**		**A(ii)**		**A(v)**		**A(viii)**	
Block	t	π_t	$\bar{\theta}_{t+1}$	π_t	$\bar{\theta}_{t+1}$	π_t	$\bar{\theta}_{t+1}$	π_t	$\bar{\theta}_{t+1}$	π_t	$\bar{\theta}_{t+1}$	π_t	$\bar{\theta}_{t+1}$
A	0	1.0294	.8312	1.1290	.8517	1.0000	.8251	1.0294	.8251	∞	?	1.0000	.8251
A	1	1.0294	.8312	1.1290	.8517	1.0294	.8312	1.0294	.8251	∞	?	1.0294	.8251
A	5	1.0294	.8312	1.1290	.8517	1.0936	.8444	1.0294	.8251	∞	?	1.1560	.8251
A	10	1.0294	.8312	1.1290	.8517	1.1193	.8497	1.0294	.8251	∞	?	1.3363	.8251
A	20	1.0294	.8312	1.1290	.8517	1.1283	.8516	1.0294	.8251	∞	?	1.7856	.8251
A	25	1.0294	.8312	1.1290	.8517	1.1288	.8517	1.0294	.8251	∞	?	2.0641	.8251
A	∞	1.0294	.8312	1.1290	.8517	1.1290	.8517	1.0294	.8251	∞	?	∞	.8251
		B(i)		**B(iv)**		**B(vii)**		**B(ii)**		**B(v)**		**B(viii)**	
B	0	1.0000	.8251	1.0000	.8251	1.0000	.8251	1.0000	.8251	∞	?	1.0000	.8251
B	1	1.0294	.8312	1.1290	.8517	1.0294	.8312	1.0294	.8251	∞	?	1.0294	.8251
B	5	1.1560	.8573	2.1725	1.067	1.3786	.9032	1.1560	.8251	∞	?	1.5447	.8251
B	10	1.3363	.8945			2.5448	1.1438	1.3363	.8251	∞	?	4.925	.8251
B	20	1.7856	.9872			24.029	5.575	1.7856	.8251	∞	?	440.27	.8251
B	25	2.0641	1.0446			166.14	34.89	2.0641	.8251	∞	?	12344.4	.8251
B	∞	∞	∞	∞	?	∞		∞	.8251	∞	?	∞	.8251

Note: From equation (4) it can be seen that $\bar{\theta}_{t+1}$ depends upon π_t. In this table accordingly $\bar{\theta}_{t+1}$ is shown against π_t.

and profits. In the latter cases, B(i), (ii), (vii), and (viii), the question is not meaningless. In those cases, B(i) and (vii), where the employers do not take any avoiding action, the ratio of wages to available income will itself rise without upper limit; and clearly at some point when the wage claims are absorbing more than the total national income something must give and the system will grind to a halt. In those cases, B(ii) and (viii), where the employers do take effective avoiding action, the wage-earners make no gains at all at the expense of profits.

The B-Cases all rest on what may at first appear to be a very unreal assumption, namely, that the real wage target at which wage-earners aim at each settlement rises continuously at a rate which is higher than the rate of increase of output per head. This means that as the years pass the real wage target rises in such a way as to bear no relation at all to the actual output per head. It is this feature which ensures that all the B-Cases show an explosion of the rate of inflation with no upper limit. The basic B-Case assumption may not, however, appear to be quite so unrealistic if it is expressed in a somewhat different manner. The behavioural psychology might be simply that at each wage settlement the wage-earners (1) claim a rise in the money wage which is sufficient to offset the price inflation that had occurred since the last wage settlement, that is, a claim that will simply restore the value of this year's settlement to what was the real claim made at last year's settlement, and (2) add to this an additional claim of $(\rho - 1)$ to represent some improvement of the real standard over last year's real standard. This has, of course, exactly the same effect as trying consciously to keep the real wage on a target which is growing at a rate $(\rho - 1)$.

In this connection it is of interest to note that A(viii), B(i), and B(ii) all result in the same explosion of the rate of inflation. The reason for this can be seen from an examination of the wage-fixing equation in the A-Case and in the two B-Cases.

In the A-Case, from equations (6) and (7) with $\gamma = 0$ and $\pi_t^e = \pi_{t-1}$ we obtain

$$W_t = \rho W_{t-1} \frac{P_t^e}{P_{t-1}} = \rho W_{t-1} \frac{P_{t-1}}{P_{t-2}} \tag{29}$$

The new wage claim made at the beginning of year t is W_t. In this case it would simply be ρW_{t-1} if no inflation is expected during year t. But if inflation is expected at the rate experienced during the past year (P_{t-1}/P_{t-2}) and if this rate is expected to rule over virtually the whole of the coming year $(\gamma \to 0)$, then the claim ρW_{t-1} will be multiplied by the expected inflation factor P_{t-1}/P_{t-2}; and we obtain equation (29). In this case we may call ρ the 'real-wage-aspiration factor' and P_t/P_{t-1} 'the expected-price-inflation factor'.

In the two B-Cases we have from equation (18) with $\pi_t^e = 1$,

$$\frac{W_t}{W_{t-1}} = \frac{P_{t-1}}{P_{t-2}} \rho \tag{30}$$

In these cases last year's claim made at the beginning of the year $t-1$ (namely, W_{t-1}), has been eroded by the past year's inflation and must be multiplied by P_{t-1}/P_{t-2} to bring this year's real wage at the beginning of year t up to last year's real wage achieved at the beginning of year $t-1$. But this in turn must be multiplied by ρ to allow for the aspired growth in the real standard between last year and this year. In this case we may call ρ 'the real-wage-aspiration factor' and P_{t-1}/P_{t-2} 'the price-inflation catching-up factor'.

In all three cases A(viii), B(i), and B(ii) the formulas for price and wage inflation are the same. From equations (2) and either (9) (with $\gamma = 0$ and $\pi_t^e = \pi_{t-1}$) or (21) (with $\gamma = 1$) we have

and

$$\left.\begin{array}{c} \omega_t = \rho\pi_{t-1} \\[2mm] \pi_t = \dfrac{\omega_t}{\lambda} = \dfrac{\rho}{\lambda}\,\pi_{t-1} = \phi\pi_{t-1} \end{array}\right\} \tag{31}$$

which we will use as the basic model of explosive inflation in what follows. In the wage equation we may call π_{t-1} the 'expected-price-inflation factor' or the 'price inflation-catching-up factor' according as we have the A-Case or the B-Cases in mind; and in the price equation we may call $\rho/\lambda = \phi > 1$, the 'quart-out-of-a-pint-pot factor' in price inflation.

While in all three cases the price and wage inflation factors (π and ω) are the same, the effect on the distribution of income between wages and profits ($\bar{\theta}_t$) will differ. In Cases A(viii) and B(ii) the wage-earners' claim is immediately and effectively offset by the rise in the cost of living, and their proportion of the national income remains unchanged at its normal non-inflationary level; but in Case B(i) the employers are asleep to the effects of inflation and merely restore their proportion of the national product for a fraction, $1 - \gamma$, of the year. For the delay fraction γ the claim of the wage earners is effective; and as in this case this real wage claim is growing indefinitely out of relation to output per head, it eventually claims the whole and more than the whole of the national income. Case B(i) may be quite realistic; it assumes (1) that at time t the wage-earners claim a rise in the money wage sufficient to catch up with last year's inflation (P_{t-1}/P_{t-2}), (2) that they add a bit to this claim to represent some increase in real income, this bit being somewhat greater than the increase in productivity ($\rho > \lambda$) so long as full employment is maintained ($L_t = L^*$) and (3) that the delay between a rise in costs and the mark-up of selling prices is not reduced to an absolutely negligible level ($\gamma > 0$).

Finally Case B(viii) is one where the erosion through inflation is, as it were, counted twice. Wage-earners demand an increase to make up for last year's slippage and also a further increase in a vain attempt to prevent erosion over the coming year. This as one might expect increases the rate of explosion of the inflation, which reaches a figure of over 1,000,000 per cent per annum by the 25th year.

VI

The models presented so far are all based on the unreal assumption that all wages settlements are made annually on 1 January. Even if one retains the assumption that all settlements are made annually (which may not be too unrealistic), it is unrealistic to assume that they are all made at the same date in the year. In fact, as will be shown in this section, if the settlements are spread over the year — some being made every 1 January, and others every 1 July, for example — the annual rate of inflation is not affected in those cases examined in Sections III and IV in which the inflation rate is constant; but in those cases in which the rate of inflation explodes the spreading of annual settlements over the course of the year may significantly raise the rate of growth of the inflation rate.*

We will illustrate the problem by assuming that the labour force is divided into two equal groups, an A group which settles each year on 1 January and a B group which settles each year on 1 July. The price level actually ruling on 1 January each year will be the average of the prices of A goods and of B goods which are ruling at the date, and similarly for the price level on 1 July.

The following Table IX may help to describe the wage rates and selling prices in the two sectors, A and B.

We denote the general price level actually ruling at time t by $\hat{P}_t$ so that

$$\hat{P}_t = \tfrac{1}{2}(P^{\mathrm{a}}_{t-1} + P^{\mathrm{b}}_{t-\frac{1}{2}})$$

and

$$\hat{P}_{t+\frac{1}{2}} = \tfrac{1}{2}(P^{\mathrm{a}}_t + P^{\mathrm{b}}_{t-\frac{1}{2}}) \tag{32}$$

---

*At the end of Section I of this appendix we pointed out that the inflation rate will, of course, be raised if wage settlements are made more frequently (e.g. once a quarter instead of once a year) in an attempt to mitigate the deleterious effect of rises in the cost of living on the real wage. The point made in this section is quite different, namely, that, even if each group of workers maintains an annual wage settlement of a given kind, the mere fact that they settle at different dates in the course of the year will reinforce any explosive tendency in an inflationary situation.

Table IX

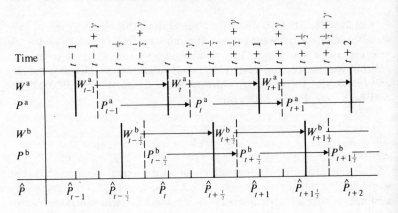

We have also, corresponding to the price equation (1),

$$P_t^{\mathrm{a}} = \mu \, \frac{W_t^{\mathrm{a}} L^{\mathrm{a}}}{Q_t^{\mathrm{a}}} \left. \right\}$$

and

$$P_{t+\frac{1}{2}}^{\mathrm{b}} = \mu \, \frac{W_{t+\frac{1}{2}}^{\mathrm{b}} L^{\mathrm{b}}}{Q_{t+\frac{1}{2}}^{\mathrm{b}}} \tag{33}$$

where $L^{\mathrm{a}} = L^{\mathrm{b}} = \frac{1}{2} L^*$, with demand-management policies keeping total employment at the full employment level, L^*.

We assume that the price of A goods is fixed by a mark-up of the costs at 1 January, the mark-up being made after 1 January but before 1 July $(0 < \gamma < \frac{1}{2})$; and similarly for B goods, where the mark-up is on July costs but is made between July and December.

In order to illustrate the case of a constant rate of inflation we now apply equations (32) and (33) to Case A(i) of Section III.

We then have, corresponding to equation (8) with $\pi_t^{\mathrm{e}} = 1$,

$$\frac{W_t^{\mathrm{a}}}{W_{t-1}^{\mathrm{a}}} = \frac{W_{t+\frac{1}{2}}^{\mathrm{b}}}{W_{t-\frac{1}{2}}^{\mathrm{b}}} = \rho \tag{34}$$

so that from (33)

$$\frac{P_t^{\mathrm{a}}}{P_{t-1}^{\mathrm{a}}} = \frac{W_t^{\mathrm{a}}}{W_{t-1}} \cdot \frac{Q_{t-1}^{\mathrm{a}}}{Q_t^{\mathrm{a}}} = \frac{\rho}{\lambda} = \phi$$

and

$$\frac{P_{t+\frac{1}{2}}^{b}}{P_{t-\frac{1}{2}}^{b}} = \frac{W_{t+\frac{1}{2}}^{b}}{W_{t-\frac{1}{2}}^{b}} \cdot \frac{Q_{t-\frac{1}{2}}^{b}}{Q_{t+\frac{1}{2}}^{b}} = \frac{\rho}{\lambda} = \phi \qquad (35)$$

But since the prices of both A goods and B goods rise in the same annual ratio, ϕ, the general price level in (32) must also rise by the same ratio ϕ, which from equation (12) can be seen to be the same as if all settlements were made on 1 January.

We will illustrate the effect on cases of explosive inflation by examining Cases B(i), (ii), and (iii). In these cases the wage-fixing equations (cf. equation (18) with $\pi_t^e = 1$) take the form

$$W_t^a = R_0 \rho^t \hat{P}_t \left.\vphantom{\begin{array}{c}1\\1\end{array}}\right\}$$

and

$$W_{t+\frac{1}{2}}^b = R_0 \rho^{t+\frac{1}{2}} \hat{P}_{t+\frac{1}{2}} \qquad (36)$$

Substituting the value of W^a from equations (36) into the equation (33) for P^a and using equation (3) we obtain

$$P_t^a = \frac{\mu(\lambda - 1)}{l} \cdot \frac{R_1 L^*}{\overline{Q}_1} \phi^{t-1} \hat{P}_t$$

But with $\gamma = 1$ or $\pi_t^e = 1$, R_1 the actual real wage of A workers at time $t = 1$ is the same as $\overline{R}_1^e$ the real wage planned by A workers for the year 1, so that from equations (5) and (10)

$$P_t^a = \frac{\overline{\theta}_1^e}{\overline{\theta}} \phi^{t-1} \hat{P}_t = \phi^{t-1} \hat{P}_t \qquad (37a)$$

if, consistently with the treatment of Cases B(i), (ii), and (iii) in Section IV, we choose a time scale such that at $t = 1$, $\overline{\theta}_1^e = \overline{\theta}$.

By a similar process from the value of W^b in equation (36) and the level of P^b in equation (33) we can obtain

$$P_{t+\frac{1}{2}}^b = \phi^{t-\frac{1}{2}} \hat{P}_{t+\frac{1}{2}} \qquad (37b)$$

From equations (32) and (37a and b) we obtain

$$\hat{P}_{t+1} = \tfrac{1}{2}\phi^t(\phi^{-1}\hat{P}_t + \phi^{-\frac{1}{2}}\hat{P}_{t+\frac{1}{2}})$$
$$\hat{P}_{t+1\frac{1}{2}} = \tfrac{1}{2}\phi^t(\hat{P}_{t+1} + \phi^{-\frac{1}{2}}\hat{P}_{t+\frac{1}{2}}) \qquad (38)$$
$$\hat{P}_{t+2} = \tfrac{1}{2}\phi^t(\hat{P}_{t+1} + \phi^{+\frac{1}{2}}\hat{P}_{t+1\frac{1}{2}})$$

With $\phi > 1$ and with positive rates of inflation, that is, with $\hat{P}_{t+1} > \hat{P}_t$ and $\hat{P}_{t+1\frac{1}{2}} > \hat{P}_{t+\frac{1}{2}}$, we can deduce from equations (38) that $\hat{P}_{t+1} < \hat{P}_{t+1\frac{1}{2}}$

Table X

t	π_t Cases B(i), (ii) and (iii)	$\hat{\pi}_{t+1}$ From Equation (40)
0	1.0000	1.0000
1	1.0294	1.0446
5	1.1560	1.2234
10	1.3363	1.4920
20	1.7856	2.2421
25	2.0641	2.7636

$< \hat{P}_{t+2}$. That is to say, as one would expect, there are also intermediate six-monthly rates of inflation.

From the third equation in (38) we have

$$\hat{\pi}_{t+1} \equiv \frac{\hat{P}_{t+2}}{\hat{P}_{t+1}} = \phi^t \left(\tfrac{1}{2} + \tfrac{1}{2}\phi^{+\frac{1}{2}} \frac{\hat{P}_{t+1\frac{1}{2}}}{\hat{P}_{t+1}} \right) \tag{39}$$

But since $\phi > 1$ and $(\hat{P}_{t+1\frac{1}{2}}/\hat{P}_{t+1}) > 1$, it follows that $(\hat{P}_{t+2}/\hat{P}_{t+1}) > \phi^t$. Suppose, however, that there were only A workers; then from Table IX it can be seen that $\hat{P}_t$ would equal P_{t-1}^a. We must therefore compare $\hat{\pi}_{t+1}$ with the value of π_t in equation (22), which is ϕ^t. Thus the spreading of wage settlements between 1 January and 1 July can be seen to boost the rate of inflation.

The reason for this is as follows. The wage settlement on 1 January this year t will depend upon the cost of living ruling on 1 January this year. But this will depend not only on the price of A goods, which are the marked-up cost of the wage settlement of a year ago, but also on the price of B goods, which are the marked-up cost of wage settlements made only six months ago. But the marked-up cost of these latter wage settlements will be at a higher level than those of a year ago for two reasons: first, because the growth of real wage aspirations will have exceeded that of output per head for an extra six months ($\phi^{\frac{1}{2}} = (\rho/\lambda)^{\frac{1}{2}} > 1$), and, second, because the cost of living six months ago will be higher than that of a year ago ($(P_{t-\frac{1}{2}}/P_{t-1}) > 1$). As a result the wages settlement on 1 January of this year will exceed the wage settlement of 1 January of last year by an extra amount due to the higher wage settlement of six months ago.

By elimination of $\hat{P}_{t+1\frac{1}{2}}$ and $\hat{P}_{t+\frac{1}{2}}$ between the three equations (38) and rearrangement of terms we obtain

$$\hat{\pi}_{t+1} = \phi^t \left\{ \tfrac{1}{2} + \tfrac{1}{2}\phi^{\frac{1}{2}} + \tfrac{1}{4}\phi^{t+\frac{1}{2}} \left(1 - \frac{1}{\phi\hat{\pi}_t} \right) \right\} \tag{40}$$

Since $\phi > 1$ and $\hat{\pi}_t > \hat{\pi}_{t-1}$, it follows that $\hat{\pi}_{t+1}/\hat{\pi}_t > \phi$. But from equation (22) $\pi_t/\pi_{t-1} = \phi$, which is the corresponding result in the absence of B workers. Thus the inflation factor itself explodes at a constant rate ϕ in the absence of B workers, but at a higher and ever increasing rate in the case of spreading of settlements between A workers and B workers.

With $\rho = 1.05$ and $\lambda = 1.02$ so that $\phi = 1.0294$, as in the numerical examples of Table VII and on the assumption that we start with zero inflation ($\pi_0 = \hat{\pi}_1 = 1$) we can by successive solutions of equation (40) obtain values for the resulting $\hat{\pi}_{t+1}$ to compare with those given for π_t in B(i), (ii), and (iii) in Table VII. This is done in Table X.

APPENDIX B

The Effect of New Keynesian Demand Management Combined with Wage Settlements Aimed at (1) an Over-Ambitious Standard of Living or (2) the Promotion of Employment

Throughout this appendix we assume that there is a New Keynesian demand-management policy which keeps the total money demand for labour on a fixed annual growth path. (1) In Section I we combine this with the type of wage-fixing arrangements that we described in Appendix A, namely, money wage claims aimed at the achievement of a certain level of real wage income. (2) In Section II we combine it with wage-fixing arrangements under which wage rates are set so as to maintain levels of employment.

A major result of the simple models examined in this appendix is that there is a danger of instability in the case of combination (1) which does not occur in the case of combination (2).

However, in this appendix we are making the very unrealistic assumption that the New Keynesian demand-management policies are one hundred per cent effective in keeping total money earnings precisely and exactly on the predetermined growth path. In reality, of course, such a demand-management policy could take the form only of financial-policy adjustments to total money expenditures, which are made with some delay in response to deviations of total money expenditures and so of the money demand for labour off the planned growth path. The basic instability problem arising with combination (1) could not, therefore, occur in the crude form described in Section I of this appendix. It points however to a problem which will be investigated with more realistic assumptions in Volume II of this work.

I

We start with the wage-fixing and price-fixing equations (31) of Appendix A, namely:

$$\omega_t = \rho_t \pi_{t-1}$$

and

$$\pi_t = \frac{\omega_t}{\lambda} \tag{1}$$

so that

$$\omega_t = \frac{\rho_t}{\lambda} \omega_{t-1}$$

We now assume that ρ_t/λ (i.e. the quart-out-of-a-pint-pot factor measuring the excess of the real-wage-aspiration factor over the labour-productivity factor) depends on the level of employment in the manner of an inflation-adjusted Phillips curve. That is to say, we assume that there is a certain level of employment $\bar{L}$ at which wage-earners will aim at a real increase in the standard of living equal to the real increase in productivity per head so that $\rho/\lambda = 1$. At levels of employment greater than this $\rho > \lambda$ and *vice versa*.

We will express this by the equation

$$\frac{\rho_t}{\lambda} = l_t^\beta \tag{2}$$

where $l_t = L_t/\bar{L}$. It is to be observed that when $L_t = \bar{L}$, $\rho_t/\lambda = 1$. This makes the quart-out-of-a-pint-pot factor which is operative at the end of year t (namely, ρ_t/λ) dependent upon the level of employment experienced during year t (namely, $L_t/\bar{L}$). The term β measures the elasticity of ρ/λ with respect to l; for example, if $\beta = 2$, then a 1 per cent increase in L would cause a 2 per cent increase in ρ/λ.

From (1) and (2) we obtain

$$\omega_t = \omega_{t-1} l_t^\beta \tag{3}$$

Let us suppose that a demand-management policy is introduced such as to ensure that the total money demand for labour increases at a proportionate rate $\alpha - 1$ so that

$$\frac{L_{t+1} W_{t+1}}{L_t W_t} = \alpha$$

which can be expressed as

$$\omega_t \frac{l_{t+1}}{l_t} = \alpha \tag{4}$$

If we express equations (3) and (4) in logarithmic form we have

$$\log \omega_t = \log \omega_{t-1} + \beta \log l_t \tag{5}$$

and

$$\log \omega_t + \log l_{t+1} - \log l_t = \log \alpha \tag{6}$$

Using (6) to eliminate $\log \omega_t$ and $\log \omega_{t-1}$ from (5) we obtain

$$\log l_{t+1} + (\beta - 2) \log l_t + \log l_{t-1} = 0 \tag{7}$$

The equilibrium level of $\log l$ is zero in which case $l = L/\bar{L}$ would be constant at unity.

The roots of equation (7) are

$$\tfrac{1}{2}(2 - \beta \doteq \sqrt{\beta^2 - 4\beta})$$

with three possible cases.

Case 1. With $\beta > 4$ the solution has two real roots and we have

$$\log l_t = A_1 \left(\frac{2 - \beta + \sqrt{\beta^2 - 4\beta}}{2}\right)^t + A_2 \left(\frac{2 - \beta - \sqrt{\beta^2 - 4\beta}}{2}\right)^t$$

with A_1 and A_2 determined by the initial conditions. The dominant root is the negative root

$$\frac{2 - \beta - \sqrt{\beta^2 - 4\beta}}{2}$$

which is < -1. This means that the level of employment will alternate from year to year with ever-increasing swings above and below its equilibrium level.

Case 2. With $\beta = 4$ the solution gives

$$\log l_t = (A_1' + A_2' t)(-1)^t$$

with A_1' and A_2' again determined by the initial conditions. Once again the level of employment will alternate from one year to the next with swings above and below its equilibrium level, and with $A_2' \neq 0$ these swings will ultimately become ever larger and larger.

Case 3. With $\beta < 4$ the roots of equation (7) are conjugate complex and the solution gives

$$\log l_t = A''(1)^t \cos(\theta t - e)$$

with A'' and e determined by the initial conditions and with

$$\tan \theta = -\frac{\sqrt{\beta(4 - \beta)}}{\beta - 2}$$

In this case the level of employment will be subject to a continuous non-damped non-explosive cyclical movement. The amplitude of the swings will be determined by A'' which depends upon the initial conditions, and the period of the cycle will be equal to $2\pi/\theta$.

It is clear that this particular combination of wage-fixing arrangements would lead to intolerable fluctuations.

II

We now assume that wage rates are adjusted in such a way as to maintain employment and for this purpose we replace equation (3) with

$$\omega_t = \alpha_t l_t^{\hat{\beta}} \tag{8}$$

The term $\alpha_t = W_{t+1} L_{t+1} / W_t L_t$ expresses the rise in the total money demand for labour which, it is announced at the end of year t, will be effected through demand-management policies for year $t + 1$.

If employment is to remain unchanged ($L_{t+1} = L_t$), then α_t would represent the rise in the money wage rate ($\omega_t = W_{t+1}/W_t$) which must occur between year t and year $t + 1$. If, however, employment is to be increased, then ω_t must be $< \alpha_t$ and *vice versa*.

The term $l_t^{\hat{\beta}}$ in equation (8) now expresses the effect of the supply–demand conditions in the labour market on the money wage rate. With $l_t = L_t/\bar{L}$, $\bar{L}$ now represents the level of the demand for labour during year t which would be just sufficient to drive the wage rate up for year $t + 1$ by an amount corresponding to α_t, since with $L_t = \bar{L}$, $l_t = 1$ and $\omega_t = \alpha_t$. If $l_t > 1$, then $\omega_t > \alpha_t$ and vice versa.

We are thus assuming a change in wage-fixing institutions which somehow or another causes wage settlements (ω_t) to pivot not around the expected change in the cost of living ($\pi_{t-1} = \omega_{t-1}/\lambda$), but around the expected increase in the money demand for labour α_t. Around this pivot the volume of existing employment and thus the general scarcity or abundance of labour will adjust the actual money wage claim, whereas with the unreformed wage system the volume of employment adjusted the real-wage aspirations of the workers.

The basic and essential change is the substitution of the pivot α_t for ω_{t-1}/λ. Two other changes may or may not have occurred. The sensitivity parameter $\hat{\beta}$ may differ from β; and the level of employment $\bar{L}$ at which the wage settlement is equal to the pivot may differ in the two cases; that is to say, $l = 1$ may represent a different unemployment percentage in the two cases.

If we now express equations (8) and (4) in logarithmic form we obtain

$$\log \omega_t = \log \alpha + \hat{\beta} \log l_t \tag{9}$$

and

$$\log \omega_t + \log l_{t+1} - \log l_t = \log \alpha \tag{10}$$

from which, by elimination of $\log \omega_t$, one obtains

$$\log l_{t+1} = (1 - \hat{\beta}) \log l_t$$

with the solution

$$\log l_t = \log l_0(1 - \hat{\beta})^t \tag{11}$$

From this one can deduce:

(1) If $0 < \hat{\beta} < 1$, the volume of employment will converge monotonically on to its equilibrium level with $\log l_t = 0$ or $L_t = \bar{L}$.
(2) If $\hat{\beta} = 1$, then the level of employment will adjust immediately to its equilibrium level.
(3) If $1 < \hat{\beta} < 2$, the level of employment will converge with damped alternations on to its equilibrium level.
(4) If $2 < \beta$, then the level of employment will alternate with ever-increasing swings above and below its equilibrium level.

One may conclude that provided that $\hat{\beta}$ lies between 0 and 2 the system will eventually produce the equilibrium level of employment, and that this will happen very rapidly if $\hat{\beta}$ has a value near unity.

III

In Table XI we give an example of an unreformed wage-fixing system in which a demand-management policy is introduced for year 1 which restrains the rise in the total money wage bill to 5 per cent per annum (i.e. $W_1 L_1/W_0 L_0 = \alpha = 1.05$). With $\alpha = 1.05$ the equilibrium position would be one with $\omega = 1.05$ and $l = 1.0$. But we start out of equilibrium. We assume that $\omega_{-1} = 1.06$ which determines the rate of price inflation during year 0. We also assume that $l_0 = 1.01$, that is, that the level of employment during year 0 is such as to cause ρ_0/λ to exceed unity. For both these reasons ω_0 (i.e. W_1/W_0) is above its equilibrium level. Starting from this disequilibrium position, the table shows over a series of years how with the unreformed wage-fixing arrangements and with values of β of 0.5, 1.0, and 2.0 there would ensue undamped unexplosive cycles of both the wage inflation factor ω and the employment factor l.

In Table XII we give an example of a reformed wage-fixing system in which a demand-management policy is announced during year 0 to be about to come into effect from year 1 so that $W_1 L_1/W_0 L_0 = \alpha$ will be kept to a level of 1.05. Once again the equilibrium position would be $\omega = 1.05$ and $l = 1.0$. But we start out of equilibrium with a high demand for labour in year 0 ($l_0 = 1.01$) which causes the wage fixed at the beginning of year 1 to be raised by more than 5 per cent ($\omega_0 = W_1/W_0 > 1.05$). The subsequent movements of ω and l are shown for values of $\hat{\beta}$ of 0.5, 1.0, 1.5, and 2.0. With $\hat{\beta} = 0.5$ both ω and l converge fairly rapidly onto their equilibrium values. With $\hat{\beta} = 1.0$, they move immediately to their equilibrium values. With $\hat{\beta} = 1.5$, they move once more fairly rapidly onto their equilibrium values but with ever diminishing swings above and

Table XI

$$\omega_t = \omega_{t-1} l_t^{\beta}, \quad l_t = \frac{\alpha}{\omega_{t-1}} l_{t-1}, \quad l_0 = 1.01, \quad \omega_{-1} = 1.06, \quad \alpha = 1.05$$

	$\beta = 0.5$		$\beta = 1$		$\beta = 2$	
t	ω	l	ω	l	ω	l
-1	1.06	–	1.06	–	1.06	–
0	1.0653	1.01	1.0706	1.01	1.0813	1.01
1	1.0629	0.9955	1.0605	0.9906	1.0401	0.9808
2	1.0541	0.9834	1.0401	0.9808	1.0197	0.9901
3	1.0433	0.9796	1.0298	0.9901	1.0599	1.0195
4	1.0359	0.9859	1.0396	1.0095	1.0812	1.0100
5	1.0355	0.9993	1.0600	1.0196	1.0402	0.9809
6	1.0424	1.0133	1.0706	1.0100		
7	1.0531	1.0207	1.0605	0.9906		
8	1.0624	1.0177				
9	1.0655	1.0058				
10	1.0608	0.9912				
11	1.0508	0.9811				

Table XII

$$\omega_t = \alpha l_t^{\beta}, \quad l_t = \frac{\alpha}{\omega_{t-1}} l_{t-1}, \quad l_0 = 1.01, \quad \alpha = 1.05$$

	$\hat{\beta} = 0.5$		$\hat{\beta} = 1$		$\hat{\beta} = 1.5$		$\hat{\beta} = 2$	
t	ω	l	ω	l	ω	l	ω	l
0	1.0552	1.01	1.0605	1.01	1.0658	1.01	1.0711	1.01
1	1.0526	1.0050	1.05	1.00	1.0422	0.9950	1.0293	0.9901
2	1.0513	1.0025	1.05	1.00	1.0539	1.0024	1.0711	1.0100
3	1.0507	1.0013	1.05	1.00	1.0479	0.9987	1.0293	0.9901
4	1.0503	1.0006	1.05	1.00	1.0511	1.0007	1.0711	1.0100
5	1.0502	1.0003	1.05	1.00	1.0495	0.9997	1.0293	0.9901

below these values. With $\hat{\beta} = 2.0$, they do not move to their equilibrium values but move perpetually above and below these values with swings which do not diminish as time passes. Indeed if $\hat{\beta}$ were greater than 2, these swings would increase in amplitude from period to period.

APPENDIX C

Two Models of Fiscal Devices for the Control of Cost-Push Inflation

I

In this appendix we will assume, as in Appendices A and B, that selling prices are set as a mark-up on the labour cost of production. But we modify the result by introducing (1) a tax/subsidy scheme designed to tax (or to subsidise) rates of increase of selling price in excess of (or falling below) some permitted rate of rise and (2) a tax/subsidy scheme designed to tax (or to subsidise) rates of increase of money wage rates in excess of (or falling below) some permitted rate of rise.

In the absence of either of these fiscal schemes we would start with a mark-up equation corresponding to that given in equation (1) of Appendix A, namely,

$$P_t = \mu \frac{W_t L_t}{Q_t} \tag{1}$$

In Appendices A and B we simply assumed that the mark-up factor μ was given at a constant conventional level. But one of the important questions in the present appendix will be whether the fiscal devices will affect the mark-up factor μ. We must, therefore, consider what it is that determines the level of μ. For this purpose we will make the following assumptions:

(1) We assume that the delay γ between the fixing of the money wage rate at the beginning of the year and the consequent mark-up of selling prices is negligible so that virtually the whole of the output of year t (namely, $\bar{Q}_t$) is sold at the price P_t.

(2) Merely for simplification of the algebra without any significant loss of generality we will assume that $\bar{Q}_t = Q_t$. In other words we assume that increases in output per head do not occur continuously throughout the year at an exponential rate l but occur with annual jerks at the beginning of each year at the annualised rate of $\lambda - 1 = e^l - 1$. Thus with a constant labour force

$$\bar{Q}_{t+1} = Q_{t+1} = \lambda \bar{Q}_t = \lambda Q_t$$

(3) We assume that there are a large number of independent producers selling their products in an imperfectly competitive market. The individual producer is small enough to assume that he cannot by his own action significantly affect the demand curve for his product; but he is selling in an imperfect market in which he assumes that the price elasticity of demand for his product (ϵ_d) is constant at some value where $1 < -\epsilon_d < \infty$.

(4) We assume that during any one year the output per worker (Q_t/L_t) in any one firm is constant however much or little labour a producer may employ, though productivity grows from year to year, so that $Q_{t+1}/L_{t+1} = \lambda(Q_t/L_t)$.

(5) We assume that there is some wage-fixing arrangement (e.g. a collective bargain between a large group of producers and a trade union) which means that each producer must take as given and beyond his individual control the wage rate, W_t, at which he can employ whatever number of workers he may decide to employ.

(6) The profit which the producer will make in year t can be expressed by

$$V_t = P_t Q_t - W_t L_t \tag{2}$$

Our final assumption is that he will maximise his profit by choosing that output at which the marginal revenue is equal to the marginal labour cost. With W_t given and L_t/Q_t constant, differentiating equation (2) with respect to Q_t and setting $dV_t/dQ_t = 0$ gives

$$P_t = \frac{\epsilon_d}{1 + \epsilon_d} \frac{W_t L_t}{Q_t} = \mu \frac{W_t L_t}{Q_t} \tag{3}$$

where

$$\frac{P_t}{Q_t} \frac{dQ_t}{dP_t} = \epsilon_d$$

Thus if $-\epsilon_d = 6, \mu = 1.2$.

It is to be observed that with these assumptions the producer will mark up his labour cost at the beginning of year t (namely, $W_t L_t/Q_t$) by the mark-up factor $\mu = \epsilon_d/(1 + \epsilon_d)$, whatever the level of demand which he expects during the year. He will set his price at $\mu(W_t L_t/Q_t)$ and produce and sell during the year whatever turns out to be needed to meet the current demand for his product at that price. With our assumptions his marginal variable cost is constant at $W_t L_t/Q_t$. Given the level of his demand curve he will sell output up to the point at which his marginal revenue $P_t(1 + \epsilon_d)/\epsilon_d$ is equal to this marginal variable cost.

II

We proceed by introducing a tax/subsidy device into the model outlined in Section I. We will consider two alternative schemes. Scheme A will take the form of setting a 'norm' or permitted rate of inflation of the prices charged by a firm for its products, with the imposition of a tax charged on any excess of price rise over this norm (or of a subsidy paid for any deficiency of the price rise below the permitted norm), calculated on the current level of the firm's output. This scheme can be represented by the equation

$$V_t = P_t Q_t - W_t L_t - T_t (P_t - \eta_{t-1} P_{t-1}) Q_t \qquad (4)$$

where V_t is the firm's profit net of any tax, T_t represents the effective rate of tax (or subsidy) on the excess (or deficiency) over the 'norm', and η_{t-1} (which we will call the expansion factor) represents one plus the permitted 'norm' rate of price inflation.

Scheme B operates not on excess price rises above a permitted norm but on excess wage-rate rises on the current amount of labour employed above a permitted 'norm' rate of wage increase, and can be expressed by the equation

$$V_t = P_t Q_t - W_t L_t - T_t (W_t - \eta_{t-1} W_{t-1}) L_t \qquad (5)$$

We will examine each of these two schemes in turn. There are, however, certain features which are common to both.

(1) We will in both cases employ as a wage-fixing equation

$$\omega_t = \rho_t \pi_{t-1} - \alpha T_{t+1} \qquad (6)$$

Basically we are assuming the wage-fixing equation of Appendix A, equation (31), in which the wage-inflation factor (ω_t) depends upon the real-wage-aspiration factor (ρ_t) multiplied by the expected-price-inflation factor or the price-inflation-catching-up factor (π_{t-1}). But we assume that this wage-setting formula may itself be damped down by the existence of the inflation tax, T_t.

Since $\omega_t = W_{t+1}/W_t$, equation (6) is concerned with the setting of the wage rate at the beginning of year $t + 1$. This will be influenced by T_{t+1}, that is, by the rate of tax which will be levied on excess inflation during year $t + 1$ and which we assume to have been announced in time to influence the setting at the beginning of year $t + 1$ of the wage rate W_{t+1}.

There are two possible reasons why ω_t may be reduced by the announcement of T_{t+1}. In the first place, the mere existence of the scheme may rationally or irrationally make workers expect a dampening down of the inflation rate, so that last year's inflation factor π_{t-1} plays a less potent role. In the second place, the existence of the fiscal device, by affecting the employer's prospect of profit may increase the employer's resistance to a wage claim and thus make workers willing to moderate the wage rise on which they would have insisted in the absence of the scheme. We will examine this possibility in the case of each model in Section V of this appendix.

(2) It is possible in each case for the government, having fixed the expansion factor η_{t-1}, to attempt then to fix the tax rate T_t at such a level that the fiscal scheme is self-balancing in revenue. If all firms were the same, this would mean that the threat of tax on excess inflation and the offer of subsidy on moderation in inflation would be just sufficient to keep the inflation down to the permitted 'norm' level. If firms were not all the same, it would mean that those who found it paid in spite of tax to go above the norm were just balanced by those who were tempted by the subsidy to keep below the norm, so that tax revenue equalled subsidy payments. We may think then of an intermediate 'representative firm' which had an incentive in this case simply to respect the 'norm'.

This case of a rate of tax/subsidy T_t which is self-balancing in revenue would correspond to the effect of a scheme whereby licenses to inflate up to the permitted norm were issued to each firm, the firms being then permitted to buy or sell the licenses from and to each other. The price T_t would then correspond to the market price of the licenses, this price settling down at a level at which those who were prepared in spite of the price to purchase additional licenses to go above the 'norm' level were equal to those who were induced by the price to sell some of their licenses and to keep below the 'norm' level. In the main text of Chapter X a number of reasons are given for the view that it would probably be necessary to operate by means of a tax/subsidy scheme rather than by a system of marketable licenses.

(3) In each of the Schemes A or B the tax rate T_t represents this year's cost of the scheme to the firm for each unit of this year's excess over the permitted norm. But this must, alas, be distinguished from the actual tax rate, T_t^*, which the authorities have imposed on a unit of excess over the norm. The distinction between T_t^* and T_t can be explained by taking Scheme A as an example.

From equation (4) it can be seen that by increasing its current price P_t by one unit the firm will pay an extra tax (or lose a subsidy) of $T_t^* Q_t$. But next year the firm may expect to have a tax-free price norm of $\eta_t P_t$ where η_t is the expected expansion factor for next year. A unit increase in P_t may therefore be expected to have a value next year in tax avoidance (or subsidy gain) of $T_{t+1}^* \eta_t Q_{t+1}$ where T_{t+1}^* is the expected level of next year's tax rate and Q_{t+1} the expected level of next year's output. We write i for one plus the rate of interest, which we may call the interest-rate factor. If $i_{t+1} - 1$ is the expected interest rate payable during the year $t + 1$, the value at year t of the future tax/subsidy value of a unit increase in P_t is $T_{t+1}^* (\eta_t/i_{t+1}) Q_{t+1}$. The present net cost, $T_t Q_t$, is the present payment of $T_t^* Q_t$ less the present value of future gain. From this we obtain

$$T_t = T_t^* - T_{t+1}^* \frac{\eta_t}{i_{t+1}} \frac{Q_{t+1}}{Q_t}. \tag{7}$$

We may call T_t^* the 'purchase' and T_t the 'hire' rate of tax. T_t^* is the tax rate payable by the firm to 'purchase' the right to a permanent increase in the sales price of its output by one unit; T_t is the tax rate payable for 'hiring' the right to such a unit increase in its price for this year only. In any scheme for the purchase and sale of a limited amount of licenses to raise $P_t Q_t$ by a unit increase of P_t, T_t would be the market price payable by one firm to another for the hire of such licenses for one year and T_t^* the market price payable for the permanent acquisition by one firm from another of a unit of such licenses. It is T_t and not T_t^* which is relevant for assessing this year's cost of this year's rise in a firm's selling price.

From (7) it can be seen that the relationship between T_t and T_t^* depends essentially upon what is expected to be the future of the scheme. If it is expected that, for reasons discussed later, the scheme will be successful in reducing the rate of inflation and so in reducing the expected rate of inflation, T_{t+1}^* may well be expected to be lower than T_t^*, in which case the difference between T_t and T_t^* will be reduced. On the other hand, suppose that T, η and i are all expected to be constant and that in addition the level of employment is expected to be constant so that $Q_{t+1}/Q_t = \lambda$. Then

$$T = T^* \left(1 - \frac{\eta\lambda}{i}\right)$$

In this case the expansion factor, η, must be kept below i/λ to avoid any positive rate of tax, T^*, from giving an incentive for firms to raise their current sales prices indefinitely, since the present value of the future higher tax-free base would outweigh the present tax cost of the rise.

A similar distinction between T_t and T_t^* must be drawn in the case of Scheme B.

III

Scheme A is designed to put the tax/subsidy directly on increases in the price of a firm's product above or below a stated norm, as is represented in equation (4).

With a given demand curve, and with W_t, T_t, η_{t-1}, and P_{t-1} given, the firm will choose an output to maximise its net profit V_t. Differentiation of equation (4) with respect to Q_t with L_t/Q_t constant and setting the result equal to zero gives

$$\frac{dV_t}{dQ_t} = P_t \frac{1 - T_t}{\mu} + T_t \eta_{t-1} P_{t-1} - \frac{W_t L_t}{Q_t} = 0 \qquad (8)$$

where μ, as before, equals $\epsilon_d/(1 + \epsilon_d)$.*

If we use the wage-fixing equation (6) and replace W_t in equation (8) with $W_{t-1} (\rho \pi_{t-2} - \alpha T_t)$ we obtain from equation (8)

$$\pi_{t-1}(1 - T_t) + \mu T_t \eta_{t-1} = \mu \frac{L_t W_{t-1}}{Q_t P_{t-1}} (\rho \pi_{t-2} - \alpha T_t) \qquad (9)$$

From equation (9) we can derive a relationship between the permitted expansion factor η_{t-1} and the tax rate T_t which will equate π_{t-1} to η_{t-1}. If we write $\pi_{t=1} = \eta_{t-1}$ in equation (9) we obtain

$$\eta_{t-1} = \mu \frac{L_t W_{t-1}}{Q_t P_{t-1}} \frac{\rho \pi_{t-2} - \alpha T_t}{1 + (\mu - 1) T_t} \qquad (10)$$

We may assume that the authorities avoid the folly of raising the tax rate to such a height that employers are prepared to take on labour only if the workers will pay a wage to the employers (i.e. if $W_t = W_{t-1}(\rho \pi_{t-2} - \alpha T_t) < 0$). It follows from equation (9), as we would expect, that a higher level of T_t is needed to reduce $\pi_{t-1} = \eta_{t-1}$, that is to say, to reduce the self-balancing level of price inflation.

In what follows we will assume that η and T are chosen in such a combination as to make $\eta = \pi$ in which case the firm pays no net tax or

*If μ, T_t, P_{t-1}, and $W_t L_t/Q_t$ are given

$$\frac{\partial P_t}{\partial \eta_{t-1}} = -\frac{T_t}{1 - T_t} \mu P_{t-1}$$

which is < 0, since for the reason given in connection with equation (11) below we can assume $T_t < 1$. This represents what may at first sight appear a paradoxical conclusion, namely, that given the tax rate T a relaxation of the restriction on the tax-free permitted rise in the price will lead to a reduction in the price. The reason is that an increase in η means that the excess of any P_t over the permitted norm $\eta_{t-1} P_{t-1}$ is reduced, so that the tax on the existing marginal unit of output produced is reduced. This raises marginal revenue. It pays, therefore, to expand output and bring down the price until the lower price compensates for the reduced tax on the last unit of output so that marginal revenue is once more equal to the constant marginal labour cost, $W_t L_t/Q_t$.

subsidy. It will nevertheless with Scheme A have an incentive to lower its price in order to avoid having to incur a tax payment if it did not do so. This can be shown as follows.

From equation (8) with $\pi_{t-1} = P_t/P_{t-1} = \eta_{t-1}$ one can derive

$$1 + (\mu - 1) T_t = \mu \frac{L_t W_t}{P_t Q_t} = \frac{\mu}{\hat{\mu}} \tag{11}$$

where $\hat{\mu} = P_t Q_t/L_t W_t$ is the new mark-up factor. Since $\mu - 1 > 0$, $\mu/\hat{\mu} > 1$. The new mark-up factor will be lower than without the tax scheme. Producers will cut their profit margin to avoid paying tax. The extent, therefore, to which Scheme A can be used will depend upon the extent to which it is considered safe to restrain the profit mark-up without damaging incentives to invest and produce. Suppose $\mu = 1.2$ and that the mark-up factor must not be reduced below $\hat{\mu} = 1.1$, which would represent a halving of the profit margin from 20 per cent to 10 per cent. Then from equation (11) one can calculate that T_t must not rise above $45 \cdot 4\dot{5}$ per cent. From equation (11) it is clear that if T_t were raised to unity, $\hat{\mu}$ would be reduced to unity and profits would be reduced to zero.

From equation (8) with $\eta_{t-1} = \pi_{t-1}$ we can obtain the new price mark-up equation

$$P_t = \frac{W_t L_t}{Q_t} \frac{\mu}{1 + (\mu - 1) T_t} \tag{12}$$

so that

$$\pi_t = \frac{\omega_t}{\lambda} \frac{1 + (\mu - 1) T_t}{1 + (\mu - 1) T_{t+1}} \tag{13}$$

If we then substitute the value of ω_t from the wage-fixing equation (6) we obtain

or

$$\left. \begin{array}{l} \pi_t = \dfrac{\rho_t \pi_{t-1} - \alpha T_{t+1}}{\lambda} \dfrac{1 + (\mu - 1) T_t}{1 + (\mu - 1) T_{t+1}} \\[4mm] T_{t+1} = \dfrac{\rho_t \pi_{t-1} [1 + (\mu - 1) T_t] - \lambda \pi_t}{\alpha [1 + (\mu - 1) T_t] + (\mu - 1) \lambda \pi_t} \end{array} \right\} \tag{14}$$

Up to this point what we have said about the effects of Scheme A are unaffected by the question of the form of demand-management policies being pursued by the financial authorities. The new mark-up on labour costs is not affected by the scale of demand for the products of industry, though the volume of output is, of course, affected. But if the real-wage-aspiration factor ρ_t is affected by the volume of employment, equations

(14) will be affected by the scale of demand. We will from this point onwards assume an Orthodox Keynesian demand-management policy such that full employment is maintained and ρ_t remains constant at ρ.

Suppose now that the authorities introduce the scheme in year 2, set $\eta_1 = \eta_2 = \eta_3$, etc. $= \bar{\eta}$, and then impose a series of tax rates T_2, T_3, etc., such as to keep $\pi_1 = \pi_2 = \pi_3$, etc. $= \bar{\pi} = \bar{\eta}$. In other words, the government proposes to reduce the current inflation factor π_0 to $\bar{\pi}$ by setting an expansion factor $\bar{\eta} = \bar{\pi}$ and then adjusts T_2, T_3, etc., at rates which keep the inflation factor down to the constant level $\bar{\pi}$.

From equation (14) we obtain

$$T_2 = \frac{\phi \pi_0 - \bar{\pi}}{(\alpha/\lambda) + (\mu - 1)\bar{\pi}}$$

$$T_3 = \bar{\pi} \frac{\phi[1 + (\mu - 1)T_2] - 1}{(\alpha/\lambda)[1 + (\mu - 1)T_2] + (\mu - 1)\bar{\pi}}$$

(15)

where $\phi = \rho/\lambda$. We consider three cases.

Case (1) is the case where $\phi > 1$ and the scheme has no direct effect on the wage-fixing equation, so that $\alpha = 0$. In this case we have from equation (15)

$$T_2 = \frac{1}{\mu - 1} \left(\phi \frac{\pi_0}{\bar{\pi}} - 1 \right)$$

$$T_3 = \frac{1}{\mu - 1} (\phi - 1) + \phi T_2$$

(16)

With $\phi > 1$ and $\pi_0/\bar{\pi} > 1$, T_2 will be > 0 and $T_3 > T_2$. From equations (14) and (17) we can obtain

$$T_t = \frac{1}{\mu - 1} \left(\phi^t \frac{\pi_0}{\bar{\pi}} - 1 \right)$$

It is clear that in this case the scheme cannot work as $T_t \to \infty$ as $t \to \infty$. The scheme cannot possibly cope with quart-out-of-a-pint-pot inflation if the scheme has no direct effect in moderating the wage-fixing equation.

Case (2) is the case where there is only expectational or catching-up inflation ($\phi = 1$) and the scheme has no direct effect on the wage-fixing equation ($\alpha = 0$).

From equation (15) we now have

$$T_2 = \frac{1}{\mu - 1} \left(\frac{\pi_0}{\bar{\pi}} - 1 \right)$$

$$T_3 = T_2$$

(17)

In this case the scheme will not involve an excessively high T_2 provided that $\bar{\pi}$ is not set at too ambitious a level below π_0. But in this case the tax rate T_2 will have to be kept at this constant level in order to prevent a renewed rise in the inflation factor. The imposition of the tax rate T_2 has given employers an incentive to reduce their mark-up (see equation (12)). This has lowered the inflation rate in year 1 and has thus reduced the expectation of inflation for the following years. But if T_2 is then removed this will restore the mark-up to its previous level, which will increase the inflation factor in the year in which the tax rate is eliminated and will thus restore the expectation of inflation and thus the actual rate of inflation.

Nor is anything to be gained in this case by arranging for a gradual stage-by-stage reduction in inflation, for example, by aiming at $\pi_0 > \pi_1 > \pi_2 > \pi_3 > \cdots \pi_{t-1} > \pi_t = \bar{\pi}$. Since

$$\bar{\pi} = \pi_t = \pi_0 \frac{\pi_1}{\pi_0} \cdot \frac{\pi_2}{\pi_1} \cdots \frac{\pi_t}{\pi_{t-1}}$$

we can obtain from equation (14), with $\rho/\lambda = 1$ and $\alpha = 0$

$$T_t = \frac{1}{\mu - 1} \left(\frac{\pi_0}{\bar{\pi}} - 1 \right)$$

which is the same value as that given for T_2 in (17), a tax rate that would have to be continued so long as π was to be kept down to $\bar{\pi}$.

With $(\mu - 1) T = (\pi_0/\bar{\pi}) - 1$, it can be seen from equation (12) that the mark-up factor would be reduced from μ to $\mu(\bar{\pi}/\pi_0)$. If $\mu = 1.2$ and if it was undesirable to reduce μ to below 1.1, then $\pi_0/\bar{\pi}$ must not be greater than 1.2/1.1, so that if π_0 were 1.15 $\bar{\pi}$ must not be reduced below $(1.15 \times 1.1)/1.2 = 1.054$ and T must not be raised above

$$\frac{(1.2/1.1) - 1}{0.2} = 0.4\dot{5}$$

Case (3). If we consider the general case with $\rho/\lambda = \phi > 1$ and $\alpha > 0$, we can see from the first equation in (14) that there exists a steady-state solution with constant values of $\pi = \bar{\pi}$ and $T = \bar{T}$ in which $\bar{T} = \bar{\pi}(\phi - 1)(\lambda/\alpha)$. Suppose then that one sets a value for π at $\bar{\pi}$ and adjusts T to maintain this value of $\bar{\pi}$. From the second equation in (14) one can see that $T_{t+1} - T_t \gtrless 0$ according as $T_t \lessgtr \bar{\pi}(\phi - 1)(\lambda/\alpha)$, so that the system will eventually approach this steady state. But care would have to be taken to choose $\bar{\pi}$ so that T did not exceed the permissible upper limit (in our numerical example of $0.4\dot{5}$) either at the outset of the operation (if T_2 must start above the final $\bar{T}$) or at its final value of $\bar{T} = \bar{\pi}(\phi - 1)(\lambda/\alpha)$.

From cases (1) and (2) above it can be seen that if the tax/subsidy scheme has no direct effect on wage claims ($\alpha = 0$), the scheme cannot cope with quart-out-of-pint-pot inflation (Case (1)). But it can modify expectational or catching-up price inflation (Case (2)). This it can do because it induces the producers to cut their profit margins so that the consequential once-for-all moderation of price inflation sets in motion a moderation of the expectational or catching-up factor in wage inflation. But this effect results only from a permanent cut in profit margins.

In cases where the scheme has some direct moderating effect on wage claims ($\alpha > 0$) the scheme can effectively moderate both quart-out-of-a-pint-pot and also expectational or catching-up inflation, but once more only at the cost of a permanent cut of profit margins.

IV

Scheme B is designed to put the tax/subsidy on increases in the wage rate which is paid over and above (or below) a permitted norm as is represented in equation (5).

With a given demand curve and with W_t, T_t, η_{t-1}, and W_{t-1} given, the firm is assumed to choose an output to maximise its net profit V_t. Differentiation of equation (5) with respect to Q_t with L_t/Q_t constant and setting the result to zero gives

$$\frac{dV_t}{dQ_t} = \frac{P_t}{\mu} - \frac{W_t L_t(1 + T_t) - T_t \eta_{t-1} W_{t-1} L_t}{Q_t} = 0 \qquad (18)$$

It is clear that the selling price will now be the marked-up variable cost which is the wage cost plus any net tax on the excess wage rate of those employed. Unless the scheme directly modifies the wage claim — unless, that is to say, in the wage-fixing equation (6) α is > 0 — the effect of the scheme will be to raise the price level if, in an attempt to restrain inflation, the permitted expansion norm η_{t-1} is set above the uncontrolled wage inflation factor $\omega_{t-1} \equiv W_t/W_{t-1}$.

Suppose that $\alpha = 0$, and assume an Orthodox Keynesian demand-management policy such that full employment is always maintained. The wage-fixing equation (6) now becomes

$$\frac{W_t}{W_{t-1}} = \omega_{t-1} = \rho \pi_{t-2} \qquad (19)$$

as in equation (31) of Appendix A. We will illustrate this case with the catching-up interpretation of the term π_{t-2} which is derived in equation

(30) of Appendix A from equation (18) of Appendix A with $\pi_t^e = 1$. This gives

$$W_t = \bar{R}_0^e \rho^t P_{t-1} \tag{20}$$

as the form of wage claim at the beginning of year t, where $\bar{R}_0^e$ is the real wage claim at the beginning of year 0, so that $\bar{R}_0^e \rho^t$ is the real wage claim at the beginning of year t and P_{t-1} is the cost of living ruling at the end of year $t - 1$.

If we substitute for W_t and W_{t-1} in equation (18) from equations (19) and (20) and rearrange terms we obtain

$$\pi_t = \mu \, \frac{\bar{R}_1^e L^*}{Q_1} \, \phi^t \left[1 + T_{t+1} \left(1 - \frac{\eta_t}{\rho \pi_{t-1}} \right) \right] \tag{21}$$

Provided that the scheme is restrictive, that is, that η_t is set at a level lower than $\omega_t = \rho \pi_{t-1}$, the price inflation factor π_t will be in excess of

$$\mu \, \frac{\bar{R}_1^e L^*}{Q_1} \, \phi^t$$

which is the inflation factor that would result in the absence of the scheme (i.e. with $T = 0$) and which, with

$$\mu \, \frac{\bar{R}_1^e L^*}{Q_1} = \frac{\bar{\theta}_1^e}{\bar{\theta}} = 1$$

corresponds to the value of π_t given in equation (22) of Appendix A. The anti-inflation tax on excess wages will in fact have increased the rate of inflation because prices will be marked up on the wage cost plus the tax on the wage cost.

The efficacy of Scheme B in fact depends upon $\alpha > 0$ in the wage-fixing equation (6). One can now imagine an effective revenue self-balancing scheme in which T and η are so chosen that $\eta = \omega$. In this case with $W_t = \eta_{t-1} W_{t-1}$ equation (18) gives the price mark-up equation

$$P_t = \mu \, \frac{W_t L_t}{Q_t} \tag{22}$$

which is the same as in equation (1) with the absence of any scheme at all.

From equation (22) we get the inflation factor

$$\pi_t = \frac{\omega_t}{\lambda} \tag{23}$$

and using the wage-fixing equation (6) we get

$$\pi_t = \frac{\rho\pi_{t-1} - \alpha T_{t+1}}{\lambda}$$

or

$$T_{t+1} = \frac{\rho\pi_{t-1} - \lambda\pi_t}{\alpha} \qquad (24)$$

A policy of setting T_2, T_3, etc., so as to reduce the inflation factor from π_0 to $\pi_1 = \pi_2 = \pi_3$, etc. $= \bar{\pi}$ would thus entail tax rates of

$$T_2 = \frac{\rho\pi_0 - \lambda\bar{\pi}}{\alpha}$$

and

$$T_3 = T_4, \text{etc.} = \bar{T} = \bar{\pi}(\phi - 1)\frac{\lambda}{\alpha} \qquad (25)$$

The scheme would not be feasible unless $\alpha > 0$; but whether or not with $\alpha > 0$ the scheme would be feasible at tolerable rates of T would depend essentially upon α being sufficiently high. Thus, suppose $\rho = 1.05, \lambda = 1.02$, and $\alpha = 0.1$. This would mean that a 10 per cent rate of tax on excess wage rates ($T = 0.1$) would be needed to moderate the percentage wage increase in any wage bargain by one percentage point ($\alpha T = 0.01$). In this case $T = 33$ per cent would keep the rate of price inflation down to 10 per cent per annum ($\bar{\pi} = 1.1$).

V

The preceding analysis suggests that the crucial question is whether the introduction of either scheme would directly moderate the wage inflation factor ω, that is to say, whether the wage-fixing equation (6) would remain unchanged or would be modified by an $\alpha > 0$. Would the mere existence of the tax rate T_{t+1} affect the setting of the wage rate W_{t+1} regardless of any effect which it might have had on the past price inflation factor π_{t-1}? What, in other words, is likely to be the effect on wage-bargaining of the mere announcement of a tax/subsidy rate on either price or wage increases?

By elimination of $W_t L_t$ between equations (2) and (3) we obtain in the absence of either Scheme A or Scheme B

$$V_t = \frac{\mu - 1}{\mu} P_t Q_t \qquad (26)$$

which expresses the profit of the firm as a proportion of its total sales on the assumption that it employs the profit-maximising mark-up for its selling price.

Similarly, elimination of $W_t L_t - T_t \eta_{t-1} P_{t-1} Q_t$ between equations (4) and (8) gives us as the maximised profit in the case of Scheme A

$$V_t = (1 - T_t) \frac{\mu - 1}{\mu} P_t Q_t \qquad (27)$$

and elimination of $W_t L_t + T_t (W_t - \eta_{t-1} W_{t-1}) L_t$ between equations (5) and (18) in the case of Scheme B gives

$$V_t = \frac{\mu - 1}{\mu} P_t Q_t \qquad (28)$$

From these three equations two important conclusions can be drawn.

In the first place, the net profit enjoyed by the firm will in all three cases be a constant proportion of the total value of its sales.

Second, this constant proportion will be the same as between Scheme B and No Scheme, whereas with Scheme A it will be only $(1 - T)$ times what it would have been with No Scheme. This is the consequence of the fact, which we already noted, that in the case of Scheme A there will be an incentive to cut the profit margin in order to avoid tax on excess price increases, an incentive that does not exist with Scheme B where there is no tax on price increases as such but only on wage increases.

The fact that with Scheme A there will be a smaller proportion of the national product going to profits could have a significant effect in moderating wage claims. We have already, in Section III, allowed for the fact that by restraining selling prices and so the rate of inflation of the cost of living it may restrain money wage claims. But an additional cause of restraint in wage-bargaining is possible if wage claims are pressed by workers and conceded by employers if profits are high, and vice versa if profits are low, quite apart from any other factors such as the level of the existing real wage or the current rate of inflation. The loss of a given amount of profit will be more serious and more strongly resisted if the total available profit is smaller. In what follows we will for this reason concentrate attention on the proportionate loss of profit resulting from a given proportionate rise in the wage rate.

From the equations (26), (27), and (28) for the level of post-tax maximised profit in the three cases, it can be seen that the effect of concession of an increased wage rate on the post-tax profit as measured by $(W_t/V_t)(dV_t/dW_t)$ is in all cases equal to the effect of the wage increase on the total value of the firm's sales, as measured by

$$\frac{W_t}{P_t Q_t} \frac{d(P_t Q_t)}{dW_t}$$

But the interpretation and the value of this term will depend critically upon the assumptions made about the institutional characteristics of the wage-bargaining procedures and about the demand-management policies of the financial authorities.

We can in all three cases assume that the individual firm, which continues to be in the same unchanged state of imperfect competition with all other firms in so far as the sale of its product is concerned, will mark up its selling prices on the occasion of a rise in its wage rate on the same unchanged principles.

With No Scheme we obtain from equation (3), with L_t/Q_t and μ constant,

$$dP_t = \mu \frac{L_t}{Q_t} dW_t \tag{29a}$$

or

$$\frac{dP_t}{P_t} = \frac{dW_t}{W_t} \tag{29b}$$

In the case of Scheme A, the employer being faced with a given T_t, μ_{t-1}, and P_{t-1} and with μ and L_t/Q_t constant, the rise in price consequent on a rise in the wage rate can be derived from equation (8) as

$$dP_t = \frac{\mu}{1 - T_t} \frac{L_t}{Q_t} dW_t \tag{30a}$$

which can be expressed as

$$\frac{dP_t}{P_t} = \left(1 + \mu \frac{T_t}{1 - T_t}\right) \frac{dW_t}{W_t} \tag{30b}$$

if we start in equation (8) from the position of a self-balancing tax/subsidy scheme with $\eta_{t-1} P_{t-1} = P_t$.

Similarly from equation (18) we can derive in the case of Scheme B

$$dP_t = (1 + T_t) \mu \frac{L_t}{Q_t} dW_t \tag{31a}$$

which can be expressed as

$$\frac{dP_t}{P_t} = (1 + T_t) \frac{dW_t}{W_t} \tag{31b}$$

If we start in equation (18) from a position of a self-balancing tax/subsidy scheme with $\eta_{t-1} W_{t-1} = W_t$.

We have now to ask by how much will the volume of sales (Q_t) fall off when, as a result of a conceded wage increase, selling prices are raised in the ways indicated in equations (29), (30), and (31)? The answer clearly depends upon what, if anything, has happened to the demand curve facing the individual firm as a result of the wage increase. If the wage increase were conceded only by the individual firm which made up a small part of an otherwise unchanged economy, the reduction in sales would be along the individual firm's unchanged demand curve with its price elasticity of ϵ_d which we have used for the expression $\mu = \epsilon_d/(1 + \epsilon_d)$. But suppose at the other extreme that the wage increase had been granted by a national wage bargain, so that all the firm's competitors would also be raising their selling prices, and that there was a reliable Orthodox Keynesian demand-management policy which ensured that the money demand for products was so raised as to maintain employment unchanged, then the quantity of sales by the individual firm would be unchanged and would be expected to be unchanged by the rises in selling prices resulting from the unchanged mark-ups on the higher wage rate. It would be as if the elasticity of a firm's demand curve *in respect of price rises due to increased wage rates*, which we henceforth denote as $\bar{\epsilon}_d$, was zero instead of ϵ_d.

From equations (26), (27), and (28) it can be seen that in all three cases money profit net of tax is a constant proportion of total sales, so that

$$\frac{dV_t}{V_t} = \frac{dQ_t}{Q_t} + \frac{dP_t}{P_t}$$

We may use the definition of $\bar{\epsilon}_d$ to write this as

$$\frac{dV_t}{V_t} = (1 + \bar{\epsilon}_d) \frac{dP_t}{P_t} \qquad (32)$$

for all three cases.

From equation (32) together with equations (29), (30), and (31) we can derive the following sets of values for dV_t/V_t and for $(dV_t/V_t) - (dP_t/P_t)$. In the case of No Scheme

and

$$\left. \begin{aligned} \frac{dV_t}{V_t} &= (1 + \bar{\epsilon}_d) \frac{dW_t}{W_t} \\[2mm] \frac{dV_t}{V_t} - \frac{dP_t}{P_t} &= \bar{\epsilon}_d \frac{dW_t}{W_t} \end{aligned} \right\} \qquad (33)$$

For Scheme A

$$\left.\begin{array}{l} \dfrac{dV_t}{V_t} = (1 + \overline{\epsilon}_d)\left(1 + \mu\,\dfrac{T_t}{1 - T_t}\right)\dfrac{dW_t}{W_t} \\[4mm] \dfrac{dV_t}{V_t} - \dfrac{dP_t}{P_t} = \overline{\epsilon}_d\left(1 + \mu\,\dfrac{T_t}{1 - T_t}\right)\dfrac{dW_t}{W_t} \end{array}\right\} \quad (34)$$

and

For Scheme B

$$\left.\begin{array}{l} \dfrac{dV_t}{V_t} = (1 + \overline{\epsilon}_d)(1 + T_t)\,\dfrac{dW_t}{W_t} \\[4mm] \dfrac{dV_t}{V_t} - \dfrac{dP_t}{P_t} = \overline{\epsilon}_d(1 + T_t)\,\dfrac{dW_t}{W_t} \end{array}\right\} \quad (35)^*$$

and

On the basis of these three sets of equations we will examine three special cases.

(i) We assume a single national wage negotiation combined with reliable Orthodox Keynesian demand-management which maintains full employment. In this case $\overline{\epsilon}_d = 0$ since there is no change in employment or output. Moreover each producer expects no change in his individual output or employment since every competing price will be raised *pari passu* with his own. The rise in price, being general, will also represent the general rise in the cost of living so that the change in real profit is represented by

$$\frac{dV_t}{V_t} - \frac{dP_t}{P_t}$$

*Making use of equations (26), (29a), and (32) we obtain for No Scheme, with $\mu - 1 = -1/(1 + \epsilon_d)$,

$$dV_t = -\frac{1 + \overline{\epsilon}_d}{1 + \epsilon_d}\,L_t dW_t$$

Making use of equations (27), (30a), and (32) we obtain for Scheme A,

$$dV_t = -\frac{1 + \overline{\epsilon}_d}{1 + \epsilon_d}\,L_t dW_t$$

Making use of equations (28), (31a), and (32) we obtain for Scheme B,

$$dV_t = -\frac{1 + \overline{\epsilon}_d}{1 + \epsilon_d}\,(1 + T_t)L_t dW_t$$

The absolute change in money profit is the same for No Scheme and for Scheme A, though the proportionate change in profit is greater for Scheme A. The absolute and proportionate change in money profit is $(1 + T_t)$ times greater for Scheme B than for No Scheme.

From equations (33), (34), and (35) it can be seen that this term will be zero, whether there is No Scheme, Scheme A, or Scheme B. Real profit will remain unchanged since in each case prices will go up in the same ratio as money costs. All that has happened is that all money prices and money costs will have gone up in the same ratio leaving all real variables unchanged. There is no reason why resistance to money wage claims should be greater with either scheme than it would be in the absence of any scheme.

(ii) Suppose, however, that there is a single national wage bargain combined with reliable New Keynesian demand-management policies so that total money expenditure, $P_t Q_t$, is going to remain unaffected by a wage concession. Since it is a national wage concession no producer need expect to be hurt any more or less than any other producer, so that each producer can expect to receive an unchanged total sales value, in which case for him $\bar{\epsilon}_d = -1$. The rise in prices will be universal so that $(dV_t/V_t) - (dP_t/P_t)$ will represent the proportionate change in real profits. From equations (33), (34), and (35) with $\bar{\epsilon}_d = -1$ we obtain

$$\frac{dV_t}{V_t} - \frac{dP_t}{P_t} = \begin{cases} -\dfrac{dW_t}{W_t} & \text{for No Scheme} \\[2em] -\left(1 + \mu \dfrac{T_t}{1 - T_t}\right)\dfrac{dW_t}{W_t} & \text{for Scheme A} \\[2em] -(1 + T_t)\dfrac{dW_t}{W_t} & \text{for Scheme B} \end{cases} \qquad (36)$$

It is clear that in this case there will be an increased incentive to resist a wage increase for both schemes compared with the situation without any scheme.

(iii) Let us assume next that the wage-bargaining is on a company level, each firm settling with its own trade union the wage rate at which it can employ as many workers as it chooses to employ. With each individual firm making up only a small part of the total economy we can assume, first, that it will be faced with the unchanged individual demand curve of elasticity ϵ_d from which $\mu - 1 = -1/(1 + \epsilon_d)$ is derived and, second, that since the prices of goods supplied by all other producers will be unaffected by its own price change, the money profit, dV_t/V_t, will represent the change in its real profit. From equations (33), (34), and (35) we now obtain, with $1 + \bar{\epsilon}_d = 1 + \epsilon_d \equiv -1/(\mu - 1)$,

$$\frac{dV_t}{V_t} = \begin{cases} -\dfrac{1}{\mu-1}\dfrac{dW_t}{W_t} & \text{with No Scheme} \\[3ex] -\dfrac{1}{\mu-1}\left(1+\mu\dfrac{T_t}{1-T_t}\right)\dfrac{dW_t}{W_t} & \text{with Scheme A} \\[3ex] -\dfrac{1}{\mu-1}(1+T_t)\dfrac{dW_t}{W_t} & \text{with Scheme B} \end{cases} \quad (37)$$

Once again it is clear that there will be a greater incentive to resist a wage claim with Scheme A or Scheme B than would be the case in the absence of any scheme.

It is of interest to compare the results in equations (37) with those in equations (36). With $\mu = 1.2$, $1/(\mu - 1) = 5$; and this means that the loss of real profit from a given proportionate wage increase would eat into real profits five times more if the wage concession were given by a single individual firm than it would if it were granted simultaneously by all competing firms against the background of a New Keynesian demand-management policy which prevented any rise in wage rates from affecting the level of total money expenditures. As compared with this, there would be no loss of real profit at all if the the wage concessions were general and given against the background of Orthodox Keynesian demand-management policies which kept the level of employment and output unaffected by wage rises.

In the real world wage negotiations lie somewhere between the two extremes of national wage negotiations and single company wage negotiations. In the case of a negotiation which covers the wages paid in all the firms in one industry but not the wages paid in other industries, the individual firm's demand curve will be raised because all the other competing firms in that industry will be raising the prices of their competing products. But the demand curve of the individual firm will not be raised as much as it would have been if the wage negotiation had been a national one. Moreover, the extent to which a rise in the sales prices of all the firms subject to a single wage negotiation will affect the general cost of living and thus the real value of the profits of the individual firm subject to the negotiation will depend upon the proportion of the total economy which is covered by the negotiation. The measure of the effect on real profit would lie somewhere between

$$\frac{dV_t}{V_t} \quad \text{and} \quad \frac{dV_t}{V_t} - \frac{dP_t}{P_t}$$

and the value of the $-\bar{\epsilon}_d$ which was relevant for those covered by the single negotiation would lie somewhere between the $-\epsilon_d$ of the single firm and $-\bar{\epsilon}_d = 0$ in the case of Orthodox Keynesian demand management or $-\bar{\epsilon}_d = 1$ in the case of New Keynesian demand management.

One can only conclude that the institution of either Scheme A or B is likely to lead to a value of $\alpha > 0$ in the wage-fixing equation (6). The actual level of α will be much affected in the ways indicated in this Section V: that is to say, by the choice of scheme, by the operative tax rates, by the extent of the various sectors of the economy which are covered by any single wage negotiation, and by the nature of the demand-management policies pursued by the financial authorities. But what the actual value of α is likely to be in any given case is a matter which this section leaves undecided, since the author of this appendix knows of no way in which its probable value can be assessed.

The Legal Background to the Restraint of Monopolistic Behaviour in the UK

This appendix contains a brief survey of the main principles of the laws restraining anti-competitive practices in the UK as they existed in 1979, when the Conservative government came into power, together with the main changes in the law resulting from the subsequent Competition Act of 1980.

There are two different forms which monopolistic, anti-competitive practices may take:

(1) They may take the form of agreements between a number of otherwise independent competing enterprises to restrict their competitive behaviour in certain ways (e.g. by agreeing not to charge prices below a certain stated level or not to produce more than a certain agreed quota of output).

(2) The market may, on the other hand, be dominated by large enterprises so that a single enterprise can itself without any agreement with other firms act in a monopolistic manner (e.g. by charging an excessively high price and restricting its output).

Controls over these two forms of anti-competitive practice are inevitably interrelated. If, for example, restrictive agreements between independent enterprises were more strictly controlled than were anti-competitive practices of a single dominant firm, there would be an incentive for independent firms to merge into a single firm in order to be freer to control prices and outputs. This suggests a possible need for a third form of control, namely, control over mergers.

In the UK these matters are subject to two separate legal regimes, the domestic law of the UK and the law of the European Community. This appendix deals with each of these regimes in turn.

A. The UK Law

The philosophy behind the UK legislation is a pragmatic one based on the belief that, while there are in general strong arguments in favour of competition, there may well be cases in which counterbalancing advantages are to be gained from monopolistic practices. This pragmatic attitude has resulted in a distinction between (1) the outlawing (under a Restrictive

Practices Court) of certain clearly defined agreements between independent producers which, because they are presumed to be against the public interest are generally prohibited, subject to certain clearly defined exceptions suitable for judicial interpretation, and (2) the assessment (under a Monopolies and Mergers Commission) on a case-by-case basis of the relative advantages and disadvantages of a particular practice by a particular single firm, without any *a priori* presumption that the public interest is best served by outlawing the particular monopolistic behaviour in question.

The UK policy also allows for the fact that it is not always sufficient to have power to control the behaviour of a dominant firm, since failure to innovate and other forms of inefficiency on the part of a monopolistic concern are hard to detect and impossible to rectify by negative controls. For this reason UK policy considers also the possibility of maintaining the competitive structure of an industry by assessment and control through the Monopolies and Mergers Commission, again on a case by case basis, of proposed mergers of independent concerns into a single enterprise.

There is an official institution, the Office of Fair Trading, served by a professional staff and headed by a Director General of Fair Trading who has extensive powers and duties in bringing matters before the Restrictive Practices Court and the Monopolies and Mergers Commission and in following up their decisions and recommendations.

(1) *The Restrictive Practices Court*

All agreements between two or more independent concerns covering transactions in goods or services and which involve restrictions concerning prices, recommended prices, terms and conditions of sales or purchases, quantities or descriptions of the products, processes of manufacture, or persons with whom or areas in which transactions may take place must be registered with the Office of Fair Trading.

All such agreements must be referred by the Director General of Fair Trading to the Restrictive Practices Court, a court which is presided over by a judge but which comprises also lay members who are experienced and knowledgeable in business matters.

The court must condemn all such restrictive practices unless they can be successfully defended by the practitioners. For a successful defence two hurdles must be surmounted. First, the court must be convinced that the agreement has one at least of a number of positive characteristics, namely: that it serves to protect the public from injury; that its removal would deny to purchasers, consumers, or users certain specific advantages; that it provides a countervailing power to the businesses concerned against a monopolistic purchaser of their products or against a monopolistic seller of the supplies which they need; that its removal would be harmful to employment or harmful to export earnings; that it is required to support some other restriction which has been judged to be desirable; or that it does not in fact materially affect competitive conditions. Second, if the Court is persuaded that the agreement satisfies one of these positive characteristics it must then go on to consider whether any detriments which may result from the agreement are such as to outweigh the satisfaction of one or more of the above conditions. Only if that is the case will the Court sanction the agreement.

Restrictive agreements are not illegal until they have been condemned by the Court; nor is it a criminal offence to fail to register a restrictive agreement which ought to have been registered. But an unregistered agreement which should have been registered or a registered agreement which has been condemned by the Court is void, so that its terms cannot be legally enforced as a contract. Civil proceedings could be taken for an injunction to put a stop to the unlawful practice and for damages by anyone who was hurt by the operation of a restrictive agreement which had improperly not been registered or which had been registered and condemned by the Court. In the latter case those who continued to operate a condemned agreement would be in contempt of court and liable to the resulting penalties.

Such is the general structure of the UK control of restrictive business practices. But there are a number of exceptions due either to the complete exemption of certain agreements from registration and control or to modifications in the requirements that they be considered for condemnation by the Court. The following is a catalogue of the sorts of agreement which, in one way or another, escape the full rigour of control:

Agreements concerning the employment of workers, which means that trade union and similar labour restrictive practices are not controlled.

Authorised agricultural marketing schemes, export agreements, and certain types of agreement protecting the use of patent rights, know-how, and trade marks.

Exclusive dealing agreements, whereby a single producer agrees with a single dealer that the producer will sell only to that dealer and the dealer will purchase only from that producer in so far as certain goods or a certain area of trade is concerned.

Agreements covering certain services and, in particular, professional and educational services; international sea transport, air transport, and road passenger transport services; and a considerable range of financial services including the borrowings and loans of building societies.

Agreements which are certified by the Secretary of State to be of substantial importance to the national economy in the promotion of efficiency or the improvement of industrial capacity.

Agreements designed to maintain authorised standards (such as standards set by the British Standards Institution; agreements between co-operative societies; agreements to hold down prices at the request of a minister; and agreements judged to have insignificant effects.

All agreements concerning coal and steel which are regulated by the European Coal and Steel Community are exempt from the UK control. For agreements in other industries the EEC law takes precedence over the UK law in the sense that the UK court must not allow what the EEC law prohibits. But it is arguable that where the EEC law is specifically less restrictive than the UK law, the UK should be able to prohibit what the EEC allows. The Director General of Fair Trading is, however, authorised in such cases not to bring the UK agreement before the UK Restrictive Practices Court, since the harmonisation of a practice throughout the community may be judged to be of greater importance than its prohibition in the UK.

(2) *The Monopolies and Mergers Commission*

In addition to the Restrictive Practices Court there is a quite separate body, namely, the Monopolies and Mergers Commission. The Restrictive Practices Court is a court of law in the full sense. Its task is to judge on the basis of the evidence supplied on the one side by the Director General of Fair Trading and on the other side by the persons defending their agreement whether in terms of the conditions laid down in the Act the agreement should be registered and, if so, whether in terms of the conditions laid down in the Act it should be condemned or not. The Monopolies and Mergers Commission is a different type of body. Its task is to investigate specific cases of business behaviour which are referred to it by the Director General of Fair Trading or by the Secretary of State in order to assess whether on a balance of considerations they involve monopolistic, anti-competitive behaviour which is against the public interest.

It is also the duty of the Director General of Fair Trading to consider the reference of proposed mergers to the Monopolies and Mergers Commission if he feels that a proposed merger raises sufficient public interest to be subject to a full investigation by the Commission. Before reaching a decision on a particular case he consults the Mergers Panel, which is a committee on which all the departments with an interest in the matter are represented.

In the case of an adverse report by the Monopolies and Mergers Commission on a practice which has been referred to it the Director General of Fair Trading will attempt to obtain an undertaking by the business concerned to change its practices appropriately; but in the absence of such an undertaking it is up to the Secretary of State ultimately to decide what action, if any, should be taken to enforce a change in the concern's behaviour. The Commission is thus not a court which is required to judge whether or not certain specific statutory provisions have been observed; but it is a body of persons, with appropriate knowledge and experience, whose task is to make a detailed investigation of the implications for the public interest of a particular business practice in a particular market situation.

Before the passage of the Competition Act of 1980 there were two important limitations to the cases which could be referred to the Commission.

First, only cases of behaviour involving a monopoly situation could be referred to the Commission; and a monopoly situation was defined as one in which the single enterprise or a group of enterprises operating together, whether by agreement or otherwise, accounted for a share of a quarter or more in the market concerned.

Second, the Director General of Fair Trading could not refer the behaviour of nationalised industries or similar public bodies to the Commission for investigation; that could be done only by the ministers concerned.

Both these restrictions have been removed by the Competition Act of 1980. The behaviour of an individual enterprise, even if it commands less than one quarter of the relevant market, may now be investigated by the Director General of Fair Trading and ultimately, if necessary, referred to the Monopolies and Mergers Commission in order to decide whether it is operating an anti-competitive practice and, if so, whether its effects are against the public interest. This covers both public and private sectors. In addition the Commission may now be asked to investigate the efficiency and costs, service, or abuse of monopoly by nationalised industries and similar public bodies, though the Commission may not question the appropriateness of any financial restrictions or objectives which have been given to the concern by enactment or by the appropriate minister.

Restrictive practices concerning labour, while they are exempt from control by the Restrictive Practices Court, can be referred for investigation to the Monopolies and Mergers Commission provided that they are not the subject of a current industrial dispute. The Commission has the duty of stating whether the practice exists and what, if any, of its effects are against the public interest; but the Commission is not required to consider remedies and the government has not taken power to control such practices. In fact no reference of this kind has been made to the Commission.

In the case of other references the Secretary of State has, ultimately, extensive power by the issue of orders to correct any action which the Commission reports to be against the public interest. He can make it unlawful: to carry out specified agreements; or to withhold supplies from specified potential customers; or to refuse to supply one type of product unless other products are also purchased; or to discriminate in the prices charged to different customers; or to charge prices which depart from a published price list; or to give preferential treatment to certain customers. He may require the publication of prices and he may regulate the prices to be charged if the Monopolies and Mergers Commission has specified prices as ruling against the public interest. Normally these powers are kept in the background and used only as an ultimate sanction if it has proved impossible to negotiate an undertaking by the enterprise in question to modify its operations in such a way as to meet the Commission's criticisms. In addition, there are powers to break up a monopoly supplier, though these powers have in fact never been used.

Proposed mergers between one enterprise and another can also be referred to the Commission for investigation if the value of the assets to be transferred from the one ownership to the other exceeds £15 million or if the transfer of ownership would create or enhance a monopoly situation, defined as a situation in which the new single concern would command a share of a quarter or more of the market for the products concerned. If such a merger is considered by the Commission to be against the public interest, the Secretary of State can by order prohibit the merger.

In judging whether a monopolistic, anti-competitive practice, or a merger is against the public interest the Commission may take into account anything which it considers relevant but, in particular, it must consider: the desirability of maintaining competition; the interests of consumers and users in respect of the prices charged and the quality and variety of supplies; the desirability of promoting through competition the reduction of costs and the development of new techniques and new products; the maintenance of a balanced distribution of production and employment in the various regions of the UK; and the maintenance and promotion of competitive activity in markets outside the UK. Other matters which the Commission has in fact taken into account in its assessment of the public interest include efficiency, the balance of payments, employment, industrial relations, the desirability of the largest company in an industry remaining in UK ownership, and the possibility of a UK industry being subject to the other interests of a foreign holding company.

(3)   *Resale Price Maintenance*

The procedures of the Restrictive Practices Court and of the Monopolies and Mergers Commission differ in many important respects, but they both allow for the fact that an anti-competitive practice may be found on balance not to be against the public interest in the particular circumstances of the case. In no case do they proceed by making a particular arrangement illegal in all cases irrespective of any judgement or investigation by Court or Commission. There is, however, one exception to this general treatment of monopolistic, anti-competitive practices in UK law. Resale price maintenance — that is to say, action taken by suppliers to cut off supplies to any dealer who sells the product at retail at a price below that which is set by the supplier — is illegal, whether the prices are maintained by agreed action between the suppliers acting jointly or by the action of an individual producer. Under the relevant statute it is possible for particular products to be exempt from the prohibition of resale price maintenance; such exemptions have been granted only in respect of the sale of books and pharmaceutical products.

(4)   *The Price Commission*

Before the passage of the Competition Act of 1980, in addition to the Restrictive Practices Court and the Monopolies and Mergers Commission, there existed a Price Commission which, under the Price Commission Act of 1977, operated in the following way. Price increases by major concerns in both the public and private sectors had to be notified in advance to the Price Commission; and the Price Commission had the power to investigate price increases, prices, and profit margins of individual enterprises whether or not these were subject to prenotification by major concerns. In general, prices were frozen during the period of the Commission's investigation, but the Commission had discretion to grant interim price increases and (until the obligation was removed by an Amendment Act in 1979) it was required to grant such interim price increases to the extent necessary to permit certain minimum profit margins. The Commission could make recommendations to the Secretary of State who could decide whether to impose restrictions on the enterprise's prices or profit margins for a period up to twelve months. The Secretary of State was not obliged to accept the Price Commission's recommendations but could not be more restrictive than the Commission had recommended. The Commission could also make observations on conduct which could be followed up in negotiation between the Secretary of State and the company or industry concerned.

The Secretary of State could order the Commission to examine any behaviour by a group of more than one supplier relating to the group's prices or charges, with similar powers to impose restrictions. In this case the restrictions could be continued for any length of time provided they were approved by Parliament for any period in excess of twelve months.

In making its recommendations the Price Commission was instructed to have regard to all matters relevant to restraining prices in so far as this was compatible with the making of adequate profits by efficient suppliers and in particular to take into account: the need of a business to recover costs incurred in efficiently supplying goods and to maintain the value of its assets; the encouragement of cost reductions and the securing of consequential price reductions; the need for profits sufficient to cover the costs of capital and to provide funds for innovation and technical progress; the need to take account of inflation in determining the value of assets; the maintenance of the quality of supplies and the satisfaction of the demands of the users of products; the need to safeguard the interests of users by promoting competition or (where competition was not possible) by restricting prices and charges; the maintenance of a balance between supply and demand for products; the avoidance of detriment to the balance of payments through price restrictions; and the need to increase the share of UK enterprises in the UK and in other markets.

The Price Commission was abolished by the Competition Act of 1980. The Conservative ministers made it clear that they had no intention of maintaining any system of price control, but rather would rely on the encouragement of the forces of competition. The Competition Act of 1980 merely enabled the Secretary of State to request the Director General of Fair Trading to make a price investigation in the case of any price that was of major public concern; but it did not confer on the Secretary of State any powers to enforce any price restrictions which might appear desirable in the light of the investigation. The already existing powers of the Monopolies and Mergers Commission to consider the setting of prices by any concern that was referred to it for report, and of the Secretary of State consequently to regulate a monopoly's prices, remained unchanged.

B.   EEC Law

The EEC law has the same twofold division as the UK law. It regulates both restrictive agreements between independent enterprises (Article 85 of the Treaty of Rome) and also abuses of monopoly power by single concerns (Article 86 of the Treaty). Under the UK law, as explained above, there is no *a priori* presumption that anti-competitive practices by single concerns are against the public interest, which is assessed on the merits of each case by the Monopolies and Mergers Commission; there is such a presumption in the case of certain restrictive agreements between independent concerns, but even in this case the Restrictive Practices Court can, over a fairly wide range of circumstances, judge that the public interest is best served by the continuation of the restrictive practices. In contrast to this the EEC law simply bans practices which impede competition and affect trade between the member countries; and this means that a practice is *ipso facto* illegal without being subject to any previous examination and condemnation. Subject to appeal to the European Court, the Commission of the EEC is the body which decides whether a particular practice does offend Article 85 or 86 of the Rome Treaty; and it has powers to levy fines on those who infringe its decisions.

(1)   *Restrictive Agreements*
Article 85 of the Rome Treaty prohibits agreements between enterprises which both impede competition and affect trade between the EEC countries, with special reference to agreements which fix prices or conditions of sale, limit production, share markets, discriminate, or make contracts subject to supplementary obligations which are not directly relevant to the transaction in question. Any such contracts are void and

cannot be enforced by the courts. The Commission has powers, subject to appeal to the European Court, to order an undertaking to cease an infringement of the Article.

Exemptions from this banning of such agreements can be granted by the Commission if the agreement concerned has been notified to it and if it is agreed that the restriction will lead to a substantial improvement in the trade concerned, provided that arrangements are such that the consumers will enjoy an adequate share of the resulting advantages. The Commission can grant block exemptions from control for certain broad classes of restrictive agreements. It has already done so in two cases, subject to limitations which ensure that trade between the EEC countries is not prevented, namely, in the case of (1) exclusive dealings (whereby supplier A sells only to dealer B who purchases only from supplier A) and (2) specialisation agreements (whereby A undertakes not to produce product X and B not to produce product Y, so that A can enjoy economies from specialising in Y and B those from specialising in X). There is also under consideration a possible third block exemption to cover legitimate forms of agreements restricting the use of patent rights.

(2) *Monopolies and Mergers*

Article 86 prohibits the abusive use of its market powers by any undertaking which enjoys a dominant market position and which thereby affects the trade between the member countries. Abusive use of such powers is described as consisting, in particular, in setting unfair prices or conditions, limiting production to the detriment of consumers, applying dissimilar treatments to similar transactions, or making the conclusion of a contract subject to the acceptance of other obligations which are not relevant to the transaction in question. As in the case of Article 85, so also in the case of this Article 86, the Commission can order an undertaking to cease any infringement which it has been judged to be making of the above provisions.

The EEC Treaty contains no specific reference to the control of mergers, but a merger could be controlled if it were judged to constitute an abuse of a dominant market position.

C.   The Relation between EEC and UK Law

The EEC law must be observed in the UK courts. In fact the objectives of the two sets of laws are very similar, as can be seen from the preceding survey, and there is little serious conflict between their results. There are cases in which the EEC treatment may be more restrictive than the UK treatment (e.g. in regard to the permitted restrictions on the use of patent rights), in which case the EEC restriction must clearly be enforced in the UK court. But there are other possible cases (e.g. in regard to the EEC block exemption of specialisation agreements which enjoy no such general exemption under the UK law) in which the UK law is more restrictive than the EEC law; and it is not clear whether it would be illegal for the UK to prohibit an arrangement which the EEC law sanctions. However, as has been stated above, the Director General of Fair Trading in the UK has the power to refrain from referring any agreements to the Restrictive Practices Court for possible condemnation if such agreements are expressly authorised as being legitimate under EEC law.

While there is little or no serious conflict of ultimate result under the two legal systems, there are, as has already been indicated, great differences of procedure. Under UK law in general no practice is illegal until it has been condemned either by the Restrictive Practices Court (in which case it is judged not simply by the effect of the particular restriction in the particular market conditions but in terms of a set of fairly precise statutory criteria concerning its form by the normal adversary procedures of a court of law) or by the Monopolies and Mergers Commission (in which case it is subject to an investigation by experts of the particular market conditions, to an impartial assessment of the general public interest, and ultimately to an *ad hoc* ministerial decision). Under EEC law the practice must generally be judged by the effects of the particular practice in the particular market concerned. This means that in all cases (except for the block exemptions given under Article 85) a detailed market investigation and assessment is desirable. However in appeals to the European Court and in decisions about EEC obligations in the UK courts, decisions which ideally need detailed expert market investigation and assessment must be taken through normal adversary court proceedings.

APPENDIX E

Further Problems of Labour Co-operatives and Capital–Labour Partnerships

The discussion in Chapter IX has been confined to those basic features of different forms of labour participation in management and ownership which are most relevant to the question whether these institutional forms provide a cure of the evils of stagflation, that is to say, whether they provide both a relaxation of excessive upward pressure on money wage costs and also, at the same time, a means of promoting full employment. There are, however, a number of other problems which arise in the operation of these forms of institutional participation by the worker which are less directly concerned with their effect on the problems of stagflation but which are nevertheless indirectly concerned, since their solution is necessary for the general effective working of these institutions and thus indirectly for their effective working as remedies for stagflation. This appendix is devoted to a brief discussion of the most important of these remaining problems.

Problem I. How would (a) a labour co-operative or (b) a capital–labour partnership deal with any part of its (a) earned surplus or (b) net value added which it ploughed back into the business without distributing it to (a) the members or (b) the shareholders?

(a) *Labour Co-operatives*

The purchase of a new machine by a co-operative should be to the advantage of all the members if the discounted cash flow from the machine (using the rate of interest at which it could borrow funds) were greater than the cost of the machine. The funds for the purchase of the machine could come from the issue of new debt or the use of the accumulation of past depreciation funds. But it might be necessary for the concern to finance capital development by ploughing back part of its earned surplus in those cases in which it had difficulty in borrowing additional funds on the market, provided that its own members were convinced of the profitability of the new investment at the rate of return that was attractive to them.

This possibility would raise no great problem if the membership of the co-operative were unchanging not only in size but also in individual persons who made up the membership. But consider a case in which elderly Mr Smith is about to reach retiring age, while young Mr Brown has just joined the co-operative. If part of this year's earned surplus is ploughed back into the concern, Mr Brown will gain from the future yield of the machine at the expense of Mr Smith who will lose part of his share of this year's earned surplus.

For this reason, if some part of earned surplus were ploughed back into the business, new debt should be issued at some acceptable rate of interest to all the existing members to represent that part of each member's earnings which had been retained in the co-operative. If this solution were adopted, it would be reasonable to allow members to sell their holdings of the co-operative debt to outsiders to enable the members to spread their risks by investing their capital in a different enterprise from their work.

(b)   *Capital–Labour Partnership*

Precisely similar problems arise in the case of a capital–labour partnership except that in this case the retained net value added would be distributed in capital shares *pro rata* to all shareholders, whether capitalist or workers.

Problem II.   Should (a) a labour co-operative's or (b) a capital–labour partnership's capital gains be added to (and capital losses be subtracted from) the computation of (a) the earned surplus or (b) the net value added?

(a)   *Labour Co-operatives*

If any part of the earned surplus that was ploughed back into the business was offset by the issue of new debt to the members of the co-operative, then the total debt would remain equal to the total accumulated investment in fixed capital. Any repayment of debt to outsiders would come out of the earned surplus and would thus be offset by the issue of new debt to the insiders. But how should an unexpected capital gain or loss on the co-operative's assets be treated?*

If the capital gain were included in the year's income (i.e. were included in the earned surplus), then it would have to be offset by an equivalent increase in the issue of new debt to the members of the partnership unless it were realised and distributed to them. Conversely, a capital loss would either have to be offset by a reduced payment of earnings to each member or offset by a cancellation of debt due by the co-operative to its members or an actual incurring of debt by the members to the co-operative. In this latter case members might on retirement find not that the co-operative owed money to them but they owed money to the co-operative.

The alternative would be not to include capital gains and losses in the

---

*The estimation of capital gains and losses as well as of the depreciation allowances for the calculation of the earned surplus raises the familiar problems of inflation accounting, since it is the co-operative's income and capital in real terms with which the members should be concerned. These issues are not considered in this book.

computation of the earned surplus. In this case there would once again be some degree of unfairness between old and young members or between present and future members. Capital gains made as a result of this year's enterprise would be to the advantage not of this year's members but of the members in future years. Or capital losses made this year would have to be made good eventually out of the productive efforts and the earned surplus of future years.

(b) *Capital–Labour Partnerships*

Similar problems exist, but with the very important difference that any capital gain or loss, if included in the current year's net value added, would not accrue only to the workers but to all shareholders, that is, to all workers and capitalists in the business. The risks of gain and loss would be much more widely spread and the problems of inclusion of capital gains and losses in the year's income would be *pro tanto* less severe.

Problem III.   Should the management of a co-operative or partnership be able to dismiss from the concern workers who wish to remain members of it?

Problem IV.   Should members of a co-operative or partnership be free to leave the co-operative or partnership even if that would be against the interest of the remaining members?

(a) *Labour Co-operatives*

As has been argued in Chapter IX, the existing members will gain from an increase in the size of the membership of an egalitarian labour co-operative if the earnings per member (EM) is less than the marginal revenue product of a worker (MRP). EM is what will be paid to the new members; MRP is what he adds to the earned surplus; if $MRP > EM$, there is a bonus to be distributed over the whole membership. Conversely, if $EM > MRP$ the remaining members would gain if one of their members were to leave the co-operative, that is to say, the remaining members would save in distribution (EM) more than the loss in the net revenue of (MRP).

But an individual worker would wish to join or to remain in the co-operative if the EM were greater than what he could earn outside the co-operative (OE). Conversely he would be unwilling to join and, if a member, would want to quit if $EM < OE$.

The co-operative is thus confronted with the six following possible situations:

(1) $MRP > EM > OE$
(2) $OE > EM > MRP$
(3) $EM > OE > MRP$
(4) $EM > MRP > OE$

(5) $MRP > OE > EM$
(6) $OE > MRP > EM$

Situations (1) and (2) do not give rise to any serious conflicts of interest. In situation (1) it is to the advantage both of the existing members ($MRP > EM$) and of any new recruits ($EM > OE$) that the membership should be expanded. In situation (2) it is to the advantage both of the remaining members ($MRP < EM$) and of any members who leave ($EM < OE$) that the membership should contract.

But in the remaining four situations there is a clear conflict of interest.

In situations (3) and (4) there is an advantage to individual members to remain in the co-operative, and indeed for individual outsiders to join the co-operative ($EM > OE$), but there is an advantage to any remaining members that individuals far from joining should in fact leave the co-operative ($EM > MRP$).

This situation is of the kind discussed in Chapter IX in connection with Table III; and it raises the question whether the management of the labour co-operative should be able to dismiss working members against the wishes of those members in the interests of the remaining members. In an egalitarian labour co-operative it would seem anomalous that the management should have the power of dismissing members who were unwilling to leave. To have this power means that all the workers are not treated equally. Some (e.g. the latest recruits) would not have the same security of tenure as the others.

But a better solution might be found if the egalitarian principle were abandoned. In situation (3) what the members of a co-operative stand to gain by a reduction, or to lose by an increase, in the size of the membership is $EM - MRP$. What the individual stands to gain by being allowed to join the co-operative or to lose by being dismissed from the co-operative is $EM - OE$. Thus in situation (3) with $OE > MRP$ the existing members ought to be able to bribe an individual existing member to leave by an annual payment B_3 where

$$EM - OE < B_3 < EM - MRP$$

Conversely in situation (4) with $OE < MRP$ an outsider should be able to buy his way in to the co-operative by an annual payment B_4 where

$$EM - OE > B_4 > EM - MRP$$

But this solution really offends against the egalitarian principle. In situation (3) the 'dismissed' member is being paid $OE + B_3$ which is greater than the EM of the remaining members; and in situation (4) the newly recruited member would be being paid a reward equal to $EM - B_4$, while the previously recruited members would be being paid EM.

In situations (5) and (6) the conflict is of the opposite kind, where individuals would be unwilling to join and desirous of leaving the co-operative (OE > EM), whereas the remaining members of the co-operative would gain by an expansion and lose by a contraction of the membership (MRP > EM).*

It would seem clear that the co-operative could not force unwilling outsiders to join the co-operative. But whether or not individual members should be free to leave the co-operative at the cost of leaving the reduced number of remaining members with the liability of meeting the whole of the burden of fixed interest and rent is a very real and difficult question. If it were possible, the position of a co-operative that was not doing well could be very unstable. Some members would be able to move out to other occupations more easily than others. As they moved out the fixed interest burden would be more concentrated and the EM would fall still further below OE for the remaining members. Others might then move out. The process could go on until the fixed interest absorbed the whole of the net value added so that EM was reduced to zero.

The alternative rule would be that a member could leave the co-operative only with the permission of the remaining members. What the individual stands to gain by leaving the co-operative or to lose by having to join it is OE − EM. What the remaining members of the co-operative stand to gain by recruiting a member or to lose by losing a member is MRP − EM. Thus in situation (5) it should be possible to arrange for a payment B_5 from the existing members to a new recruit which would induce the new recruit to join the co-operative or to an existing member to persuade him to stay, where

$$OE - EM < B_5 < MRP - EM$$

And in situation (6) it should be possible to arrange a payment B_6 to the co-operative by any individual member who wished to leave, sufficient to induce the existing members to release him, where

$$OE - EM > B_6 > MRP - EM$$

But once again rules of this kind imply that members are not always treated equally. Thus the solution in situation (5) would imply that one member was paid EM + B_5 while others received only EM. Moreover, any such arrangements might well undermine morale by encouraging individual members to threaten to leave, simply in order to bargain for specially favourable treatment.

*This is the sort of situation which could rise from a deterioration in the market price at which the co-operative's product could be sold. Because of the fixed cost of interest and rent the earned surplus might well fall in much greater proportion than the MRP so that EM fell below MRP.

(b)   *Capital—Labour Partnership*

Similar problems arise with the important difference that it would be much easier to allow working partners complete freedom to leave the partnership if they so desired, since any loss to the partnership would be shared among all shareholders, that it, among those who had provided the capital as well as among the workers, and would no longer fall exclusively on the remaining workers.

Problem V.   How would differentials be set between the earnings of workers in (a) a labour co-operative and (b) a capital—labour partnership?

(a)   *Labour Co-operatives*

It will probably be recognised that such differentials (e.g. between skilled and unskilled workers) should exist. If so, two questions arise. First, how should the members of the co-operative decide what the differentials should be? Second, given a set of differentials, how will that affect the operation of the co-operative?

We will first consider the second of these equations and then, in the light of the effect of a given set of differentials, consider on what principles the differentials should be set.

Consider then a case in which there are three different grades of labour, 1, 2, and 3, with N_1, N_2, and N_3 representing the number of members of the co-operative in each grade. The easiest way to think of the effect on the distribution of the earned surplus of a differential in payment in which a member in grade 2 is paid twice as much as a member in grade 1 is to imagine the same payment being made for each unit of 'effective work' done and to assume that an hour's work by a grade 2 worker is twice as 'effective' as an hour's work by a grade 1 worker. We can then allot to each grade a multiplier, α_1, α_2, α_3 such that $\alpha_1 N_1$, $\alpha_2 N_2$, and $\alpha_3 N_3$ represent the number of units of 'effective work' produced by grades 1, 2, and 3, respectively. The absolute values of the α's are immaterial; all that matters is the relationship between them. Thus if $\alpha_3/\alpha_2 = 1.5$, an individual in grade 3 is treated as producing 50 per cent more 'effective work' than a worker in grade 2 and will accordingly be paid 50 per cent more. We can then calculate an average earning per unit of 'effective work' done, namely, $\overline{EM}$ where

$$\overline{EM} = \text{the earned surplus} \div (\alpha_1 N_1 + \alpha_2 N_2 + \alpha_3 N_3)$$

The payment to a worker in grade 1, 2, or 3 will then be $EM_1 = \alpha_1 \overline{EM}$, $EM_2 = \alpha_2 \overline{EM}$, and $EM_3 = \alpha_3 \overline{EM}$, respectively.

In considering the question whether it would pay the other members of the co-operative to take on more or to dismiss existing workers in any one grade, we can apply an analysis similar to that used for a single body of homogeneous workers in discussing Problems III and IV. Each grade of labour will be making its own marginal contribution to the co-operative, that is, will have its own MRP. It will pay all the members in the co-operative to increase or to decrease by one individual the members in grade 1 according as $EM_1 \lessgtr MRP_1$. The individual in question will want to be a member or not to be a member according as $EO_1 \lessgtr EM_1$. And similarly for the other grades.

We turn then to the question on what principles the differentials represented by the α's should be set. The easiest way to think of the problems involved in this decision is to imagine a labour co-operative with a set of differentials which is fully satisfactory to everybody, and then to imagine a change in circumstances that will introduce a conflict of interest among the members of the co-operative. Suppose then that we start with the happy state of affairs in which $OE_1 = EM_1 = MRP_1$ for grade 1 workers; and similarly for workers in all other grades. In each grade no individual wishes to leave or to join the co-operative, and in the case of each grade there is no advantage to the other members that there should be any change of numbers in that grade. Suppose then that there is a change in technology which causes MRP_1 to rise and MRP_2 to fall (e.g. typists could do much of the work of skilled compositors). It will be to the advantage of the membership of the co-operative as a whole to reduce numbers in grade 2 and to increase numbers in grade 1; it will be to the advantage of outside grade 1 workers to join if the differential α_1 is raised; it will not be to the advantage of workers in grade 2 to leave; but the disadvantage to the membership as a whole of maintaining the numbers in grade 2 would be reduced if the differential α_2 were reduced.

This example serves to illustrate the fact that the setting in a labour co-operative of differentials between grades of labour raises the same fundamental questions as those discussed in connection with Problems III and IV. Do the other members have the right to dismiss redundant workers in grade 2? Or do they have the right to reduce the differential paid to workers in grade 2 below the level that was previously agreed between all the members to be appropriate? Or do existing members in grade 2 have an inalienable right until age of retirement to work in the co-operative at the originally agreed rates of differential in the distribution of the earned surpluses?

One possible set of solutions to these problems raises just the same issue as was discussed in connection with Problems III and IV, namely, whether or not the co-operative is prepared to abandon the egalitarian principle and to contemplate situations in which workers of the same grade are employed simultaneously at different rates of earnings. If, for example, in the case examined above it were the rule that the unwanted members in grade 2 could not be dismissed, it might be possible to bribe them to leave for outside employment. Or, failing that, it would be possible to let the members in grade 2 run down by retirement. But as this happened would it be legitimate to replace some of the retired members in grade 2 with new recruits in grade 2 but at a lower differential, α_2, than had previously been applied to the workers in grade 2? If the technological change affected grade 2 workers throughout industry, it might well be that the OE_2 of grade 2 workers had fallen and that new grade 2 workers would gladly join the co-operative at a lower differential than previously. But if the pre-existing members in grade 2 had the right to continue in employment at the old and higher differential, this would mean old and new grade 2 members working side by side at different rates of earnings.

In fact the change requires the substitution of grade 1 for grade 2 workers. This calls for a fall in the price of grade 2 relative to the price of grade 1 workers. If the egalitarian principle is abandoned the substitution might take place in a labour co-operative by applying it to new members but not to old members. It could be argued that the existing members in grades 1 and 2 had agreed to share on old differentials α_1 and α_2 and should continue to do so, although new recruits in grade 1 will be offered a better α_1 and in grade 2 a lower α_2. But in this case will it be ruled that, except on terms agreeable to the other members of the co-operative, existing members in grade 1 are not free to leave the co-operative, simply because they no longer like the old terms and that the old members in grade 2 cannot be dismissed or have their earnings cut simply because their fellow members now find that they are overpaid? If it were considered necessary to allow grade 1 workers to leave without any penalty, it might well be necessary to raise the α_1 and so the EM_1 of existing grade 1 members in order to retain their services. If at the same time it were considered necessary to maintain the α_2 and so the EM_2 of grade 2 workers, the substitution would involve an additional charge on the other members who would have to finance the increased EM_1 without any off-setting reduction in the EM_2.

A rule that existing members could retain their original shares would have one great advantage. It should mean that many of the demarcation rules and other restrictive labour practices would be dissolved; if any existing member was in any case entitled to retain his existing holding of shares he, like everyone else, would only gain by being willing himself, and by allowing every other partner, to work freely and without restriction at any task in the partnership which offered the highest MRP. But, as we have argued, this would have to be combined with arrangements which allowed new recruits to be taken on on terms that were not necessarily as favourable as those that applied to existing members, the value of whose special skills had, for example, been eroded by technical progress. This means that conflict would arise if any group of workers felt that the special restrictive demarcation rules attaching to their work should be maintained in the interests of the future members of their 'guild' — if, for example, existing compositors felt that their skilled tasks must be protected from inroads by other types of worker not in their own interests (since their own shareholdings would not be at risk) but in the interest of the future earnings of their sons on whose entrance to their 'guild' they had been relying.

(b) *Capital—Labour Partnership*

The problems of differentials for different grades of labour are essentially the same for capital—labour partnerships as they are for labour co-operatives.

In connection with Problems III, IV and V it is worth noting that even if the egalitarian principle is not abandoned, the necessary adjustment in the economy could still be brought about if it was easy for new competing co-operatives or partnerships to be formed to undercut the old existing co-operatives.

Thus consider the case of a co-operative in which $OE < MRP < EM$. The outside individual would be better off in the co-operative ($OE < EM$), but the existing members will not want to accept him ($EM > MRP$). The outsider can hope to improve on his low OE *either* by being accepted into the existing co-operative at a reward EM', such that $OE < EM' < MRP < EM$, *or* alternatively by finding a number of similar disadvantaged individuals and setting up a new competing co-operative to take advantage of the conditions which allow the existing co-operative to afford so high an EM.

Or consider the case of a change of technology which in any given co-operative has raised the MRP_1 of grade 1 workers and lowered that of grade 2 workers, so that $EM_1 < MRP$ and $EM_2 > MRP_2$. The situation can be put right *either* (i) by the existing co-operative, while maintaining the EM_1 and EM_2 for existing workers, taking on new grade 1 workers at a reward higher than EM_1 and taking on any new recruits in grade 2 at a reward lower than EM_2 *or* (ii) by grade 2 workers, who can no longer find employment at EM_2, and grade 1 workers, who want to earn more than EM_1, getting together and setting up a new competing co-operative.

Problem VI.   In what conditions would workers qualify for employment benefit in an economy consisting of (a) labour co-operatives or (b) capital—labour partnership?

(a) *Labour Co-operatives*

Members of such a co-operative are self-employed. If they leave their work in the co-operative, in what circumstances will they qualify for unemployment benefit? Consider a case in which the market turns against a labour co-operative to such an extent that some of the workers in the co-operative are receiving an income which has fallen very low. Will they be free to leave their work (having in effect lost their livelihood in their present occupation) and to claim unemployment benefit? It would seem right and proper that when a worker's income in a co-operative fell below a certain figure he should be free to leave and to take unemployment benefit. But could all persons who left a co-operative take unemployment benefit?

In short could unemployment benefit (UB) be counted as an alternative outside earning (OE) available to any worker in a labour co-operative?

It is helpful to consider the position in a capitalist-entrepreneurial regime. Suppose that in such a concern MRP < UB so that the worker would be dismissed if any wage equal to or greater than UB were demanded. It would appear very reasonable to treat it as a case of loss of job which qualified for UB.

Consider then the implications of adopting in a regime of labour co-operatives the criterion that UB should be available for any worker who could not find or be placed in a job in which MRP > UB. If the regime was not based on the egalitarian principle and if the unemployed were always anxious to take any job in which their earnings (EM) would be greater than the unemployment benefit (UB), it would then be possible to treat UB simply as a full-back OE which any worker could choose if he so desired. For if UB < MRP the employment of the worker in the co-operative will lead to an excess of income of MRP − UB which can be divided between the new member and the existing members. It will be to the advantage of all concerned to employ the new member.

The limited problem of the work-shy would remain. It is possible that a situation would arise in which UB < MRP but UB > MRP − D where D is the excess of reward in work over income out of work which the work-shy would require to induce him to work. This limited problem is similar to that encountered in a capitalist-entrepreneurial regime. Would those administering the system of unemployment benefit have sufficient evidence to ensure that UB was not paid to anyone to whom the offer of an equivalent or higher EM in an existing co-operative was available?

The problem is, however, not quite so straightforward if the egalitarian principle was adopted in the regime of labour co-operatives. A situation can well arise in which EM < UB < MRP (cf. situation (5) on page 220 above). Such a situation might be one in which a labour co-operative was being built up. The existing membership is small relatively to the capital that, for reasons of economies of scale, has to be installed. The EM is thus low because of the heavy debt per member. An expansion of the membership may bring success. It would not be feasible for the administrators of unemployment benefit directly to measure the MRPs of different concerns; and even if they could, it would not be reasonable to insist on a worker giving up his UB for a lower EM.

There are only two possible solutions. The first is to rely on the possibility of new members being attracted to give up their UB for the low EM on the expectation of a much higher future EM as the co-operative developed. The second, more probable and perhaps more sensible, solution is the abandonment of the egalitarian principle and the employment of more workers either as wage hands at a fixed wage (W) or as members with an earnings equivalent to W, such that EM < UB < W < MRP.

(b)   *Capital-Labour Partnership*
The same analysis applies.

Index

Advisory, Conciliation and Arbitration Service (ACAS), and enforcement of terms of employment 77
  function 81
  and trade union bargaining 67
Agricultural Wages Boards 61
agricultural workers, movement of redundant 40
agriculture, effect of productivity increases in 40
alternative accommodation, difficulty of 42
anti-competitive practices, forms of 207
arbitral bodies, *see* Advisory, Conciliation and Arbitration Service *and* Central Arbitration Service
  for pay disputes 158
arbitral body, and employment-promotion criteria 158
  need for a single 110–12
arbitration, not-quite-compulsory 108–18
  promotion of employment through 108–10
Australia, wage-fixing in 104

balancing conditions against pay 38
blacking by workers in trade disputes 75–6, 79, 82
bonus payments 101
breach of contract, action against 76
  civil proceedings for damages 81, 82

capital gains and losses of labour co-operatives 218–19
  of capital-labour partnerships 219
capital intensive production technology 126
capitalists, admission to capital-labour partnerships 137
capitalist-entrepreneurial concerns, control of monopolistic action 123–4, 125
  and expansion 132
capital-labour partnerships, admission of capitalists to 137
  and conflicts 135
  differentials in 135
    setting 225

management and dismissal of workers 219–22
members dismissed or leaving 219–22
problems of 217–26
qualification for employment benefit 225–6
central arbitral body, disputes under 105
  terms of pay award 105
Central Arbitration Committee (CAC) 61, 67, 77, 81
Central Bank, and the gold standard 24–5
  responsibilities 10
central redundancy fund, employers' rights 63
centralised, income policy 98–109
  wage-fixing 100–2
  wage guidance 98–100
closed shop 64
  post-entry and pre-entry 68, 69, 70, 94, 157
  statutory provisions 67–70
Codes of Practice in labour relations 70
collective agreement terms, enforcement of 78
collective bargaining 67, 109
  and redundancies 67
  in wage-fixing 61
company-by-company wage bargaining 150
comparability, principle of 38
  of rates of pay 37–9
compensation, redundancy 63
  for unfair dismissal 66
Competition Act (1980) 207, 210, 213, 214
competition, to control profit margins 159
  EEC law regarding 214
  forces of, and the free-enterprise system 44
  imperfect, in wage-fixing 44
conflicts between labour and capital 135
contracts of employment, lay-offs and short-time 63
  and service 58–61

contracts of employment *contd.*
    statutory provisions affecting 61−6
co-operatives, *see* labour co-operatives
cost inflation eroding profits 17−18
cost of living, effect of oil prices on 28
    wages and 33−5
        to maintain 15
cost-push inflation, fiscal devices for
    control of 188−205
Cousins, Frank 31

demand, stimulating 23
demand-management policies 8, 9, 10,
    11, 155
    and wage settlements 182−7
    techniques and stimulation of the
        economy 25
    and wage-fixing 21−6
Department of Employment and redun-
    dancies 64, 67
Depression of 1930, conditions in
    22−3
differential(s), problems 135
    setting in labour co-operatives and
        capital-labour partnerships 222−5
Director General of Fair Trading 96,
    208, 210, 211, 213, 216
distribution of income, measures for
    influencing 18
domestic expenditures, control of 7−9

earned incomes 32
earned surplus, problem of 217−18
    of labour co-operatives 119, 122,
        123, 124
economic growth and prosperity, period
    of 24
economy, and stagflation 1
    UK (1970s) 153
egalitarian labour co-operatives 219
    expansion problem 132n
    principle, implications of 124−6,
        128, 129
employee, dismissal of non-union 64−5
    claim for damages for unfair dismissal
        66
employer(s), and closed shop 67−70
    and employee terms of contract 60
    and information to trade union 67
    monopolistic and monopsonistic
        powers 48, 49, 52, 91
        measures for reducing 56
employers' associations, funds exempt
    from claims 72
    officials legal action against 72−3

employment, benefit, qualification for
    in labour co-operatives 225−6
    conditions for 94
    continuity of 63
    effect of high and stable level of 9
    expansion of 132
    full 3, 7
    individual contracts of 58−61
    promotion of 11
        through arbitration 108−10
        wage award for 106, 107
        wage rate adjustment 185
Employment Act (1980) 67, 68, 69,
    70, 74, 80, 93
    and dismissal of employee 64−5,
        66
    and picketing 78, 79
    and trade union immunity 73
Employment Appeal Tribunal 80
Employment Policy White Paper for
    full employment 24
energy, industrial, reduction needed 29
European Coal and Steel Community
    210
European Court 216
    appeal to on restrictive practices 214
European Economic Community (EEC)
    law for monopolistic behaviour
        214−15
    precedence in law 210
    relations between UK law and
        215−16
Exchequer, Chancellor of, policy
    dilemma 4
expansion, of demand 25
    to mop up unemployed 131, 132
expected-price-inflation factor 176

Fair Wages Resolution 78
family allowances 86
financial restraint policy 12
fiscal devices for the control of cost-
    push inflation 188−205
fringe benefits 102, 140
    as wage increases 148
full employment 3, 7, 8
    meaning of 13−15
    rate of unemployment (FERU) 15

Germany, economic policy 4
    inflation in (1920s) 1−2
Gold Standard 25
government fiscal policy and cost of
    living 34
    intervention in competitive market
        47n

Great Slump (1930s) and Great Stag-flation (1970s) differences 4, 5, 153
Gross Domestic Product 7
groups of workers and muscle power in wage claims 30
guaranteed work agreement 62
guideline norms for wage-fixing 100

housing controls and movement of workers 97
  inefficient use of 97

imperfect labour market, single employer in 49–55
imports, costs of, causing inflation 16–17
incentives, employer and employee 86
income, distribution 36
  increase and productivity 3
    tax on 139
  redistribution 19
  and wages 15–20
  and wealth distribution 56
incomes policy 155
  centralised 98–107
  effects of 9
independent trade union and collective bargaining 67
individual worker, industrial action of, legal claim against 76
industrial action, and contract provisions 59n
  effects on wage earners 31–2
  to raise prices 123, 126
  resources for 27
industrial tribunals 65
  functions of 80
inegalitarian labour-capital partnerships 133–4
inflation, changes to reduce 160–1
  fiscal devices for control of 138–52
  Germany and 4
  of 1970s, cause of 16
  price 1, 16
  reducing value of wages 27–8
  in stagflation 1, 4
  and wage costs, effect of 159
injunctions against trade union action 82
'In Place of Strife' 82
interest rate, factor 191
  reduction 23

Jackson, Tom, and wage-fixing 31
job evaluation 38
Joint Industrial Councils, Statutory 61

keeping-up-with-the-Joneses syndrome 30
Keynes, John Maynard 4, 153
  economic policies *see* Keynesian versus the monetarists 11
Keynesian, full employment policy 154
  models of economy 22n
  policies and full employment 3
  technique of demand management 23–4
Keynesianism, orthodox and new 8–11

labour, competitive principle in 95
labour contracts, collective 59
    individual 59
  current demand for and inflation 13
  increased mobility of 95–7
  market, competition in 85–96
    treatment of unemployed 85–6
    reasons for intervention in 85–8
  monopolies and wage increases 24
  movement to jobs 87
  organisations, uncontrolled monopoly bargaining 33
  redeployment 90, 91
  restrictive practices 95
  wage rate, competition for 15
labour-capital partnerships 156–7
  conflicts in 134–6
  participation in profits and management 137
labour co-operatives 156–7
  admission of members 124–5
  and capital intensity 126–7
  competitive, the case for 119–37
    as a cure for stagflation 127–31
  crucial role of 131–3
  decisions of shareholders in 135–6
  differential setting 222
  egalitarian contrasted with capitalist entrepreneurial concern 129–31
  large, direct economic incentives 123
  management and the dismissal of workers 219–22
  member's dismissal or leaving 219–22
  monopolistic powers, control of 123
  problems 217–26
  promotion problems 135
  qualification for employment benefit 225–6

labour co-operatives *contd.*
  role of 122
  and the scale of production 121–4
  small, and direct economic incentives 122
  and stagflation 126
  and trade unions 121
labour-intensive production technology 126
labour-productivity factor 183
lame ducks in demand-management policies 25–6
lay-offs and short-time in contracts of employment 63
legal, background of monopolistic behaviour 207–16
  immunities in trade disputes 74
  provisions, adjudication and enforcement 80–3
length of notice in agreement 62–3
living standards, increases in, effects of 25
  over-ambitious rise in 27
low-paid workers, exploitation of 19, 42
  improvement in conditions for 42
  move to higher paid 42
low pay, cure for 42–3

market competition and wage claims 26
mark-up factor and fiscal devices 188–9
Mergers Panel 210
miners' wage increases, effect on governments 32
mobility to better paid job 96–7
monetarist policy 11
monetary and bugetary policies, devising 7
money selling prices, stabilisation of 155
money wage rate, factors determining 165
  and distribution of income 156
  direct effect of schemes on 149–51
Monopolies Commission 216
monopolies, control of 17
  and mergers, EEC law 215
Monopolies and Mergers Commission 74n, 96, 208, 210–12, 213, 214
  factors in judging 212
monopolistic, action by trade unions, exemption from 72
  behaviour in the UK, legal background to restraint 207–16
  cartel formation, prevention of 44

incentive to restrict output and sales 47–8, 52
and monopsonistic features of the real world 47
organisations of workers' wage claims 26
power of employers 48, 51
powers of labour organisations (UK) 58–84
  of trade unions 48
practices 71n
  counterbalancing advantages from 207–8
monopoly wage bargaining, uncontrolled, effect of 31
monopsonistic, incentive to restrict scale of employment 48
power 86
  of employer 48, 49, 52
movement of persons, removal of impediments for 18
movement of workers, unemployed during 23

National Coal Board 32
national, income (1925–39, 1965–79) 5
  pay awards 105
  product and wage claims 165–6, 170, 173
  wage rates 101
nationalisation 159
  and price control 17
net national income 16
net sales as tax/subsidy base 142
net value added 119n
  problem of 217–18
New Keynesian, approach policy 155–6
  demand management combined with wage settlements 182–7, 204, 205–6
  principles 99, 100
  strategy 8–11
non-accelerating inflation rate of unemployment (NAIRU) 13, 14, 15
North Sea Oil, revenue from 29
not-quite-so-compulsory arbitration 108–18

Office of Fair Trading 208
oil, crisis, effect of 3, 28–30
  price rises and cost of living 16
  uses not tied to employment levels 29
Orthodox Keynesian, approach policy 155

demand management inflationary implications 159–81
  of full employment 195, 197, 202, 206, 215
  policy 22
  principles 98, 100
output, and employment (UK) depression 154
  increase in pay for 39
overmanning 96
overtime wage rates 101

patent rights, EEC and UK law 215
pay, criteria for wage fixing 42
  determination, difficulties of 101, 102
  disputes, arbitral body for 158
  fixing rates of, *see* wage-fixing
  increase above norm, tax on 152
  rises, factors for 101
    as incentives 41
  settlement arbitration 111
pension funds securities 32
perfect competition, the fairyland of 45–7
Phelps Brown, Sir Henry, arbitration proposal 105–6
Phillips-curve effect 161
  inflation-adjusted 183
picketing 78–80, 92
  Code of Practice for 79
  and highway obstruction 80
  the police and 79–80
  secondary and tertiary, action against 79
pickets, legal actions against 73, 79
piece rates 101
police duties and strike picketing 79–80
politics and income distribution 20
pollution, government intervention for 47
poverty, reasons for 19
pressure groups and wage claims 27–8
Price Commission Act (1977) 213
Price Commission, The 213–14
price control 17, 159
    schemes, administrative problems 143–4
  inflation, cause of 16
    current rate 13
    exploding 28
    factor 163
    scheme for control 140–3, 146–7
      efficacy of 146–7
  fixing to avoid inflationary losses 173, 175

price-inflation-catching-up-factor 176
private sector wage increase, effect of 32
producer market, invasion of 47
producing in an imperfectly competitive market 47
production technology, capital-intensive 126
productivity deals between employee and employer 43
productivity, difficulties with increases in 39–40
  growth in stagflation 3
  improved, linking rates of pay with 39–42
products, reduced demand for affecting employment and wage rates 21–2
profit(s), margins, excess, restraining 18, 159
  role of 18
profit-sharing schemes 156–7
property, dispersal of ownership 18
  incomes from 16
public service workers' wage increases, effect on public 32

qualifications, control of 94–5
quart-out-of-a-pint-pot factor 176, 183
  inflation 195, 197
  syndrome 28

rates of pay, central body for 157–8
real income, oil prices and 29
real profit margin deflation 35
real-wage-aspiration factor 168, 170, 183, 196
real wage inflation 35
recession, world, cause of 154
reduced costs and reduced prices 42
redundancies 67
  alternative employment in 63
  attitudes to 14
  payments 116
  statutory rights of 63–4
relativities, adjustment of 102–4
resale price maintenance 212
restrictive agreements 209
  escaping control 209–10
  injunction for 209
Restrictive Agreements (EEC law) 214–15
restrictive practices, concerning labour, investigating body for 211
  in labour co-operatives 136
  prevention 44
  removal of 96

Restrictive Practices Court 207–8, 208–
        10, 212, 213, 214, 216
    and business practices 96
Restrictive Trade Practices Act 71n
retail price index 1

sanctions, problems of 115–17
school leavers and employment 14
Secretary of State, powers in restrictive
        practices 211, 212
self-balancing fiscal scheme 144–6
self-employment, avoidance of statutory
        requirements 60
    and employees, distinctions between
        60
    tax advantages 60
    and trade union restrictions 60
selling prices, marking-up wage costs
        163, 164
    restraint of effect of 200
    scheme to control inflation of 151–2
short-time working in contract of
        employment 63
single   enterprise,   anti-competitive
        practice 207
skills, problems with differences 135
social, benefits and tax 86
    security provisions in trade disputes
        83
Social Security Act (1980) 83
stagflation 1–20, 96
    action for cure of 20
    causes and consequences of 2–5
    and oil prices 29
    problems of 153, 154
state benefits, improvement of, effect on
        unemployed 27
state intervention of lower paid 43
statutory provisions affecting employ-
        ment contracts 62
strike weapon in income distribution
        20
strikes, financing of 116–17
    sympathetic 75–6, 79, 82
striking against an award 116
supplementary benefit 27
    as a loan 115–16
    in strikes 83
sweated labour 42
sympathetic striking 75–6, 79, 82

tax/taxation,   advantages   to   self-
        employed 60
    and cost of living 34
    on excess inflation 190, 191
    on increases in income 139
    rate, reduction of 23

social benefits and 86
tax/subsidy, on output 190
    scheme on selling prices 188
    schemes   and   unemployment
        138–9
    in wage rate 197
technology, modern, actions of groups
        in 26
torts against trade association officials
        72–3
trade disputes, criminal acts in 81
    defined 73
    and legal immunity 74–5
    legal protection for action 71
    legislation 72
    subjects covered 74
trade union(s), activities, time off for
        67
    bargaining power 58
    bashing 157
    and closed shop 67–70
    damages for expulsion from 81
    dismissal for activity in 65
    exemption from, restraint on monop-
        olistic action 70–7
    expulsion   from,   when   reasonable
        117
    factors changing 20
    formation of 66–7
    funds, exempt form legal claims 72
        immunity of 117
    and income distribution 20
    information from employer 67
    injunctions against 82
    membership 67–70
        agreement 68
        refused 69–70
    monopolistic powers 26, 52
        and wage fixing 157
    and monopsonistic powers 48
    officials, legal action against 72–3
    policies in stagflation 3
    powers, general limitation of 92–5
    protection of worker 56–7
    religious objection to joining 69
    statutory provisions for not joining
        64
    varied powers in wage bargaining
        31
    and wage claims 13–14
    wage fixing power undermined 22
Trades   Union   Congress   (TUC),   and
        Bridlington principles 73–4
    and trade union membership 69
transport charges under nationalisation
        and labour co-operatives 122

Treasury, The, responsibilities in inflation and deflation 10

Treaty of Rome, Articles 85 and 86 on restrictive agreements 214

See also European Economic Community

unemployed, setting up new co-operative 131–2, 136

and tax 86

workers and co-operatives 132

unemployment benefit 27

effect of decrease in 161

and imports 155

and inflation, choice between 1–2

interwar (UK) 25

post Second World War 25

pressure on labour market 22

in stagflation 1–2, 7

unfair dismissal, compensation provision 65

statutory provisions 64

United Kingdom, and EEC law, relations between 215–16

law on monopolistic behaviour 207–14

United States Act of Congress and employment 24

unsocial hours, wage rates 101

value added per unit of output, tax on 140

Value Added Tax (VAT) 141–2

on excessive increases 138

wage(s), annual settlements 177 ff.

bargaining, on company level 204, 205

of individual employer 26

bargains, extension of scope of 77

claims, exceeding rise in output 27

over-ambitious 26–8

real wage 165, 173

target 169

and the cost of living 33–5

costs, linking productivity with 39–42

and oil costs 29

percentage increase 13

Councils 42, 61

differentials 33

leap-frogging processes in 30

and distribution of income 15–20, 30–3

explosion causing inflation (1970) 16

income, distribution of 15–20, 30–3

increases, and employment 12

linked to productivity 38–40

inflation, a scheme for control of 147–9, 152

on rate of inflation 173, 175, 177

negotiations, large unions and 30–1

and profit, distribution of income between 16

rates and cost of living 34

increases in, impact on prices 22

increasing to trade level 93–4

norms 35

and relief of poverty 19

restraint, effect of 10

setting of 18

taxing increases in 138

role of competitive forces 157

settlements, company and local 101

designed to achieve over-ambitious real wage 159–81

expectations after 161

over-ambitious and inflation 160

wage-fixing, arrangements, necessity of 44–5

reform of 20

bodies, statutory 61

case for decentralised 88–91

criteria for 37–43

and demand management 21–6

effects on unemployment and inflation 21–36

for employment promotion 36

and full employment 8–9

and incomes policy 11

institutions and promotion of employment 15

intermediate system 104–6

policies and inflation 9

through trade unions 157

Webb, Sidney and Beatrice quoted 108–9

Weighell, Sidney and wage fixing 31

workers, actions of, causing economic loss 26

capital resources since 1930s 27

leaving or dismissal from co-operative or partnership 219–22

legal immunities in industrial action 77

movement and comparability 37–8

prevention of monopsonistic exploitation 56, 61

risks in labour co-operatives 127

and wage differentials 30

world recession 4